CONTAGION

OTHER BOOKS BY DARREN W. RITSON:
Ghost Hunter, True Life Encounters from the North East
In Search of Ghosts – Real Hauntings from around Britain
Haunted Newcastle
Paranormal North East – True Ghost Stories
Supernatural North
Haunted Durham
Ghosts at Christmas
Haunted Berwick
Haunted Northumberland
Haunted Tyneside
Haunted Carlisle
Paranormal County Durham
Haunted Wearside
Newcastle East Through Time

OTHER BOOKS BY MICHAEL J. HALLOWELL:
Herbal Healing – A Practical Introduction to Medicinal Herbs
Ales & Spirits
Invizikids
Mystery Animals of Northumberland & Tyneside
The House That Jack Built
Christmas Ghost Stories
South Shields Through Time
Paranormal South Tyneside

CO-AUTHORED BY DARREN W. RITSON & MICHAEL J. HALLOWELL
The South Shields Poltergeist - One Family's Fight Against an Invisible Intruder
Ghost Taverns
The Haunting of Willington Mill

CONTAGION

In the Shadow of the South Shields Poltergeist

DARREN W. RITSON
&
MICHAEL J. HALLOWELL

Foreword by Colin Wilson

THE LIMBURY PRESS

For Colin Wilson

This First Edition published by
The Limbury Press
43 Neville Road
Limbury, Luton
Bedfordshire
LU3 2JG
www.limburypress.co.uk

Copyright © Darren W. Ritson & Michael J. Hallowell 2014

Darren W. Ritson & Michael J. Hallowell have asserted their right under the Copyright, Designs & Patents Act, 1988 to be identified as the authors of this work.

All rights reserved. No part of this publication may be reproduced, stored in a retrieval system, or transmitted, in any form, or by any means, electronic, mechanical, photocopying, recording or otherwise, without the prior consent of the publishers.

This book is sold subject to the condition that it shall not, by way of trade or otherwise, be lent, resold, hired out or otherwise circulated without the publisher's prior consent in any form of binding or cover other than in which it is published and without a similar condition, including this condition, being imposed on the subsequent purchaser.

ISBN 978-0-9565228-9-4

Typesetting & Design by The Limbury Press

Printed by imprint**digital**
Seychelles Farm
Upton Pyne
Devon, EX5 5HY

CONTENTS

A Word From Mike Hallowell   6
Acknowledgements   7
Foreword   9
Introduction   14
Authors' Note   18

CHAPTER

1	Defining Moments	19
2	The Poltergeist at Work	23
3	Principles of Contagion	27
4	Shadows	35
5	Investigation at Jarrow	38
6	Polt Parallels	43
7	The House on Pallister Street	75
8	Catalyst	79
9	The Haunted Loom	90
10	Friends & Family	97
11	The Authors' Experiences	99
12	Time and Time Again	106
13	"I'm Sick of the Bastard!"	115
14	Echoes of Lock Street	126
15	The Incubus	135
16	"Get off Me!"	155
17	Standby: The Polt Power Source?	170
18	"My Name is Legion, For We Are Many".	173
19	Enfield and Other Cases: Contagion and Parallels	176
20	Textual Innuendoes	186
21	Contagion; The Desire to Survive	191
22	Conclusions	200

Index   204

A WORD FROM MIKE HALLOWELL

At the end of this book the reader will become aware of my reversion to Islam, a religion which is misunderstood by many, but which has a long history of studying and "dealing with" a variety of so-called paranormal phenomena. My reversion has led me to see this book from a different perspective – ironic, considering I co-authored it. Even the cover – which Darren and I were both delighted with when we composed it back in 2009 – is something which I would have wanted to be different had I embraced Islam earlier. Regardless, although my views have shifted in some respects regarding the nature of the poltergeist phenomenon and its origins, the book stands as a witness to how I saw the phenomenon at that time, and also a testimony as to how easily our understanding can be radically altered by a watershed experience; in my case, a spiritual conversion. Darren and I have discussed in-depth how my reversion to Islam could potentially affect our working relationship as co-authors of books regarding strange phenomena. We have both concluded that, far from diminishing our ability to work together, it will in fact enhance and enrich it. Darren is one of the few authors in this field who, from my perspective, is able to take a truly detached and objective look at the enigmas and mysteries which fill our world. I believe that only a handful of other writers in the field could have accommodated such a radical change in my perspective without jettisoning me into literary oblivion as a working partner. For that I will always be in his debt. As someone who now looks at the poltergeist phenomenon from an Islamic perspective, my reversion has opened up a whole new vista to be explored. Darren and I are already planning on how this can be incorporated into our next collaborative work.

ACKNOWLEDGEMENTS

The late *Colin Wilson*, for kindly agreeing to write the foreword for this book, and for his welcome advice and encouragement; *Darren Olley* and *Lez Cottrell* for co-operating with the authors and generously supplying them with information regarding their experiences; *Derek** and *Mandy**, tenants of the house in Pallister Street, for graciously allowing the authors into their home to carry out an investigation, and for permission to use one of their photographs; *Doreen**, for sharing her story with Darren; *Drew Bartley, Fiona Vipond, Jim Collins* and *Paul Collins* of G.H.O.S.T for their assistance in investigating the Newcastle poltergeist case; *Freda** and *Arnold Longthorne**, for their courage and co-operation; Gemma, Jo, Liz, Rosie and friends for their co-operation during the Newcastle investigation. *Guy Lyon Playfair* for supplying material and anecdotal accounts included in this book, and also for his permission to use several photographs taken during the Enfield investigation by both himself and fellow investigator, *Maurice Grosse*; *Kelly Barton** and *Les McFallen**, for describing to Mike their bizarre encounters; *Mark Winter*, paranormal researcher, for his kind assistance during the investigation at Pallister Street; *Minnie**, who was gracious enough to invite us to her home and share with us her disturbing experiences. *Paul McDonald*, Curator of Newcastle Keep, for his kind support; *Rebecca* and *Karen*, who volunteered to take part in the Newcastle poltergeist investigation; *Rhianne D'Morgyn*, psychic and medium, for her valuable assistance in investigating the Jarrow and Ashington cases; *Steve Taylor*, from *Alone in the Dark Entertainment*, for introducing the authors to a number of new poltergeist cases which are detailed in this book; *Stuart* and

Lauren Smith, for allowing Mike into their home to investigate the case of the Boldon Colliery poltergeist; *Tony** and *Linda**, for giving the authors the opportunity to investigate the strange (and often disturbing) phenomena at their home in Middlesborough. *Victoria Nesbitt, her family and colleagues*, for their co-operation during the investigation into the "haunted loom" at the craft shop at Blyth.

FOREWORD

It was forty years ago, in 1969, that I wrote a chapter called 'The World of Spirits' in my book *The Occult*. In the years since then, I have probably unlearned as much as I have learned about the nature of the poltergeist, and even now would hesitate to say I understood it. But I would still say that the present book is as sound an introduction as any in existence.

The two investigators, Darren and Mike, are from Tyneside in the north east of England. It happened in the home of a young couple, Marc and Marianne, living in Lock Street, who had a son called Robert. On one occasion, the entity dragged a chest of drawers out of Robert's bedroom on to the landing; on another, hung his rocking horse by its reign from the ceiling. A large toy rabbit was found in a chair with a box-cutter blade its hand. Obviously, the poltergeist wanted to create fear, and it succeeded. Ritson and Hallowell's first book about the case, *The South Shields Poltergeist*, is not recommended for nervous readers late at night.

One of the basic questions that every psychical investigator faces is where the entity is getting its energy. In the 19th century, when many such cases were recorded, there seemed little doubt: it was from the fear of the victims involved. In a famous case in the Rue des Noyers in Paris, when the 'ghost' smashed all the windows and threw objects around, a medium (spirit-communicator) got it to admit that its energy came from the 'electrical nature' of a maidservant, who was providing it. The girl was apparently unaware of this; 'She was the most frightened of all' said the ghost.

This is an extremely interesting answer, since the investigators succeeded in ending the Lock Street haunting by getting the victims to switch off all electrical appliances at night.

In the first part of the 20th century, most investigators concluded that poltergeist energy was sexual in nature, having noted how often there was a pubescent adolescent – labelled 'the focus' - in the haunted house. And the high esteem in which Freud was held in those days meant that the unconscious mind of the 'focus' tended to get blamed for the manifestations. It was a view I myself held when I wrote *The Occult* in 1956. What changed my mind was when, in August 1980, I drove to Pontefract, in Yorkshire, to look into a poltergeist haunting that had started in 1966. Phillip, the son of the house, had just reached adolescence when pools of water began to appear on the kitchen floor. (Poltergeist phenomena often start in this way.) After a month or so it stopped, and started up again when the daughter of the house, Diane, reached adolescence. Then objects began to fly around, crockery was smashed, and Diane was often thrown out of bed by an invisible entity.

But it was when she described to me how the poltergeist had dragged her upstairs, with a grandmother clock on top of her, that I realised beyond all doubt that it was not her unconscious mind that was responsible, but some kind of 'spirit'. What kind of spirit? The researcher Guy Playfair, the author (with Maurice Grosse) of the classic *Enfield Poltergeist*, quotes a Dutch medium, Dono Gmelig-Meyling, as saying that the Enfield house was crowded with spirits from the local graveyard. In other words, the spirits of the dead.

Now in a later chapter of this book - (15) - the authors have some other interesting suggestions to make. A widow living in Ashington was also a medium, and had noted that she was not alone in the house. The entity ran its fingers through her hair and would even caress her thigh in bed. A friend named Steve Taylor remarked that he was wondering whether the visitor was not a poltergeist but an incubus. Then there is the following interesting passage:

'The word *incubus* is Latin, and drawn from *in,* which literally means "above" or "on top of", and *cubo,* which means "I lie upon", "a burden" or "a weight". This in itself highlights the predatory disposition of the entity, which, according to legend, is said to be a sexually driven monster which preys upon women.

Foreword

The female equivalent of the incubus is the succubus, who allegedly preys upon men in a similar manner.

'Supposedly, the incubi are demons of tremendous power and great age. They were even feared by the ancient Sumerians and Babylonians, who believed that they could also control storms, lightning and thunder.

'According to tradition, incubi constantly attempt to engage in sexual activity with women. Their reasons for this are two-fold. Firstly, they do so because they enjoy it, and secondly because engaging in sexual intercourse with human females is the means by which they procreate. During the act of intercourse, the incubus will draw or "suck out" energy from its victim – energy upon which it feeds to perpetuate its own existence.

'There are two prevalent theories about the nature of both the incubus and the succubus. In some traditions they are said to be two separate genders, male and female, in exactly the same way that humans are similarly divided. In other traditions, however, the concept is a little more complex. One Mediaeval view was that both incubi and succubi are genderless, and are merely two different presentations of the same entity. In other words, the entity will appear as either male or female depending on the type of sexual activity it wishes to engage in. Some scholars suggested that the demon would first appear as a succubus – normally in the guise of a voluptuous female – and have intercourse with its male victim when he was asleep. As soon as the victim ejaculated, the demon would then metamorphose into its male form, as an incubus, and select a female victim. During intercourse with the woman, the demon would ejaculate the sperm it had "collected" from the male victim and the woman would become pregnant. The child, although human in appearance, would actually be a demon in disguise who would then go on to promulgate the species in exactly the same manner as its parents. Even though the sperm used in this bizarre form of conception was taken from a human male and the mother was a human female, the resultant offspring was almost always a demon. However, sometimes the resultant offspring would not be fully demonic but actually half-demon and half-human. Such hybrids were known as *combions* or *cambions,* and were believed to possess enormous supernatural powers.

'There are a number of different ways in which an incubus

can, allegedly, be identified. When the demon engages in sexual intercourse with a human female victim, its penis is said to feel either incredibly cold or uncomfortably hot. In appearance, the incubus is said to take the form of a hideous dwarf with misaligned and deformed features. Some say that before it materialises in fleshly form it appears as a small but intense light that will dart through the air at great speed like a firefly, or as a metallic sphere. In yet other traditions it is said to appear as a swan, a dog, a goose, a dragon or even a large fish.

'Dealing with an incubus is not easy, and over the millennia numerous defence strategies have been employed with varying degrees of success. In the Christian tradition, predictably, exorcism has been the preferred option. The Roman Catholic Church has said that attending confession may also be helpful, along with making the sign of the cross, which demons are said to dislike intensely. Unfortunately, even thinking Christians have admitted that such tactics are basically useless. Testimony exists that incubi actually have no fear of exorcisms, couldn't give two hoots about the sign of the cross and, on occasion, have actually drunk holy water and spat upon the Bible in front of their victims.

'One of the most frightening beliefs regarding incubi is that, as previously stated, they "suck out" the life force from their victims. If an incubus is allowed to do this repeatedly, so it is said, the victim will endure a rapid decline in health and, eventually, die if the demon is not prevented from engaging in its rapacious behaviour.'

Later, Mike asks her: 'Have you ever seen elemental spirits in your garden – pixies, gnomes, elves...?', to which the lady replies: 'Oh yes, there are elves out there - and gnomes'. This interested me because I am apparently one of the few writers. on the paranormal who is willing to concede that such things may exist. In fact, chapter five of my book *Poltergeist* is devoted to fairies and elementals. One case that always impressed me is vouched for by my friend Lois Bourne in her book *Witch Among Us.*

Lois is a 'witch' in the sense of possessing odd psychic powers, of whose reality I have not the slightest doubt. She is an extremely sensible and down-to-earth lady. And in her book, among many stories that psychical researchers will find credible enough, she tells a story that will obviously cause most readers to doubt her truthfulness. Staying on holiday at a cottage at Crantock, in Cornwall, she met another member of a wiccan coven, and spent an evening at her home. The woman's husband, Rob, asked her if she would like to see a goblin. One appeared, he said, among the rushes of the millstream at Treago Mill every morning at sunrise, and if she wanted to see him, she had to be up early. The next morning Lois and her husband Wilfred joined Rob at the mill gate, and they crept up to the stream.

'I have never been able to decide, and still cannot decide, whether I really saw that goblin, or if Rob made me see it. Whatever it was, there, sitting on a stone calmly washing his socks, was an elfin creature with a red hat, green coat and trews, one yellow sock on, and one in his tiny hands in the process of being washed. I remember thinking at the time in my sleepy befuddled but practical way 'what an atrocious colour combination'. Suddenly he saw us and he disappeared . . . 'Now do you believe me?' asked Rob. I have known Lois for years. I may be gullible and she may be a liar, but I believe her. She is not the type to invent such a silly story. And neither is her husband Wilfred - who also saw it - the type to support a downright lie. In short, I firmly believe that the world is full of living beings who are invisible to us, and the poltergeist is only one among many.

Somewhere is this book Darren speaks of Mike's impatience with doubters, and I am reminded of a comment of William James's friend Professor James Hyslop, who said: 'I regard the existence of discarnate spirits as scientifically proved and I no longer refer to the sceptic as having any right to speak on the subject. Any man who does not accept the existence of discarnate spirits and the proof of it is either ignorant or a moral coward. I give him short shrift, and do not propose to argue with him on the supposition that he knows nothing about the subject'. These are words that every psychical researcher should learn by heart.

Why is this book called *Contagion*? Because one of its basic arguments is that poltergeists are not "one-offs", as researchers (including myself) used to assume, but seem to be capable of spreading like an infection - a startling idea new to poltergeist lore.

Colin Wilson
Cornwall, May 2009

INTRODUCTION

In 2006, the authors of this book made a life-changing decision; to investigate an alleged case of poltergeist infestation in an otherwise normal family home in the town of South Shields, Tyne & Wear. The only caveat that needs to be added to this fact is that, at the time, they had absolutely no idea that what they were about to do would change their lives to such an incalculable degree.

In their book about the affair, *The South Shields Poltergeist: One Family's Fight Against an Invisible Intruder*[1], they spoke of how every paranormal investigator dreams of their "big case"; a circumstance so bizarre and so verifiable that it truly seems to prove that the world is not just stranger than we know, but – as Heraclitus the sage (or Isaac Newton, according to some) once said– stranger than we possibly *can* know. The authors well and truly stumbled across their "big case" with the South Shields Poltergeist. Over the course of several months, they found themselves confronting a vicious – nay, sadistic – entity that seemed to break all the known rules that govern our universe. The poltergeist was invisible – well, most of the time – and also cunning and violent. It could throw objects around, send death threats to mobile phones via text messages and, when it felt so disposed, slash the flesh of those it chose to.

During the period of time in question the authors realised that the case they were investigating was truly extraordinary, possibly even unique. They believed that the world should know about it, and were convinced that both the poltergeist and their investigation of it would go down in the history of psychical research as a ground-breaking case. Renowned author and researcher Colin Wilson kindly recognised the book as "one of the great classic works on the poltergeist", a comment which the authors truly appreciated. To this day the authors have not changed their minds about how significant the South Shields case really was. Long before the entity dissipated into the ether, hopefully never to return, Darren and Mike began to write their book about the affair. *The South Shields Poltergeist* ended at the point where the bizarre phenomena that had plagued the family so intensely seemed to have stopped. Perhaps naively, the authors believed that a long, incredible chapter in their professional lives was drawing to a close. True, they would never be the same again, but they remained convinced that eventually new cases would beckon and they would be able to move on with their lives. It was not to be. Like a dark, brooding presence the shadow of the South Shields Poltergeist continued to haunt the investigators as it had once haunted the family it terrorised; just not in the same way.

Darren and Mike have learned many lessons from their experience during the South Shields investigation. They have learned that human nature can, when plunged into the correct set of circumstances, be every bit as dark and untrustworthy as the poltergeist itself. They are now less trusting of those they meet in their professional lives and see the society they are part of in a far less favourable light. The lessons they have learned should be taken on board by every paranormal investigator.

In February 2008, whilst the authors were lecturing to a class of university students who had an interest in the subject, Mike spoke bluntly of how he now finds it difficult to be tolerant of sceptics who dismiss the poltergeist experience out of hand. He struggles to be polite towards cynics who have never been in close proximity to a poltergeist let alone witnessed its devastating handiwork. How can they speak with such authority on a subject of which they have had no personal experience?

The poltergeist phenomenon is normally seen by new or inexperienced researchers as a purely paranormal one; strange things happening to or around ordinary people that simply cannot be explained. However, there is another aspect of poltergeist infestation that seasoned investigators often give weight to, and it's sometimes referred to as *contagion*. This is, allegedly, a process whereby the bizarre antics of the poltergeist spread outwards from the home of the principal experients and start to effect others around them; extended family members, friends, colleagues and investigators who choose, or accidentally wander into, the arena of metaphysical conflict. Like a communicable disease, the poltergeist phenomenon can attach itself to others. The only small mercy is that those who are seemingly subjected to such contagion normally do not suffer poltergeist phenomena to the same degree as the principal experients at "Ground Zero". As the contagion spreads, it seems to become diluted.

One part of the poltergeist phenomenon that often goes unrecognised even by experienced researchers is the destructive effect that the polt experience can have on other aspects of people's lives. The poltergeist is not only a little–understood entity that frightens its victims. The poltergeist also has an almost unbridled ability to cause devastation in the fields of employment, relationships, physical well-being and emotional/mental health. If you think, as the authors once did, that the presence of a poltergeist merely generates fear in its victims and leaves the other aspects of their lives untouched, then, putting it bluntly, you are deluded. The poltergeist infects its victims and those around them in the same way that the HIV virus infects those who contract it. It soaks itself insidiously into every fibre of their being, leaving no part or aspect of its victims untouched. Poltergeists do not only affect people; they infect whole families and even communities.

The truth is that, despite the authors' optimism, the South Shields Poltergeist came back – and with a vengeance. This time, Darren and Mike would be once again forced to do battle with their old foe, but under the auspices of radically different rules of conflict. This book is essentially the story of their ongoing struggle against the invisible intruder that once resided at Lock Street – an intruder that had, since the days of their first encounter with it, grown far stronger, more cunning and infinitely more dangerous.

What you are about to read in the following pages is a true account. The authors are well aware that some readers will find the notion of the poltergeist's return under such bizarre circumstances extremely hard to believe. In anticipation of this, they have proposed a number of different hypotheses to explain

Introduction

why the entity that they thought had disappeared for good was able to re-enter their lives with such consummate ease – and why the authors were once again singled out as targets for its dark malevolence.

During the authors' first investigation, the poltergeist sent a chilling text message to the mobile phone of one of the principal experients. It said, quite simply, "I'm back". They now grimly acknowledge that, at least in part, those words were meant for them. The South Shields Poltergeist *was* back – and it was far from finished with the two researchers who had so rudely interrupted its depraved existence.

The South Shields Poltergeist case has sent powerful ripples coursing throughout the world of paranormal research. Both in the UK and abroad, the authors' first joint book has caused incredible debate, much of it heated. Drawn into the fray have been academics and armchair enthusiasts, TV personalities and film producers, newspaper journalists and psychic mediums, legal experts and radio presenters.

And through it all, the grim legacy of the South Shields Poltergeist has been sustained. Perhaps, now that the full truth is about to be told, it can finally be laid to rest.

Darren W Ritson & Michael J Hallowell
2014

AUTHORS' NOTE

The events related in this book are entirely true. However the names of some experients have been changed, along with other incidental details, to protect their anonymity. Pseudonyms have been marked with an asterisk thus - * - at their first appearance.

One
DEFINING MOMENTS

The authors, like every reader of this book, can look back over their lives and pinpoint defining moments that were, to use a modern expression, *watersheds*; that is, points of no return or events that change one's life permanently and irredeemably.

Mike remembers the passing of his grandparents, and the day when he fell prey to an undiagnosed heart condition which took him to the brink of death. Darren, for his part, recalls the time when he first saw his baby daughter, Abbey, seconds after she was born. A taxi driver, whilst taking Darren to the hospital, commented, "You don't know what love is until you see your newborn child for the first time". Darren later reflected on how true those words were.

Both of the authors, however, will testify that they share a common defining moment in their lives; the day, in July, 2006, when they were first invited to investigate the South Shields Poltergeist.

Darren and Mike are experienced paranormal investigators. They have written many books, articles and columns on both ghosts and the hunting of them as well as about other paranormal phenomena. Diligently they have travelled the length and breadth of the British Isles – and sometimes beyond – in the search for evidence that there truly is some form of existence beyond this Vale of Tears. Both would admit candidly that they haven't been disappointed, although they know full well that not every insubstantial wisp of mist or shimmer of light is proof positive that there is more to this life than flesh-and-blood alone would testify.

Paranormal investigation is in some respects akin to the

exploration of an uncharted wilderness. Those who delve into the darkest reaches of the Amazonian Basin, for example, never know just what (or who) they'll encounter. If they're lucky, they may stumble across a hitherto unknown arachnid or two, or even a new variety of orchid. Perhaps a brightly-plumed bird of uncertain provenance may wing its way overhead, reinforcing the fact that, despite civilisation's relentless march across the natural world like a cancer, there are still some wondrous things left to discover.

Sometimes, of course, explorers stumble upon discoveries of an altogether darker nature; a bacillus or parasite, perhaps, that devastates their digestive system or covers their flesh in obscene lesions. They may even run into a hitherto unknown carnivore that displays no reluctance whatsoever when it comes to dining on humans.

Well, it's a tough job, but someone has to do it.

The authors aren't suggesting for one moment that paranormal researchers are subject to the same dangers as explorers, either by nature or degree. However, they know full well that their chosen field of endeavour may certainly be no bed of roses, either. Turn on your TV, and at any given time you'll possibly find at least half-a-dozen channels airing programmes dealing with the supernatural. Stage-bound psychics may be passing on messages from the deceased, and studio-based reporters will be revealing details of the latest UFO sighting. Society, in the main, has a thirst for the unknown. Of course, you can't believe everything you see on TV, in much the same way you can't trust everything you read in the papers. But it isn't all bunkum. Beyond the media-hungry snake-oil salesmen who peddle their psychic wares to the highest bidder, there is a truly unknown world that usually lies just beyond our senses. Sometimes, researchers who may have spent decades investigating low-level hauntings may find themselves catapulted into the uncharted regions of this world unceremoniously.

In the main, the authors have been fortunate. Their forays into the dimly-lit world of paranormal phenomena have caused them relatively little grief. True, Mike believes he once came uncomfortably close to the legendary Bigfoot when he was sailing down the Dorcheat Bayou in Louisiana, and Darren was rather unnerved on one occasion when he recorded some very sinister sounds in a deserted Scottish prison. But they have never been forced to confront anything truly malevolent or face up to an entity that could quite possibly, if it so wished, do them great harm both physically and psychologically.

Except once, that is, when they were invited to go to the house in Lock Street.

In their previous volume, *The South Shields Poltergeist: One Family's Fight Against an Invisible Intruder*, the authors described in graphic detail how a young family was almost hounded out of its home by an invisible, brooding entity that seemed hell-bent on snatching from them every ounce of happiness they possessed. The authors found themselves in the daunting position of trying to help the family deal with this nightmare situation. Over a period of months the poltergeist danced merrily with the investigators, leading them into a number of blind alleys as they desperately searched for a way to overcome its terrible influence. It proved to be an expert in psychological warfare. One minute it would pass itself off as the spirit of an innocent toddler, the next it would manifest itself as an old woman or a tall, black-clad man with sallow features and a grim countenance. At times the investigators didn't know whether they were dealing with a single entity, or two, three, four or more.

In October, 2006 the authors sought the advice of a colleague who, without pouring cold water on the idea that the entity was indeed a poltergeist, suggested that it might in some way be feeding on electricity. The householders were asked to turn all of their electrical equipment off at night instead of just leaving them on "stand-by", and, lo and behold, it worked. Almost overnight the poltergeist vanished almost completely, leaving behind an exhausted but very much relieved family who, with the authors' help, slowly began to pick up the pieces. This, too, was a defining moment in their investigation of the South Shields Poltergeist.

And there were more to come. In their first book, the authors attempted to clarify the true essence of the poltergeist. They desperately wanted to understand the nature of the beast they were dealing with. In some respects they were successful. They came to see how the polt would time its intrusions to perfection, calculating perfectly when to strike for maximum effect. They noticed how, after protracted bouts of activity, it would seemingly rest, as if exhausted. They also discovered ways in which they could make it angry and provoke it into action. Day by day, as they came to understand the activities of the poltergeist better, they were able to chip away at its defences until, one day, it left its abode in Lock Street for pastures new.

But if the authors were successful in unmasking the polt in some respects, they struggled in others. On reflection, they can see that what they discovered were things relating to what a poltergeist does, but not truly what a poltergeist *is*. They still held to their original belief that the poltergeist was essentially a form of latent energy that builds up inside its "host" before externalising itself and creating havoc in its environment. They still believed that the trigger factor to a poltergeist infestation in most cases was intense stress within the host, and that if the cause of the stress was neutralised then the polt would likely disappear.

All of the above may or may not be true; but again, on reflection, the authors can see that they made a number of unwarranted assumptions that prevented them from understanding the nature of the poltergeist more accurately. Part of this book will be devoted to rectifying this defect. As the reader will see, there were a number of incidents that forced the authors to re-evaluate their understanding of one of the world's most baffling – and terrifying – enigmas. What they discovered made them more disturbed, not less. If they believed that the entity known as the poltergeist was truly malign before, they now came to see that it could, at the apex of its power, be nothing short of terrible.

Two
THE POLTERGEIST AT WORK

Towards the end of the authors' investigation of the South Shields Poltergeist, a series of incidents occurred which, like everything the entity did, were both bizarre and intimidating. These incidents did not cause the authors to re-evaluate their understanding of the poltergeist, but with hindsight they should have done.

One of the principal experients at Lock Street, Marc, worked as a chef at a residential establishment in Newcastle upon Tyne. Coincidentally, his partner Marianne, the other principal experient, also worked at the same location but in a different capacity.

Marianne told the authors that, on one occasion, she'd entered the kitchen area where Marc worked and noticed that he'd placed a stack of dinner plates on a work surface. There was nothing at all unusual about this, and so she didn't give the matter a second thought. She then turned around and switched on an electric kettle before leaving the kitchen. As she made for the door, something caught Marianne's eye. The pile of dinner plates was now upside down. This startled her, as they had only been out of her line of sight for a matter of seconds. Someone – or something – had apparently lifted up the entire stack and inverted it. She knew that no one had entered the kitchen area whilst she was there, and later stated categorically that due to her close proximity to the workbench it would have been impossible for someone to do this in absolute silence and without drawing her attention. It took her very little time to realise that the polt was at work.

Over the next few days, other incidents took place of a similar nature. Plates, cups and saucers would be moved around – sometimes when neither Marianne nor Marc was present. On one occasion an entire collection of cutlery was removed from its normal resting place and deposited upon a work surface – again, whilst the witness's back was turned for mere moments.

According to Marc and Marianne, it wasn't long before other members of staff began to report strange things happening. One worker kept shutting a window, only to find it open minutes later. This happened repeatedly within the space of an hour. Whether Marianne suggested to her colleagues that these bizarre phenomena may have been the work of a poltergeist or not we do not know, but she told the authors that, on one occasion, every employee in the building had became sufficiently unnerved to the point where they all vacated the premises and stood outside one of the secondary entrances. As they huddled together discussing the situation, a pair of scissors plummeted from above and hit the ground with a clank. The only place the scissors could have came from, the couple suggested, was an office window directly above where the workers were standing. Marianne knew that the office was not in use – something she substantiated when she immediately re-entered the building and checked.

Perhaps the most bizarre incidents that took place at that location were witnessed by Marc. On one occasion, Marc had been walking along a corridor when a door in front of him suddenly slammed shut. Several other times that morning the same thing happened – the door would either slam shut or at the very least move without any human assistance. Marc actually filmed the door moving with the camera facility on his mobile phone. On another occasion, also at his place of work, he filmed a figurine on a shelf moving back and forth several inches – also without any human intervention. When these incidents occurred at Marc and Marianne's workplace, the poltergeist activity at their home had to all intents and purposes ceased. The authors were forced to consider the possibility that their efforts to rid the family home of the entity had been largely successful, but that the polt was now focussing its attention on the experients' place of work where it could carry out its activities relatively unhindered. The thought crossed Darren's mind that the "stand-by" electricity that the polt had been utilising at the Lock Street abode had been essentially cut off, thus forcing the polt to find its energy source elsewhere - perhaps at the principal experients' workplace. This idea seemed to be reinforced by the notion that poltergeists, unlike ghosts, are "person-centred" as opposed to "place-centred". Had the polt simply "followed" the couple to work and became active there because the investigators had made life difficult for it at Lock Street? It seemed a reasonable proposition.

But there was one thing about the events which took place at Marc and Marianne's workplace which intrigued Mike and Darren deeply. They had told them of the time when the cutlery had been removed from its normal resting place and deposited upon a bench. This immediately rang a metaphorical bell with them, and reminded Mike of a case he had investigated several years previously.

On July 29, 1999, the manager of a well-known restaurant in South Shields contacted Mike and asked him if he would visit his premises. The staff were being "frightened by something", and he wasn't sure what to do about it. Quite simply, it seemed as if the place was haunted.

There were essentially four different phenomena presenting themselves at the restaurant. Firstly, staff would report hearing footsteps coming from the upper floor. On investigation, however, they would find no one there. Secondly, the workers were becoming increasingly frustrated at the number of artefacts and objects that were suddenly going missing. The chef had "lost" several expensive knives, crockery was disappearing and, on one occasion, two wineglasses disappeared from a table right in front of the astonished diners. The third phenomenon concerned a number of candles. It was customary for waiters to place a lighted candle on each table to give the restaurant a warmer, more romantic ambience. After the diners had left, a member of staff would blow the candle out. However, on an increasing number of occasions staff found that the candles would automatically re-light themselves. I asked the manager whether he and the others could have been the subject of a practical joke, for self-igniting candles can be purchased quite cheaply from novelty shops. He rejected this suggestion outright. He had bought the candles personally, and could vouch for the fact that they were of the conventional kind and not "joke items".

However, it was the fourth phenomenon that intrigued Mike when he compared it to what had happened to Marianne and

Marc in their workplace. The restaurant manager told Mike that the previous evening the chef had been working in the kitchen - alone - when he turned around and found to his astonishment that all the cutlery items had been removed from the large trays where they rested and placed upon a workbench. This frightened him, because he was alone in the room and, according to the manager, it would have been quite impossible for someone to enter without his knowledge, let alone displace a veritable mountain of steel cutlery without being seen or heard.

Later, when Mike was told about a poltergeist doing exactly the same thing in front of Marc, he was intrigued by such an uncanny parallel. Had it not been for the fact that both incidents bore the hallmarks of paranormal activity, one would have been forced to assume that a mischievous human being was responsible. Further, such a specific act - removing cutlery from a tray and placing it upon a bench - would normally lead one to believe that *the same* person had been responsible.

As Mike mused upon the two incidents further, he realised that there were other parallels. The South Shields Poltergeist had a fascination with candles, and Marc had stated that, on one occasion, he had blown out a candle which "it" (the poltergeist) had lit only for it to promptly and mysteriously re-ignite. At that time Mike had forgotten about the parallel incident in the restaurant years earlier. The South Shields Poltergeist also used to make objects disappear, too, including tea cups and beer glasses. Finally, just like the entity in the restaurant, one could often hear "it" walking around upstairs. All in all, then, in many respects both entities had matched each other's antics perfectly. And yet, the authors were still working on the assumption, which seemed quite natural at that time, that not one but two poltergeists were at work.

This enigma was to be pivotal in both Mike and Darren radically re-appraising their understanding of the poltergeist enigma.

Three
PRINCIPLES OF CONTAGION

In the physical world, the process of infection and contagion is well understood. Our planet is literally teeming with untold numbers of bacteria, viruses, fungi and protozoa which can, under the right conditions, invade our bodies and cause sickness. All invading microbes have the ability to compromise our immune systems to some degree. Sometimes, the damage will be so slight that we may be unaware that anything is wrong. Other times, such infections may kill within hours. The methods used by invading organisms to find their way into our bodies vary. Some are airborne and can be inhaled. Others are transferred from one person to another when body fluids are exchanged. Some are ingested with tainted food and water. However, the relevant factor is that, in almost all cases, the recipients of an invading microbe will, if the organism is allowed to take hold, display the same set of symptoms. This is why medical personnel can sometimes identify infections purely by observing the visible symptoms even before blood tests are carried out.

No one would now doubt the reality of physical infection. We also know of ways in which the rate of infection can be slowed down or even halted altogether. Good hygiene, inoculation, medication such as antibiotics and anti-viral agents – all of these have a part to play. However, we should remember that it isn't that long ago when the entire concept of communicable disease was dismissed as nonsense by the world's most eminent medics. It was the Persian Avicenna who first understood the concept and popularised it back in the 11th century. Avicenna was also the first person to suggest quarantine as a means of reducing the spread of disease. But it was not until the time of Louis Pasteur, in the 19th century, that the idea of contagion as we understand it became widely accepted.

It seems, then, that as long as we restrict ourselves to observing the physical world we will get little or no opposition when we suggest that disease can be spread from one person to another, or from one infected substance to a living organism. But it is different when we enter the realm of the non-physical. Take a stroll across the psychic or spiritual landscape and you will find scientific open-mindedness far, far less accessible.

However, if we just pause for a moment and give the matter some thought, we will see quite easily that the concept of contagion is obviously not something that is restricted to the world of the flesh. Surely we all know of cases where a depressed person has, through their behaviour and actions, caused those they live or work with to become morose too. Conversely, the presence of an upbeat, positive-minded person can cause those in close proximity to embrace a better outlook. When we say that a person's presence is "a breath of fresh air", what we mean is that when they are present those around them feel better. How often have we heard a person's sense of humour described as "infectious"? Emotions, then, can be contagious also.

On a broader front, we also must recognise that ideas and concepts can be contagious. Communism, capitalism, socialism, racial hatred (or tolerance), sexism, atheism, theocracy and democracy are all ideas that, for good or ill, had their origins in a fixed place and time and spread out far and wide, sometimes "infecting" many millions of people across the globe. Sometimes, cultural traits can infect entire generations of a particular family. A good example of this is the scourge of domestic violence. It is well known that the children of perpetrators of domestic violence are more likely to engage in such behaviour themselves during adulthood. Domestic competence is another good example. Mike's wife is an excellent cook, and still uses recipes given to her by his paternal grandmother. These recipes were given to her by her own mother, and so on. Contagion or infection may be a good thing or a bad thing, then, but it is certainly not restricted to the invasion of living organisms by microbes. In its broadest sense, contagion can simply be described as "the spread of things". We may not always understand the mechanism, but it happens nonetheless.

When we enter the world of poltergeist infestation, then, we should not be too surprised to find evidence of contagion there, too. After all, our own world is filled with contagion – physical and non-physical – and the poltergeist operates within our world to a very large degree. What we need to do is look for evidence of such poltergeist-based contagion and, if we find it, determine what form it takes.

It has long been recognised by researchers that those in close proximity to the victims of a current poltergeist infestation may also become "infected" by the phenomenon, although rarely as intensely. Such contagion is normally both transient and mild. However, the symptoms are usually enough to allow witnesses to conclude that something strange indeed is going on in their abode.

As the authors were investigating the South Shields Poltergeist, they believed they witnessed numerous incidents of such contagion. A detailed account can be found in their book *The South Shields Poltergeist – One Family's Fight Against an Invisible Intruder*, but it would seem appropriate to briefly recount the incidents here.

On Wednesday, 31 August, 2006, when the poltergeist infestation at Lock Street was at its most intense, Mike received a call from a friend. The call was made to Mike's mobile phone just before 2am, but by the time Mike retrieved his phone to answer it, it had stopped ringing. Mike rang his friend back, and was mystified when the man denied making any call to him whatsoever. His phone had been sitting on the dashboard of his car and he hadn't used it in hours. However, when he checked his call log he discovered that his phone *had* made a call to Mike's mobile just before 2am. The obvious mystery was how that phone had, without any human intervention, rung Mike's mobile in the wee hours of the morning. But there was a deeper mystery. Later that morning, when his friend paid Mike a visit, it transpired that at the very time the call was made to Mike's phone, his colleague had been driving past Lock Street – *the abode of the South Shields Poltergeist.*

Of course, it might just have been an extraordinary coincidence, but it certainly made Mike think. As Mike and his friend chatted in the garden, Mike heard his mobile phone ringing in the house. He dashed inside to retrieve it, but once again just didn't get there in time. He looked at the screen and saw "1 MISSED CALL" It was from the very friend he'd just left sitting in the garden. Mike walked outside, holding his mobile in front of him, saying, "You're calling me!"

Mike's friend immediately pulled his mobile phone from his pocket. It was switched off, and yet somehow it had rung Mike's own mobile phone. Just then, Mike received a text message saying that a voicemail had been left for him. He punched in the retrieval number and, to his astonishment, found that the "message" was actually a recording of the conversation that his friend and he had just had in the garden!

Another example of such contagion occurred on 24 September. Mike and Jackie were at a house-warming party held by their two friends from Orion TV, Bob and Marrisse Whittaker. Mike and his wife stayed over at their friends' home after the party had finished, and during the night they were startled by a tremendous crash upstairs where Bob and Marrisse were sleeping. They later found out that when the couple had awoken with a start, they were amazed to see a phosphorescent ball of green light hovering in their room. Bob and Marrisse had been to the house in Lock Street earlier to interview Marianne, one of the principal experients.

One of the most sinister examples of contagion concerning the South Shields Poltergeist occurred when the authors sent examples of handwriting left by the polt at the house in Lock Street to a respected graphologist for analysis. As she looked over the pictures in the garden of her London home, she suddenly became aware of a "presence" behind her. She said she could "sense" that the presence was that of a tall man wearing a long, dark coat. Her description was identical to that given by Robert*, the young child who lived in the house at Lock Street, who had also seen the entity on numerous occasions. The graphologist was deeply disturbed by this incident.

Those at "Ground Zero" - the Lock Street home of Marianne, Marc and Robert – had been subjected to a sustained, incessant barrage of poltergeist activity. However, many of those around them – family members, friends and investigators – had also experienced brief periods of poltergeistry shortly after visiting the house in question. Some, like Mike's friend, had not even visited the house up to that point, but merely drove past it. It was as if the polt was able to infect those who, directly or indirectly, had somehow been in contact with the family at the centre of the disturbance.

The concept of poltergeist contagion is not a new one, but it seems reasonable to suggest that the mechanism by which such contagion takes place has little or nothing in common with the means by which physical diseases are transmitted from one person to another. Poltergeists are not bacteria or viruses, but it seems that they can still infect those with whom they come into contact. The common denominators in such cases seem to be either close physical proximity to the person who is the focus of the main infestation, or, alternatively, a direct or indirect link with them. In the case of the latter, it seemed to the authors as if the poltergeist was able to reach out through a chain of individuals. A good analogy is the way in which a "round robin" e-mail can be sent by one person to another, who then may forward it on to his or her own friends, and so on. There may be no direct contact between the first sender of the e-mail and the last recipient – they may even live on different continents – but everyone who receives the e-mail will "experience" the same message. All that is necessary is that each person in the chain is connected to one other person in it. Poltergeist contagion is uncannily similar. All that seems to be necessary for a person to experience polt contagion is that they are part of a chain of people which, directly or indirectly, leads back to the principal experients.

Having established a *prima facie* case that poltergeist contagion does seem to take place, the next question would logically be, how? As far as the authors can see, there are two possibilities. We may call these hypotheses *passive contagion* and *active contagion*.

Passive contagion is the process of infection at work, but without a driving intelligence behind it. If a person happens to be suffering from, say, Hepatitis A – an incredibly virulent infection – they may drink from a glass and leave traces of the virus on the rim. If someone else inadvertently drinks from the same glass, they could easily be infected with Hepatitis A themselves. This is passive contagion, because the person responsible did not knowingly infect the person who drank from the glass afterwards. They did not intend for them to be infected and devised no dastardly plan to make such a thing happen. The virus itself did not knowingly infect the person either. There is a process at work by which the infection was transmitted, but no guiding intelligence making it happen. Active infection is different, and requires a guiding intelligence to complete the transference of a disease from one person to another. A perfect example involves the dreaded HIV virus. Often the disease is passed on passively, by a person who is not even aware that they are infected themselves. Neither the recipient nor the "donor" knows that the risk of infection is present, because neither of them are aware that one of them is already playing host to the deadly virus. However, from time-to-time reports appear in the press of individuals who, knowing full well that they are HIV-positive, still engage in high-risk sexual activity with others. In some cases, criminal charges have been brought against those who have purposely infected others with HIV. One such case involved a man who deliberately engaged in sexual intercourse with a former partner. Later he confessed that he had *wanted* to infect his victim with HIV so that, "he could suffer like I was suffering". Such cases, tragic though they are, are examples of *active* contagion; the infection is not accidental – it is designed to happen. The authors think that both forms of contagion may be at work in the poltergeist phenomenon.

Although our knowledge of the poltergeist is at best nebulous, we can see that it seems to operate by a set of "rules" or at least *behavioural patterns*. The poltergeist will throw objects around in a family home, but it will not apply for a nursing job in a local hospital. It will make banging and thumping noises in a bedroom, but will not sing opera at the Albert Hall. Like human beings, the poltergeist is imbued with characteristics that identify it for what it is – a poltergeist. There's an old saying, "If it walks like a dog, barks like a dog and wags its tail like a dog – well, it's probably a dog". The same principle holds true of the poltergeist.

The problem with the poltergeist is that it represents a type of existence that we know little about. Probably, its type of existence is unique. It isn't physical, and yet it operates comfortably within the physical world. In fact, it often seems to manipulate the physical world far better than humans can. It isn't a purely psychological phenomenon, either, as the poltergeist undoubtedly enjoys some form of objective reality. Enigmatically, though, it operates very much on a psychological level. Because we are dealing with a phenomenon that is unlike any other we have encountered, it makes it extremely difficult to be predictive. By way of example, let us imagine that, tomorrow, a new species of monkey was discovered in North Africa. In one sense it could be said that we know absolutely nothing about the new species as we have only just encountered it, but on another level it can be said that we know quite a bit about it. For starters, we know that it is a monkey and we can predict with confidence that, although it is an entirely new species, it will exhibit many traits found in other types of monkey. We can also predict that it will share many common characteristics of mammalian life. It will eat, breathe, procreate and sleep, for instance. We are able to predict these things because it has a context in which it can be set, and that context tells us much before we have even studied the new species in any way. The poltergeist is different, because we simply have no firm context in which we can set it at all. All we know about it are the few characteristics of its behaviour that we have been allowed to see in cases that have been studied. These characteristics tell us something, but they do not allow us to make any predictions about aspects of its existence that we currently know nothing about. We are, to use a Biblical maxim, "seeing through a glass but darkly".

Although we cannot make safe predictions about the unknown aspects of the poltergeist phenomenon, we can hypothesise a number of potentials. For instance, the poltergeist phenomenon may include forms of passive contagion whereby certain types of connection with an "infected" person may cause others to be subject to polt-like experiences. This form of contagion may be passive because the poltergeist, whatever it may be, has not *deliberately* caused the contagion to occur. Perhaps there is an unknown but entirely natural process at work which triggers such contagion without the poltergeist deliberately causing it.

But there may also be a form of active contagion at work, too. Because our knowledge of a poltergeist's abilities is so incomplete, we must concede that it may well be able to deliberately precipitate such contagion under certain circumstances. For all we know, an "infected" person may open up a doorway of opportunity for a poltergeist to infect others when they establish certain types of connection with them. In ways we do not understand, a poltergeist may be able to *initiate* the process of contagion when a poltergeist host establishes contact with a previously uninfected person. If one sends an e-mail to a friend, it can influence that friend and that friend only within the context of the initial communication. However, if that friend then sends a reply that contains the visible address of another person previously unknown to us, it opens up a doorway of opportunity for us to then contact that person also. Why? Because a set of circumstances has been created which allows us to operate, to do things that we were hitherto unable to do. The same may be true of a poltergeist. By making contact with others, the infected person may be creating a set of circumstances which allows polt-contagion to take place. We may not understand the mechanism of such contagion, but that doesn't mean that it cannot happen. It simply means that there are natural processes at work in this world that we have not yet grasped.

In the final analysis, all we can say with certainty is that people who are connected in some way to victims of poltergeist infestation may then become victims of the enigma themselves. We do not know how it happens, but the authors have seen enough during their research to convince them that it *does* happen, whether we understand it or not.

Four
SHADOWS

As the case at South Shields seemed to be drawing to a close, Darren and Mike began to focus more on their manuscript of *The South Shields Poltergeist – One Family's Fight Against an Invisible Intruder*. They had witnessed the poltergeist at work in the Lock Street house directly, and also a degree of *contagion* when the entity had cast its psychic net further afield and invaded the lives of others less directly connected with the case. Now, the traumatic events were petering out and the experients were seeing the polt cast its last throw of the dice. It seemed to be over – almost.

The publishers scheduled the release of the book for March 30, 2008, and the authors set about creating a collection of pictures to accompany the manuscript. As the weeks went by, both Darren and Mike began to research new cases.

In January 2008, Mike received a call from Steve Taylor, the proprietor of a business called Alone in the Dark Entertainment [AITDE]. Based in Newcastle-upon-Tyne, AITDE specialises in hosting events that mostly have a paranormal theme; ghost walks through Newcastle city centre, corporate events, murder mystery nights, and hen/stag parties. Steve and his colleagues had been organising an evening of paranormal and psychic entertainment which was to be held simultaneously in three well-known public houses – all of them, of course, reputedly haunted - and he wanted the authors to play an integral part in the proceedings.

The three public houses all faced the River Tyne on Newcastle's historic quayside and stood adjacent to each other; *Bob Trollop's, Offshore 44* and *The Red House*. The idea was to pack the three inns full of people who had an interest in the paranormal and give them a night to remember. Psychic mediums would be on hand to provide readings for those who wanted them, and, later, Darren, Mike and another medium would investigate a disused part of one pub that was reputedly haunted by a rather bad-tempered spirit. They'd go up in the dark, night-vision cameras strapped to their heads, and the live-action footage would be relayed down to a series of large screens below. The authors fully accept that this sort of activity cannot be classed as serious paranormal research, and Steve Taylor never claimed that it was meant to be anything other than entertainment. Darren and Mike have no problem taking part in events like this, providing that they aren't presented as something they're not. The "walk in the dark" upstairs was meant to be good fun, scary fun and enthralling. If anything truly paranormal did take place, then it would be an added bonus. Essentially, the whole point of the exercise was to open people's minds to the idea that the world is probably a stranger place than they imagined, and send them away with both a smile on their face and a question or two in their mind.

Entirely coincidentally, AITDE had organised the event to take place on March 30, which was the same day as Mike and Darren's book on the South Shields Poltergeist was being released. The event was not the book's official launch party, but Steve rightly thought it made sense to use the AITDE event to promote the book, and of course the authors agreed. Steve therefore asked Mike and Darren if they would be prepared to give a talk on the South Shields Poltergeist case at the event.

Before the event took place, Steve contacted Mike again and told them that a man from Jarrow, which is not too far from South Shields, had e-mailed him and asked him for some help. Apparently, the correspondent and his family had been disturbed by a series of bizarre incidents that had taken place at their home. At first they'd dismissed them as coincidences, but eventually they reached the point where they could no longer accept that a rational explanation would make sense of things. Something decidedly irrational was going on in their home, and it was worrying them intensely. Steve asked Mike if he'd be prepared to visit the family along with the respected psychic medium Rhianne D'Morgyn. Mike agreed, and asked if it would also be permissible for Darren to attend.

Something struck Mike as strange. The family at Lock Street had comprised of a young couple and one young child. The family at Jarrow also comprised of a young couple and one young child. Also, the events that had been taking place at the Jarrow house had been very similar to those that had occurred at South Shields; knocks, bangs and other strange noises, coupled with incidents of objects being moved from one place to another without anyone in the household being responsible. Of course, most poltergeist infestations begin this way, so the parallels in the symptoms were not surprising in themselves. It just seemed odd that the two families should be so similar. It was probably nothing more than coincidence, he assumed, and henceforth didn't give the matter any further thought.

The event on March 30 went well. The major hiccup in the proceedings was that specialist equipment purchased by AITDE from Japan did not function as planned, and it was no longer possible to do the "walk in the dark" upstairs in the disused part of the pub. Nevertheless the authors' talk on the South Shields Poltergeist went down very well indeed. Afterwards, the crowd milled around and relaxed – buying beer and wine from the bar in copious amounts and generally enjoying themselves. Numerous guests approached Mike and Darren during the night and asked them questions about the South Shields case, which of course they were happy to answer.

One chap, called Norman, said that he'd once had an "unpleasant experience" with a poltergeist.

"It even pinched food from the refrigerator!" he added, as an afterthought.

"It wasn't a pie, by any chance was it?" enquired Mike.

"I think it was, now you come to mention it. Why do you ask?"

"Because the poltergeist at South Shields pinched a pie from the fridge there, too".

"Wow!" said Norman, "What a coincidence!"

"Mmmm...it is, isn't it?" responded Mike, not entirely convinced.

Five
INVESTIGATION AT JARROW

The house at Pallister Street*, Jarrow, seemed completely unremarkable from the outside. It was a terraced dwelling in a street which comprised of a mixture of privately owned and rented residences. Mike was familiar with Jarrow, as he used to go to school there. The school had long since gone, being replaced by a modern housing estate. Other than that, relatively little had changed since he had last visited the place in 1973. Indeed, his local tuck shop was still there, providing local kids with candy and other goodies as it had done for decades. Returning to the location was something of a nostalgia trip.

Earlier in the evening, Mike had packed his bag with various bits and pieces that he always took with him on investigations; a camera, a digital sound recorder, a notebook and a pen. He then took a bath, dressed and fixed an egg and tomato sandwich. At 6pm Darren arrived, and his bag was positively heaving with investigating equipment. Then, at 7pm, Steve Taylor turned up and without further ado they set off for Pallister Street, which was approximately fifteen minutes drive away.

The date of the investigators' first visit to Pallister Street was March 10, 2008. By the time they arrived it was dusk, but they had no trouble finding the house. Only the number on the door distinguished it from all the other residences. It was, as noted earlier, entirely unremarkable from the outside.

Derek* and Mandy* were a pleasant couple. Both were in their early twenties, and they had a young daughter called Ella* who was still less than a year old. Unfortunately, Ella had a really heavy cold and found it difficult to stop coughing. Regardless, she managed a gentle smile as the investigators entered the dining room. Mandy immediately offered her visitors coffee, whilst Derek opened up and told the investigators a little more about what had been going on.

The story had begun when the couple lived in their previous home, a rented flat not too far from their current dwelling in Pallister Street. On several occasions both Derek and Mandy had felt a "presence" in the flat that was hard to articulate, but, they said, "felt very, very real". Both said that whenever they felt the "presence" it did not engender positive feelings in them. It made them nervous and uneasy. They never actually *saw* anything, but they just "knew that something was there".

Several weeks after the couple had become aware of the presence in the flat, other, more disturbing incidents took place. One evening in April 2007, whilst Mandy was heavily pregnant, Derek went into the bathroom and was startled to see that the window was wide open. As the weather was quite inclement, there was no way that either Derek or Mandy would have opened it themselves. They were baffled. Then Derek noticed that something else was wrong. The plastic panel that lined the side of the bath had become detached, and was now simply leaning *against* the bath instead of being fixed in place. With some difficulty, he replaced the bath panel after closing the window. Darren, at this point, thought back to an almost identical incident involving a bath panel that had occurred at the house in Lock St. It, too, had been detached from the bath, and hearing this account made Darren focus more intently upon the strange coincidences that he'd noticed can occur within the realms of poltergeistry.

Several days later Derek again entered the bathroom, but, just as he did so, he thought he could hear his mobile phone ringing. He left the bathroom and went to retrieve his phone, but to his consternation found that it was no longer ringing. He checked the call log, and was puzzled to find no missed calls listed. Just then, he heard the sound of running water from the kitchen area. He walked into the kitchen and was greeted by the sight of the cold water tap over the kitchen sink blasting water into the basin at full pelt. He quickly switched it off. Neither Derek nor Mandy had been in the kitchen, and even if they had, why would they have left the tap fully turned on like that?

"Look, it wasn't like the tap was just *dripping*, or anything", said Derek. "The water pressure in the cold tap was really strong, and when it was turned on fully the water would spray everywhere. That's the way it was when I went into the kitchen. It would be ridiculous to turn on the tap that fully, let alone walk away and leave it like that".

One day in July, after Ella was born, both Derek and Mandy had a disturbing experience in the early hours of the morning. At approximately 3am, Derek awoke for no apparent reason; or at least, he thinks he did. He can't be absolutely sure. To this day he has difficulty recalling whether he was actually awake or asleep, but he distinctly remembers – either in reality or in a dream state – sitting up in bed and looking towards the bedroom door. It was open. To his horror, he could see someone standing in the doorway, silhouetted by the moonlight coming in through the window. Derek said that the person was definitely a male, and that he seemed to be wearing a shroud of some kind with a hood over his head. The really weird thing was that the man's face – or what little he could see of it – was yellow in colour. Slowly, the person staring down at him with hollow eyes just disappeared. Derek was terrified, but, working on the presumption that he was indeed awake, attempted to go back to sleep.

The following morning, Mandy told Derek that she also had experienced something rather disturbing during the night. Although she's not sure of the time it occurred, Mandy endured a short period of sleep paralysis. She had woken up, but found herself unable to move. She lay there, completely paralysed and frightened, until slumber once again overtook her.

Although the steady rise in anomalous incidents disturbed the couple, the worst was yet to come. After the birth of Ella, Derek and Mandy had got into the habit of visiting two close friends on a regular basis. On one such occasion, Sunday September 30, 2007, they returned to their flat and immediately noticed "the presence" that had disturbed them on numerous occasions previously. However, it was when the couple entered their bedroom that they were truly shocked.

The room was incredibly small, and only just wide enough to hold a double bed. In fact, to get into bed Derek and Mandy had to literally crawl across the mattress before climbing under the covers. Strewn across the bed were a pillow, an item or two of clothing, a pair of baby shoes and a rag doll. The couple could not remember whether some of the items had been on the bed when they left the flat, but were adamant that the rag doll and the shoes had not been. However, the most bizarre part of their experience was the fact that baby Ella's cot had been lifted from the floor and placed in the centre of the couple's bed, its legs at perfect right-angles to the mattress it was standing on. Now Derek and Mandy were *really* frightened. After composing themselves, Derek took a photograph of the cot *in situ,* an action for which the authors later complimented him.

The following day, Derek happened to be talking to a neighbour. Troubled by the events of the previous evening, he mentioned some of the strange occurrences that had taken place in their flat. To Derek's surprise, the neighbour then told him some things about the previous tenant that he hadn't known, but which later made him wonder whether they were connected with the experiences which were now beginning to frighten both he and his wife.

According to Derek's neighbour, their flat had previously been rented by a single person; a man who had a severe alcohol problem. The condition had consumed him to such an extent that his health was in an extremely poor state and his behaviour had become decidedly erratic. On occasions, neighbours had been forced to report him both to the police and the local authorities. The man had, seemingly, also been in the habit of leaving his bathroom window open even during bad weather, prompting the question as to whether the mysterious incident when Derek had found the same window open was in some way connected. One of the symptoms that often accompanies alcoholism is raging thirst. The alcoholic tenant of the flat that the couple now lived in had also experienced this, and was forever drinking water from the kitchen tap. The neighbour testified that as the man slowly descended into an almost permanent alcoholic stupor, he took to leaving the cold water tap in the kitchen running permanently as he simply couldn't be bothered to keep turning it on and off. To most people this would seem bizarre, but to the mind of a person whose thinking processes have been so severely damaged by drink it may have made some sort of sense. Derek couldn't help but wonder whether this was connected to the incident when he found the cold water tap in the kitchen fully open, even though neither he nor Mandy had turned it on.

Although neither Mandy nor Derek had mentioned this, Mike

also wondered whether the previous tenant had, in the latter stage of his alcoholism, became jaundiced due to liver disease. This could also have been connected to the ghostly personage that Derek saw standing in the doorway of his bedroom – someone whom he described as having a decidedly "yellow face".

As Derek recited the litany of strange events that had occurred in their previous flat to Darren, Steve and Mike, it was obvious to the investigators that he was deeply troubled – and he had not yet begun to tell them about what both he and his wife had experienced in their current dwelling. At this point, Darren asked if he could set about his regular itinerary of scouting out the various rooms in the house and setting up numerous pieces of equipment. Derek agreed. However, Mike's role would be to interview the couple whilst the other two investigators went about their business. Darren switched on his portable dictation machine on which the interview would be recorded and placed it in the centre of the dining room table. Then both Darren and Steve made their way up the narrow stairwell to the first floor. As they departed, Mike's mind was catapulted back to their first visit to Lock Street. There, too, he had interviewed the couple whilst Darren had went upstairs to set up his camera and other ghost-hunting tools of the trade.

As the tape rolled, Mike started to question the couple about their experiences. Within minutes it became painfully obvious to the researcher that something decidedly odd was going on. With every question posed, the muscles in Mike's stomach tightened further. With every answer provided by the couple, it dawned upon him with ever-growing clarity that he had walked this metaphorical road before. In fact, Mike *knew* what the answers to his questions would be before the couple even articulated them. To be frank, he didn't like what he was hearing one little bit.

After the interview had finished, Mike took Darren to one side and asked to speak to him privately.

"I'm not going to tell you what's on the interview tape, mate; just go home and listen to it. Make sure you're sitting down when you do – because what you hear will knock you for six".

Six
POLT PARALLELS

Slowly, almost painstakingly, Derek and Mandy recited the litany of strange incidents that had occurred since they had left their old flat and moved into their new home in Pallister Street. There had been many.

As had been the case in their previous home, the couple were again plagued by a "sense of presence"; a disturbing sensation that they were not alone. The feeling was not a constant one. Sometimes, days would go by and both Derek and Mandy would sense nothing. Then, without warning, the house would be filled with a dark, brooding atmosphere that was difficult to describe but nonetheless perfectly tangible. The effect that this had on both Mandy and Derek was not identical. Mandy, usually in the company of Ella, would feel frightened and vulnerable. Derek, for his part, would simply become depressed and moody.

In the first days of the couple's residence at Pallister Street, the "presence" was the only thing they noticed. But then "it" started to play tricks. One evening, Derek and Mandy were sitting at the dining room table when the door to a recessed cupboard suddenly swung open. Thinking that the movement may have been caused by a draught, Derek simply walked over to the door and shut it again. No sooner had he sat down than the door swung open a second time, but only more forcefully. This time the couple became afraid. Desperate to find a rational explanation, Derek ran his hand up and down the adjacent door which led into the kitchen, hoping that he would feel a draught which would explain why the cupboard door had "blown open". There was no draught. Whatever had opened the door, it had not been simply a gust of wind.

Several days later, Derek began seeing things "out of the corner of my eye". When the investigators asked him to describe exactly what it was, he was unable to tell them.

"I'm not really sure, to be honest. Suddenly I'll just be aware of something on the edge of my line of vision. It's just like a faint shimmer, or movement, but as soon as I turn my head it'll be gone. I can never see it clearly".

Mandy was having similar, although not identical, experiences. For a fraction of a second she would see what looked like the "shadow of a man" standing in the corner of the room, but before she had time to focus on it, it would disappear. It reminded Mike of the "subliminal messages" that American companies were alleged to splice into movies back in the 50s; a split-second instruction that read something like, BUY POPCORN NOW or BUY HOT DOGS NOW. The message – so the story goes – was only flashed onto the screen for .15 of a second, and did not register with the conscious mind of the cinema-goer. However, it remained on the screen just long enough for the *subconscious* mind to digest it – and prompt the unwary victim to go to the refreshment booth and stock up on goodies during the interval. To our knowledge, the story is nothing more than an urban legend and probably never occurred. However, the analogy holds good when compared to Mandy's experiences. The only difference is that the visions of "the shadow man" *did* remain long enough for her conscious mind to embrace them, but not long enough for her to focus on any detail.

Perhaps the most disturbing events were what the couple referred to as "the voices". Sometimes, when they were downstairs, they would hear what sounded like "deep, male voices" coming from upstairs. They could never make out the words, but there was no doubt in their mind that they *were* human. On other occasions they would hear footfalls in the bedrooms upstairs. Several times Derek dashed up the stairwell and searched the bedrooms, but he never found anything untoward.

The cupboard door opening, the voices, the "shimmers" detected just on the outskirts of the peripheral vision...these all occurred regularly if not frequently. However, there were also a number of "one-off" incidents that didn't fit any particular pattern. In most poltergeist cases, the infestation will begin with unexplained "bangs" or "raps" of unknown provenance. Mandy and Derek's new home was subjected to such phenomena, but on a very random basis. When the unexplained noises did occur, they were not similar to others. Regardless, they disturbed the couple to a great degree. Other incidents included a number of household objects, including a coffee cup and a book, being moved from one location to another, although Derek admitted it was just possible that either he or Mandy may have moved them and simply forgotten. There were other incidents that the couple related to Mike during their taped interview earlier. These, of great significance, will be dealt with in a later chapter.

As the conversation with the couple continued, there was a knock at the door. It was Rhianne D'Morgyn, the psychic medium brought in to the investigation by Steve Taylor. Rhianne is young, attractive and does not fit the stereotypical public image of a spirit medium. She has a bubbly personality and an infectious sense of humour. As soon as she entered the living room she smiled and introduced herself to the couple's young daughter, Ella. After some casual chit-chat she then asked if she could have a look around the house to "see what she could pick up". Just prior to her arrival, Mike had placed his digital sound recorder in Ella's bedroom upstairs in an effort to record any anomalous noises that may have presented themselves to the investigators. This act later sparked a great deal of amusement amongst the researchers, as the reader will soon see.

Darren, Steve and Rhianne wandered upstairs, whilst Mike continued to talk to the couple downstairs in the dining room. Rhianne says that it's important to sense spirit energies when she "reads" a dwelling, and whilst standing on the landing at the top of the stairs she confessed to feeling rather uneasy. She also said she felt somewhat disorientated, as if she was "tipping over". Mike was intrigued, as he'd felt exactly the same sensation in that location earlier. A short discussion ensued with Darren and Steve. Then, just as Mike was ascending the stairwell to join them, Rhianne announced that it was getting a little crowded and that she needed some space. The other investigators were asked to go back downstairs whilst she went about her business.

Later, Rhianne said that she could sense the presence of a number of spirits, including that of a rather portly woman who had suffered from heart problems and may well have died in the house. She made no comment as to whether she believed that these spirits were in any way connected with the paranormal phenomena taking place within the home. Mike's instinct at the time was that there was probably no connection, but he couldn't be sure.

Later in the evening, after the bulk of the preliminary investigation was over, everyone gathered in the dining room for a final review of the night's events. As the conversation proceeded, it was suddenly interrupted by a loud *thud* that seemed to come from upstairs. Mike quickly ascended the stairs and did a quick check in each room. Everything seemed to be in order, but one thing caught his eye. Derek and Mandy have a computer in their bedroom which stands on a small desk. Mike noted that the desktop was visible on the screen, and that no screensaver was active. There were only two reasons for this that he could think of; either the computer was not configured to employ a screensaver when not in use, which is unusual, or someone had just recently used the computer and the screensaver had not yet engaged itself. He made a mental note to look into this further on their next visit.

Mike made his way back downstairs and rejoined the others. However, after a few minutes Steve Taylor looked startled and said that he was sure he'd heard a voice coming from upstairs. Rhianne said that she'd heard something too, but that she couldn't be certain what it was. Darren did a quick check upstairs, but everything was in order. Later, Mike asked him if he'd noticed whether the computer's screensaver had been activated when he'd entered the main bedroom, but Darren couldn't recall.

During the conversation, the couple's young daughter, Ella, was sitting happily in her high chair eating. Her cough seemed to have subsided somewhat, and she appeared to be quite content. Then, however, Mike noticed a change. The toddler sharply turned her head towards the corner of the living room where the TV stood, and stared. Then she became quite animated and stretched out her hand, as if trying to reach for something- or perhaps someone. Mandy noticed this, too.

"Does she often do that?" asked Mike.

"All the time", replied Mandy. "It's as if she can see someone and is reaching out to them. Sometimes her head turns and it's as if she's following someone as they walk across the room. It's weird".

Mike and Darren really liked Derek, Mandy and Ella. They were a happy, contented family unit. However, both investigators felt that there was something decidedly odd about their home in Pallister Street, and the "vibes" they were picking up inside the dwelling were decidedly negative ones. Later, they'd find out why.

The day after the investigation, Mike listened to the audio recording he'd made in Ella's bedroom. At first, all he could hear was the sound of Rhianne, Darren and Steve chatting outside on the landing. Mike listened intently as Rhianne related what she was "picking up" psychically, before giving Darren a number of "spirit messages" that she had received and felt obliged to pass on to him. Then Mike heard a faint but distinct *click*. The conversation continued, interspersed by several more *clicks*. Darren, Steve and Rhianne then walked into Ella's room where Mike's audio recorder was. Now that they were standing in close proximity to it, the recording seemed to be much sharper. More *clicks*, only louder this time. At one point, a succession of clicks interrupted the conversation; indeed, they were so loud that he was amazed that none of those present in Ella's room had commented upon them at the time. Unless they hadn't heard them, of course, which was a puzzle in itself. Later, Mike replayed the sounds to Darren, who was just as mystified as his colleague.

"It's strange. I can't recall hearing anything like that at all. Hey...just a minute! I've just remembered, when Rhianne, Steve and I were talking on the landing my digital camcorder was running. I'll have to check through the footage and see if anything showed up. Who knows...maybe we'll find out *exactly* what those clicks were", Darren said.

Darren's words were prophetic. The researchers did indeed find out the cause of the mysterious clicking sounds. Rhianne, the medium, happened to be holding a ballpoint pen as she chatted to Darren and Steve. At one point on the footage she can be seen absent-mindedly clicking the top of the pen as she conversed. Nothing more than the sort of idiosyncratic nervous habit that all humans display every day of the week, then, and certainly not the poltergeist at work! Darren and Mike were slightly disappointed that the noises had not been something more exotic, but laughed heartily at the irony of the situation.

"It's the first time I've ever encountered a ballpoint *pen*tergeist!" quipped Mike. Darren subsequently groaned at Mike's attempt of a joke.

Although there was nothing at all unusual to be heard on the audio recording made by Mike – except for the "pentergeist", that is - Darren had still to listen to the recorded interview made earlier. On returning home on the night of the first visit, Darren unpacked his ghost-hunting equipment and put it away in his office, making sure to leave out his video camera and dictation machine. It was rather late when he arrived home that evening - much later than he had anticipated - and Jayne, his partner, had already gone to bed as she had an early start at work the following morning. Quietly, Darren crept around the house trying not to awaken Jayne or their daughter. Finally, he decided to make himself a bite to eat before going to bed. A sandwich, made with some chicken left over from lunchtime, seemed like a good idea. As Darren buttered two slices of bread, he was disappointed to hear footsteps coming down the stairwell. *Damn,* he thought, *I must have woken up Jayne after all.* Then, a sudden "sense of presence" overcame Darren and he just *knew* that an angry Jayne was standing in the kitchen behind him ready to let him have it with both barrels for disturbing her slumber. Cringing, and thinking he was in for an ear-bashing, he turned to say sorry for waking her up - only to find no one there. Other than himself, the kitchen was empty. Darren walked into the hall, stood at the bottom of the stairwell and stared upwards into the shadows.

"Jayne...?" he called out

No answer.

"Jayne...you there?"

Still no answer. Puzzled, he then began to climb the stairs wondering what was going on. His heart was beating loudly in his ears, and he was suddenly overcome with an overwhelming feeling that Jayne was still sound asleep in bed. He opened the bedroom door, peered in and - sure enough - there she was lying sprawled across the king-size double bed, fast sleep. Darren was glad that he had not disturbed her, but he couldn't help but wonder just who had came down the stairs and stood behind him in the kitchen. He knew that *someone* had been there. And then it dawned on him. *My God*, he thought to himself, *I hope I haven't brought anything back home with me.*

Rather nervously, Darren ate his food, brushed his teeth and went off to bed. Before he knew it morning had arrived, and all was normal. Darren and Jayne rose from their bed to the sound of their daughter Abbey shouting and singing from her room. She had been awake since 5am, and was impatient to go downstairs and watch children's TV before heading off to spend some time with her child-minder, as Darren and Jayne both had to go to work.

"Good night last night?" Jayne asked.

"Yeah, interesting..." Darren replied, studiously omitting to mention the incident that had taken place in the kitchen the night before.

Several days came - and went. Because Darren is a very busy man due to both work and family commitments, he didn't have an opportunity to listen to the tape-recorded interview made at the house on Pallister Street until the following Sunday afternoon. Jayne had taken their daughter out to see "mamar" as she called her grandmother, and Darren had the day free. As soon as he had the time, he retrieved the dictation machine from his study and took it downstairs.

Darren put the kettle on and made himself a cup of tea. Then he walked into his living room with note pad and pen, sat down and pressed the "play" button on his recording device. The reels on the tape recorder began to chug round and round and soon a gentle hissing noise could clearly be heard. Darren sat and waited, and waited, and waited some more. No interview, but merely the steady hiss of what sounded like a blank tape. Puzzled by this, Darren fast-forwarded the recording only to find nothing at all. Annoyed and upset, he concluded that somehow he must have stuffed up the recording and never actually taped anything. Then a thought struck him; prior to coming home, the tape had been tested and the interview was definitely there. So where was it now? Darren remembered listening to a small part of the recording before rewinding the tape (side A) back to its beginning so listening to it another day would be made easy. He then double-checked the cassette recorder and took out the tape. To his utter surprise he found that not only had the tape been fast

-forwarded to the end of side A, the tape itself had been turned around inside the machine so side B was ready to play. Side B was blank, and that is why the constant *hiss* was heard rather than the recorded interview. But how could that have happened? Darren distinctly recalled re-winding side A of the cassette after the recording at the house, but he was 100% certain that he hadn't turned the tape over.

Later he commented, "I just don't make mistakes like that. I'm very meticulous with what I do and I would have remembered doing something like that. Furthermore, there was no need for the tape to be on side B as it was completely blank. It just doesn't make sense".

This odd occurrence set Darren thinking about the night he had returned from the infected house. He had experienced several enigmatic incidents. He recalled the footsteps he'd heard coming down the stairs, and also the "sense of presence" he'd experienced in the kitchen. Had some kind of paranormal activity actually taken place within his own home? If so, there was only one explanation that sprung to mind; *contagion*. Darren had told Mike that he had been free from contagion during the last investigation at South Shields although this was not strictly true. Darren *had* been subject to attentions of the Lock Street polt at his home, but for reasons that will be made clear later in this book, had kept it all to himself. Once again the thought overwhelmed him like a dark, brooding cloud. It dawned on him that if this *was* the case, and contagion *had* been experienced again, albeit only a little, then the entity at Pallister Street might very well be a poltergeist. Although the investigation at Pallister Street was only in its early days, this thought disturbed Darren. He decided to rewind the tape back to where it had originally been left, at the beginning of side A, and play it. This time, the interview that Mike had carried out with Derek and Mandy was there. Darren sat anxiously, waiting to hear what had transpired during the conversation. After a short pause it began.

"You've lived in the house since October last year?", Mike asked.

The reply was in the affirmative.

"Have you ever had, previous to that, together or separately, a history of any paranormal experiences of any kind? Nothing of any major importance... but anything paranormal, no matter how big or small...anything you may have thought was a bit weird?"

"We'd never seen anything...but we have heard stuff before", answered Mandy.

"Things did happen at the old flat," added Derek.

"Of course this will remain confidential and is strictly for our records only, but have either of you ever suffered from temporal lobe epilepsy or anything like that?"

"No", both Derek and Mandy replied.

"Right.... Okay", said Mike, as he prepared to ask his next question.

At this point on the recording, Darren and Steve can be heard excusing themselves as they left to conduct some experiments on the first floor of the house. Mike continued with the interview.

"Have either of you ever been diagnosed as bi-polar?"

"No".

"Have either of you ever been in a serious accident of any kind, like a car wreck, for example?"

"No"

"You see, all these things have in the past been known to actually trigger hauntings...I won't go into specifics but it...erm, its complicated...but they are relevant. How long were you in the house before the first incident happened?"

"I had the first experience in the first week when I got that feeling at the top of the stairs", said Mandy. Derek then added, "When we moved in, we had to be put up in a hotel for three days and it was basically straight after that we just felt... uncomfortable".

"Why were you in a hotel?"

"Because we had a gas leak," said Derek.

"Do either of you belong to religious families or anything like that?"

"No", both Mandy and Derek replied.

"Right, what was the very first thing to happen here?" asked Mike.

Derek answered first:

"Well I would say the first thing to happen to me was after we had been here a month or so, and I was down here in the living room on my own when I saw a black sort of shape slowly pass by. So I went upstairs rather quickly; that was my first odd experience".

"So, what was yours?" Mike asked Mandy.

"It was, just after a week or so of living here...when I felt a horrible feeling at the top of the stairs. I had never had anything like that before..."

"Like a sense of presence?"

"Yeah...it was horrible, and then..."

"It might be difficult for you, but if you can, try to cast your mind back and tell me how far apart were those two incidents?"

"I would say just a few weeks," responded Mandy. "I never said anything at all to Derek about my experience, as I was staying at a friend's at the time and she thought I was just being silly, so I said nothing to anyone else".

"Did Derek mention his experience to you, then?"

"Yes" said Mandy.

"OK then...if you can cast your mind back...it might be difficult, but don't worry if you can't...but if you can, could you recall whether around that time there was any sort of stress in your house at the time of the sighting? Had you just had a row, were you worried about anything in particular, unpaid bills, debts, trouble at work, anything that may induce a form of stress or anxiety?"

Derek paused, and then said, "I think the only time we suffered from stress was when we were planning the wedding...but that was last December; that sighting happened well before then".

Later, after hearing this part of the interview, Darren commented, "Although the wedding was in the December, they said the sighting happened before that. Doesn't stress occur *prior* to weddings during the preparation for the big day? They moved into their new home in the October – two months before the wedding. To me that would suggest they were, like most people, probably stressed out during the wedding preparations, and that is the period during which Derek saw the 'black shape" move across the room".

Mike continued the interview.

"And what about you Mandy...were you undergoing any form of stress at this time?"

"No...we had just moved in, so we were quite happy".

"So there was nothing at all at the time that was upsetting you, then?"

"No".

"Have you noticed any particular pattern to the things that have happened - like certain areas of the house, or certain times within the day?"

"Well", said Mandy, "the place I normally feel it most is at the kitchen door, the passage, and the top of the stairs on the landing".

"Mine is the kitchen door too", added Derek, "and the landing...and sometimes the main bedroom upstairs...but its mainly the landing for me".

"Okay, so that was your first two experiences...so if you could just explain...how did it develop from there after you saw the black shape, and had the strange sensation at the top of the stairs?"

"Well, to be honest we have both been very scared since, really...and we talk about it every day", said Derek. "There are little bits and bobs [relatively minor occurrences] happening every day now...like Ella...she'll be looking at the door and there is nothing there...and she's smiling and laughing one minute then she gets very serious".

"Have you noticed any of the household items being moved around, like...have you seen them in one place one minute, and then notice them elsewhere in the house?

"Yes....", replied Mandy, "we had a little air freshener thing that had a little fan inside...we left it operating one time and when I returned to turn it off I found there was no bottom on it; it had been taken off somehow - it had to be pulled quite hard to get it off – and we found the bottom smashed all over the floor".

"That's very, very interesting".

"Not only that", said Derek, "but the air freshener was found on a different shelf to the one we left it on; it couldn't have fell and landed the way it did".

"We have also heard things moving while we have been upstairs, too, and we have also heard things in the kitchen - noises that we can't explain", said Mandy.

Derek had also heard noises, but of a different kind.

"I have also heard my name being called out too, every few weeks or so when I am in the house... in fact it happened just 30 minutes before you, Darren and Steve came tonight."

"Where did the voice come from?"

"From upstairs. I was on the PC at the time, and I even replied to it by saying, *What?* It wasn't Mandy, so God knows who it was"."When you think about all the incidents that have happened, do you get any warning that something may be about to occur, or is it with no warning whatsoever?"

"It's always a surprise", said Derek." I sometimes get little feelings...like, its hard to explain; sometimes when sitting upstairs I'd be fine, and then I'd be really scared...as though I am sensing something like someone standing really close behind me".

Mike paused for a moment, and then spoke.

"Now, this probably sounds as though I am splitting hairs, but...you'll get the gist of what I am getting at and see the point. Obviously these things that are happening, we have no reason to doubt you and there could very well be some sort of paranormal activity. There's something going on that is making them happen. Now obviously these things are unnerving...and probably sometimes really scary because there is something going on in the house and you can't control it. It's like someone messing around, just in the same way as if you had a real flesh-and-blood person in the house that you did not want there, wandering around doing stuff without your permission. So we fully understand that. Now the thing is, although you are scared, are you scared because you don't know what is going on, or what is causing it, or is it that whatever it is that is happening seems *designed* to scare you? Do you know what I mean? You see, what I am saying is that...are the things going on in the house frightening you because they appear to be *attempting* to frighten you – can you see what I am getting at?"

On reflection, Mike feels that he didn't articulate his question particularly well. What he was trying to do was establish exactly what it was that was frightening the couple. Was it simply the thought of something occurring in their home that they couldn't explain, or did they feel that whatever was happening was being *deliberately engineered* to scare them?

"Yes, I know what you mean", replied Mandy. "It seems like...you see we are not easily scared; well I'm not, so whatever it is must be *going out of its way* to frighten us...and it's working".

"Okay, can you give us some examples of things that it has

done that would make you think that 'it' was deliberately going out of its way to frighten you?" asked Mike.

"Right", said Mandy. "When we were in the bedroom and we heard something running about in the loft…it was like the sound of a person running about…*thump, thump, thump, thump*".

"Has it ever done anything, or shown any sense of aggression to you in any way, or done anything that makes you think that, whatever it is, it's angry or aggressive? Or is it just confusing you…do you know what I mean?"

"I would just say definitely yes", interjected Derek. "There have been times when I have been in the kitchen…when I open the door and suddenly the door next to the kitchen just flies open".

"But has it ever done anything that makes you think it is angry, like *slammed* anything, or crashed about in an aggressive manner?"

"Yes", Mandy added, "we've heard bangs and thumps coming from upstairs, *deafening* ones too; you would think someone was up there stamping on the floor…that, to me, sounded *very* aggressive. In fact, that night we were going to call the police as we were that convinced there was an intruder in our house. We heard banging from above…that moved around, and then it sounded like it came down the stairs. The *thump, thump, thump*, as it came down the staircase…but there was no one there, and we were terrified. You could say there was an intruder in the house, but an invisible one…"

Darren, at this point, nearly spat out a mouthful of his tea all over the living room floor; he could not believe what he was hearing, the words *invisible* and *intruder* being used in the same sentence. *Talk about spooky coincidences*, he mused. At that time the authors' *book The South Shields Poltergeist – One Family's Fight Against an Invisible Intruder* hadn't even been released. It was just plain weird that Mandy should have chosen to use two words lifted directly from the title of the book. Still, it could have been nothing more than a bizarre coincidence. He also knew that Mike must have cottoned on to what Mandy had just said on the tape – if it really was a coincidence, it was an uncanny one.

The interview continued.

"Do you know anything about who lived in the house before

you?"

"We know...where they live *now*," Derek replied.

"But do you know anything *about* them?"

"Not really, just that they were a normal, nice family"."Mandy, you mentioned earlier on, before the tape recorder was taping, that you felt something touch you on the leg; again that is something that is frightening, but have you ever felt any other of your body parts being touched – say, for example, something like fingers running through your hair?"

"Erm...Just when I walked in from the kitchen one time, and I thought Derek touched my behind in a saucy-but-fun way...but he said it wasn't him".

"Have you ever experienced other household objects moving around, either seeing them move with your eyes or finding things out of place?"

"Well", replied Mandy, "it's kinda hard to notice really...with having Ella around, things are everywhere most of the time".

"What about your lights...do they ever flicker, or do you have problems with the electricity in the house?"

"Funny you should say that", said Mandy, "The light in the hallway is always "blowing", and we have to keep changing the bulbs and fuses".

"Okay...have you ever come home to find a light on that had been left off, or a light off that had been left on?"

"Don't know...we don't really keep a record...and I can't remember any such instances anyway", said Mandy.

"Nah..." added Derek. "Most things we notice are mainly the noises and that, and the *sensing* of stuff."

Then Mandy mentioned something that struck the investigators as odd.

"It's just the constant dreams, the nightmares I am always having. *They* get me!"

"Dreams? That's interesting" said Mike. "Can I ask you - only as far as you feel comfortable - can you give me some examples of your dreams please?"

"The first one...seemed so real, but it *must* have been a dream. In the dream I was asleep...then...then I [dreamt that I] woke from it to find I was sitting in bed, although the bed was in a different place. I looked over to where the computer chair is...and it moved about three feet across the floor by itself. I couldn't remember if it was real, or if it was a dream, so I just put it down to being a dream."

"In another dream, I came downstairs and went into the kitchen. When I opened the door something invisible pushed me hard, and I fell into the wall behind me. It was terrifying".

"And this *was* a dream?"

"Yeah, I always dream that I am asleep, and I wake up…when it happens".

"Have you ever suffered from any sleep disorders such as narcolepsy or cataplexy, or anything like that?"

"No, I don't think so", Mandy said.

"What about *sleep paralysis*, when you wake up and find you can't move, and it feels someone is holding you down in your bed?"

"*Yeah*…that *has* happened to me a few times", Mandy said. "The worst one I've had - it was a *night terror* - was when I woke up one night. This happens quite a lot, and I found I could not move a muscle. It felt like someone was holding me down; it was a horrible feeling…the worst bit was when I heard a man's voice growling and whispering right in my ear", said Mandy. "I woke up crying that night".

"Can you remember what was said…. in your ear?"

"No, I couldn't understand it" Mandy replied.

"It's funny you mention that", added Derek, "because I remember a night in the old flat when we both had a night terror at the same time and we were *both* paralysed in our beds. We looked at each other in sheer fear but could do nothing about it".

"Have you ever felt as though someone was straddling your chest, during these experiences?" Mike asked.

"Yes, I have had that a few times", Mandy interjected, "Not all the time, but sometimes…I have even been pulled out the bed…I mean, *that* can't be a frigging dream, *can* it?"

"This is going to sound bizarre…but have you ever awoke from your slumbers to find that you are wearing different garments from the ones you put on to go to bed?"

"No".

"Have you ever awoke from your slumbers to find that you are covered in scratches or bruises, etc?"

"I'm *always* waking up covered in bruises, aren't I?" said Mandy.

"All the time", confirmed Derek.

"Once I even woke up covered in scratches", added Mandy.

"That's very interesting".

Mike's interest in scratches, and whether they'd ever woken up wearing different clothing, was prompted by his determination to make sure that the investigators weren't dealing with another phenomenon entirely; a peculiar set of circumstances known by UFO researchers as the *Alien Abduction Phenomenon*. People who claim to have been abducted by aliens – and there are literally millions of them – have occasionally claimed that when they woke up after an abduction experience they found themselves wearing apparel different to that they went to sleep in. On a number of occasions they have even claimed that the clothing they woke up in didn't even belong to them at all. However, waking up with scratches is also a common symptom of poltergeist infestation. A really peculiar link to the UFO phenomenon lies in the fact that UFO experients often report poltergeist-like symptoms in their home either just before their sighting, just afterwards – or both. Mike personally investigated just such a case back in 2005. He eventually wrote the story up in his popular WraithScape column *in The Shields Gazette.*

In February of that year, Mike was delighted to get a call from Kelly Barton* of South Shields, Tyne & Wear, telling him that she'd filmed some rather odd objects in the sky. Within two hours he was ensconced upon her living room sofa listening to a very intriguing tale indeed. She surely *had* filmed something rather extraordinary – more of this later - but let's not run ahead of ourselves.

Kelly's strange tale actually began several days previous to her unusual encounter. With hindsight, she now suspects that something truly odd was happening even then, and that the links in the subsequent chain of events may indeed have been connected.

On Monday 14th February, Kelly and her partner Les McFallen* were relaxing in the lounge watching TV when, without warning, they heard the alarm clock go off in the bedroom of their oldest daughter, Julie*. It was 9.30pm, and the alarm should not have activated till the following morning. Les went upstairs and switched it off, noting that Julie was still sleeping. Strange, perhaps, that the noise hadn't woken her.

On Tuesday, Wednesday and Thursday nothing untoward happened, but Friday proved to be a different kettle of fish, as they say. In the early hours of the morning Kelly woke up with a start. The first thing she noticed was that the room was unusually cold. She was just about to go back to sleep when she heard a noise – the sound of her oldest daughter, Julie, running along the passage towards her room. Kelly waited a few seconds, obviously expecting Julie to enter. Nothing happened. Curious, Kelly got out of bed and opened the door. No one was there. She checked on both her daughters, and found them to be sound asleep. Whatever or whoever had made the noise, it hadn't been Julie - and yet Kelly is convinced that it was *exactly* the sound of Julie running along the corridor that she'd heard.

The following morning, Les had been messing around with a novelty gadget that he'd had for years; actually a small machine that makes daft noises – don't ask what kind – but it's the sort of thing guaranteed to liven up a party that's been marinaded in alcohol for several hours. Their two children loved to play with the gadget, as it would inevitably make them laugh hysterically every time they switched it on.

At some point Les left the machine on the bed and went downstairs. Suddenly, just like Julie's alarm clock, it burst into life even though no one had touched it. Les went upstairs, switched off the gadget and brought it downstairs. Neither he nor Kelly could explain why it should have mysteriously burst into life. Les placed it on the window ledge in the lounge and thought no more about it; until later that day when, to their surprise, it suddenly switched itself on again. At the time, the entire family had been in the kitchen.

Sunday got off to an interesting start. The heavy grating which underpins the fire in the lounge suddenly decided to disgorge itself and land with a clump upon the hearth. Other, similar incidents followed for which no obvious explanation was forthcoming.

To sceptics, these incidents probably seem like trivial coincidences for which rational explanations can be found if we only look hard enough. Believers may assume that what the family were experiencing could be labelled as a haunting or a poltergeist infestation. However, to those who believe in the inherent connectedness of all paranormal activity, strings of odd occurrences like this may be seen as the precursors to something far more profound. This was certainly true in the case of the McFallen family.

It is known that those who see UFOs are often subject to strange occurrences just before and/or after the incident. These may include missing time – where the witness inexplicably cannot account for several hours of their life – and poltergeist-like phenomena wherein objects may move without being touched and strange noises can disturb the tranquillity of an otherwise peaceful home. Many experients are subjected to what some researchers call "the Oz Factor"; a strange sense of being "disassociated". Many describe this state as "dreamlike" or "unreal".

Monday 21 February was, according to Kelly Barton, "a normal day". The preceding days had *not* been entirely normal, for the McFallen family had, as detailed, been subjected to a string of unusual occurrences in their home; electrical appliances suddenly bursting into life, strange noises, and so on. Kelly had just returned home from picking up her oldest daughter, Julie, at school. Whilst Julie and her younger sister, Ivy*, were playing in the lounge Kelly went into the kitchen to make the tea. It was, she remembers, 4.30pm precisely. At this juncture the authors will let Kelly narrate the story in her own words:

"The weather had been very volatile that day; cold with snow, sleet and hail showers and bursts of sunshine in between. As I went into the kitchen I noticed that the sky was very dark and completely overcast. I knew another shower was coming and mentioned it to the girls as I went through.

"I suppose I always look at the [north-facing] window when I go into the kitchen", Kelly told me. "It's actually facing you as you enter. Anyway, something caught my eye as I looked out, and I could see eight bright lights in the northern sky above the rooftops behind the house. They were in a rather straggly line – apart from one which was above one of the others.

"They were moving smoothly and at different speeds to each other, but all quite slowly. They were not in formation or moving together, but rather independently of each other. They were all travelling in the same direction, though, which was westwards.

"I noticed the white-coloured lights were bright and shaped

like hockey pucks. They didn't seem close – in fact I got the feeling they were a few miles away, maybe over the River Tyne.

"I ran to open the back door and watched them for a couple of seconds before realising that we'd had the camcorder out and charged up to film the kids in the snow the previous day. I turned to find it. Luckily, it had been left on the breakfast bar behind me, so I picked it up and started filming out of the back door.

"I could see the lights with my naked eye very clearly but I couldn't tell if the camcorder was picking them up as it seemed to have trouble focusing. I carried on filming for maybe twenty seconds as they travelled westwards. They seemed to go further away and I lost sight of them over the rooftops. At the same time a hail shower had started, so I stopped the camera and stepped back in the doorway.

"The shower lasted for about ten to fifteen seconds. After a few seconds I saw one light coming back heading east so I started filming again. Then I saw a second light, slightly higher than the first, which travelled eastwards for a shorter time then seemed to go downwards behind the housetops.

"The birds had started flying again after the hail, and I filmed them for a while, trying to compare them with the objects but could not see any similarities in movement or appearance".

"One of the main things that struck me was that the brightness of the lights was not altered by the two extremes in weather conditions during the time period I watched them".

What Kelly caught on film is anyone's guess, but computer enhancement tentatively verifies her statement that the objects were "shaped like hockey pucks". They were certainly not helium balloons, seagulls or conventional aircraft, the authors would venture.

When Mike interviewed Kelly she clearly recalled the date and time of the incident. To reiterate, it was Monday, 21 February, 4.30pm. Basic information like this is useful, as it helps investigators correlate a sighting with others that may have taken place at the same time.

The question was, had anyone else seen the flotilla of shining, puck-shaped objects that Kelly had immortalised on film?

At exactly the same time as Kelly was filming her real-life flying saucers in South Shields, two members of an East Boldon family were sitting in their living room chatting to a friend. Without warning, an "intense white light" seemed to "burst through the window" and illuminated the entire room for about two seconds. The family and their friends dashed to the window and looked out, but everything seemed perfectly normal. Intriguingly, Mike discovered later that his own mother, wife and son had witnessed this same "intense flash" when he was out of the house. They too lived in the Boldon area.

More intriguingly, a woman shopping in South Shields town centre spotted "several bright lights" in the sky. She watched them drift slowly behind a cloud, fully expecting them to reappear on the other side seconds later. They never did. This sighting also took place at 4.30pm, although there was some ambiguity about the day. The witness said she was "75% certain" she'd seen the objects on the Monday – the same day as Kelly saw her UFOs – but admitted that it could have been the following day. The woman was happy to share her story, but did not want to be identified.

The flash of light seen by the East Boldon witnesses is intriguing, for it came from the opposite direction to where Kelly's "flying saucers" were seen. This phenomenon is puzzling, and doesn't fit into any commonly-recognised category of UFO.

The puck-shaped objects seen by Kelly and the lights seen by the witness in South Shields are not so problematical. As UFO researchers will know, they are often referred to as Daylight Discs and are quite common.

Kelly Barton's footage is some of the most intriguing the authors have ever seen, and Mike appreciated the fact that both she and Les were happy for him to take a copy of it away for analysis. He urged them not to destroy or wipe the original recording.

Before Mike left, he asked Kelly if he could jot down some background details; full names, ages, careers, current illnesses, and so forth. As Kelly talked and Mike scribbled down notes, little Ivy hurtled around the living room at break-neck speed on a small, plastic tricycle. Mike remarked to Kelly how he wished he had her energy. Before long she tired, collapsed on the settee and fell into a deep sleep.

Kelly continued to furnish Mike with details about her background and family life. As she did so, a small, electronic toy belonging to Ivy suddenly burst into life. It had been lying on the floor next to Ivy's "trike", and neither Kelly nor Mike was within arm's reach of it.

"See what I mean?" exclaimed Kelly. "This sort of thing has happened a lot recently".

What connection is there, if any, between the UFO sighting and the bizarre occurrences that troubled the family in the preceding days? If there is a connection, does this imply that it had already been "ordained" in advance – by whom we can only speculate – that Kelly would see and film those mystery objects? Or, could it be that the preceding paranormal phenomena in some way "set up" Kelly psychologically, and perhaps psychically, for the forthcoming sighting? Such philosophical meanderings only serve to lead us into the uncharted regions of the Enigma Zone, of course. Perhaps the only thing we can say with any certainty is that there may very well be a connection, as other UFO experients have been subject to similar phenomena on numerous occasions in the past. However, the exact nature of such a correlation between UFO sightings and the poltergeist phenomenon is still unknown.

Mike later wrote up the family's experience in his *WraithScape* column in *The Shields Gazette.*

Another poltergeist case Mike investigated – and a far more disturbing one – took place near Ryhope back in 1995. Here, there were no UFO-related incidents, but the "scratches" phenomenon was once again apparent.

Mike and his wife Jackie were friendly with the couple. They lived in a converted farmhouse in a pleasant neighbourhood, and life seemed to be reasonably happy for the family until a terrifying series of incidents forced them from their home for several weeks.

The woman in the house, Freda Longthorne*, received a call from a friend one afternoon. The friend told Freda that she was going to attend a show hosted by a celebrity TV medium that evening, but didn't want to go alone. Would Freda be prepared to accompany her, she wondered?

At first Freda was reluctant and refused. She had no interest in spiritualism, and would have much preferred to stay at home and watch TV. However, her friend was persistent and eventually Freda capitulated. She got dressed and made her way to the theatre in Sunderland.

"To be quite honest, I was bored", Freda confessed later. "I just sat at the back and really heard nothing that interested me. Afterwards, I just drove home and thought nothing more about it. Arnold (a serving police officer) and I just had something to eat, watched some TV and then went to bed. He never even asked what the show had been like – I don't think he was interested either, to be frank".

The following morning, Freda and Arnold awoke. Over breakfast, something seemed to have piqued Arnold's attention and he asked Freda "whether the show had been successful".

"Well, I don't think so", answered Freda. "Nothing funny happened that I recall".

"Well, I hope you're right", responded Arnold, "Because I'm beginning to wonder whether you might have brought something home with you".

Puzzled, Freda asked Arnold exactly what he meant. The story he related to her was startling indeed. After they'd both gone to bed the previous night, Arnold and Freda had both fallen asleep. Then, at about 2am, Arnold suddenly found himself wide awake for no apparent reason. Almost immediately, his attention was drawn to a small, glowing light, green in colour, that seemed to be hovering in the corner of the room. As he stared at the object, dumbfounded, it steadily increased in girth until it was approximately the size of a football. Arnold also noticed that there were parts of the orb that were slightly darker than others. He later commented that, "it was as if there was a shape inside the light, but I just couldn't make out what it was".

Just as suddenly, the light disappeared and Arnold was left in the darkness, trying to make sense of what had just occurred. Before going back to sleep – something which he found difficult, naturally, given what had just occurred – Arnold noticed something else. Beside his bed there was a chest of drawers, and on top of it stood an alarm clock. Suddenly the alarm clock burst into life, and Arnold was sure he heard the voice of his disabled daughter shout "Daddy!". According to Arnold, it sounded as if her voice was coming from within the clock itself, over the top of the electronic alarm. It was then that the thought entered his mind – could this bizarre occurrence have something to do with his wife's attendance at the mediumship demonstration earlier?

There really wasn't much that Freda could say. Maybe Arnold had simply had a bad dream. After breakfast the couple went about their business and dismissed what had happened from their minds.

But then it happened again, the very next evening. Arnold and Freda had gone to bed as usual, and after a short while they'd fallen asleep. Then – again at exactly 2am – Arnold found himself awake. The sphere of green light was back in the corner of the room. And it was growing.

Essentially, the sequence of events was an exact repeat of what had occurred the previous evening – but with one difference. Arnold noticed that the "dark patches" within the sphere were more clearly defined now. He couldn't make sense of them, but he felt that he should be able to recognise whatever it was within the light. Before he could make such an attempt, however, the light faded out again as it had done the night before.

The following morning, Arnold – who has sadly died since - told Freda what had happened. This time, she was worried and was beginning to regret going to the display of mediumship at the theatre. Now, for the first time, she was beginning to wonder whether something at the event had "attached itself" to her. At lunchtime the gnawing fear was still with her, and she found herself unable to eat.

On the third night, the orb returned to the farmhouse at its now established time of 2am. This time the "object" within the light was far, far clearer. Arnold could see that it was a human face. Reluctant though he was to do so, he felt honesty was the best policy; he shared his experience with Freda, who was now becoming very, very frightened. The fear she was enduring had killed her appetite, and she didn't eat a thing all day.

On the fourth night, the light returned and the face was clearer still. It was that of an old woman, and she was staring at Arnold intently. He was becoming rather scared too, now, and things weren't helped when the shape within the sphere metamorphosed into a bell shape. Now, instead of just being able to see the old woman's face, he could also see her shoulders. It dawned on Arnold that, with every passing manifestation, the orb of light was slowly but surely becoming more human in shape and size. His stomach turned when he wondered whether, if things persisted, it would eventually materialise into a fully anthropomorphic shape.

Arnold realised that the couple needed help. The problem was that he had no idea where they could get it.

Arnold and Freda breathed a huge sigh of relief the next evening when, for the first time, they both enjoyed a night of undisturbed sleep. However, if they thought that the nightmare was over, they were wrong. It was only just beginning.

Two days later, Freda had just started to pick at her food again, although it was obvious that she'd lost some weight. The day passed uneventfully, and around 11.30pm the couple went to bed. The following morning they both woke up refreshed, but, as they both lay in bed, Arnold related to Freda that he'd had "a really weird dream" during the night.

"You're not going to believe this", he said, "but I actually dreamed that I was wandering around on all fours in the back garden, eating the grass on the lawn! How weird is *that?*"

Freda laughed. Then, Arnold decided to get up and dress. As he sat up and swung his legs over the side of the bed, Freda glanced at him and said, "Arnold, what's wrong with your hands?"

Arnold stared down at his fingers, and gasped in astonishment. His nails were black – ingrained with soil, mud and tiny flecks of green vegetation. His fingers were also covered in scratches. It looked for all the world – and here's the chilling irony – as if he'd been crawling around on a wet lawn. Alarmed, Arnold raced downstairs and checked the doors. They were all locked, the security alarm was still activated and there was no mud or soil to be seen in the hallway or anywhere else, for that matter. Surely, if he'd been sleepwalking then he would have left traces of his midnight perambulation out in the garden? But there were none. There was, in fact, no evidence to suggest that Arnold had left his bed at all after getting into it – and yet his hands were caked in dirt.

This was the second case that Mike knew of in which one of the principal experients had "dreamed" they had been crawling around in the garden. His wife knew of another couple who had gone through something nigh-identical, also after seeing orbs of light in their room, one of which contained a face. The parallel was so extraordinary that Mike became convinced that the same "guiding intelligence" may well have been at work – although he just couldn't see how.

The following morning Arnold again found his hands covered in soil. But this time, unaccountably, his arms – from his wrist up to his elbows – were also covered in deep scratches. What compounded the mystery was the fact that Freda, who was still not eating and was now "a bag of nerves", had hardly slept a wink and knew that Arnold had never left his bed.

Freda was still hardly eating and her weight had dropped dramatically. Neighbours were starting to comment on her milk-white complexion and how poorly she looked. On the night in question, the couple had slept quite well. The following morning, Arnold rose early and checked his hands. They were clean. He washed, shaved, dressed and then left the house to go to the police station for his shift.

Later that day, Freda arrived at Mike's house. Jackie made some tea and the couple listened patiently as Freda poured out her story. She looked ill, and her features were drawn. Whatever was going on in her home, Mike knew that she certainly wasn't faking it. She was absolutely terrified and said resolutely that she wasn't going to go back into her home ever again. That evening, her entire family moved in with Arnold's brother in Darlington. It would be weeks before she'd pluck up the courage to re-enter the house.

Over the coming days, Freda kept in touch with Mike and Jackie by phone. She fed them snippets of information – anything that she thought might help Mike unravel the mystery of why her family had been "targeted" in such a horrific manner. For instance, she discovered that two brothers who had lived in an adjacent cottage many years previously were known to have "dabbled in the occult", and had seemingly been adept at using an ouija board. Their former bedroom looked directly upon the bedroom that she slept in with Arnold. Could there be a connection? Mike felt that it was unlikely. Why would this have brought such calamity not to the house the brothers had lived in, but instead to the dwelling nearby? And why only now? They had lived there for years without any bother. It had only been after Freda's visit to the show at the theatre that they had been subjected to poltergeist-like phenomena.

Over the ensuing weeks, Jackie and Freda became good friends. Jackie made suggestion to Freda that she felt might help.

"Freda, maybe if you go back into the house with a different attitude – a positive attitude, you know, that this thing isn't going to beat you – it might just go away. Have you ever thought about redecorating...maybe giving your home a makeover? Perhaps you should just draw a line in the sand and forget the past".

Freda thought that this was a remarkably good suggestion, but had reservations about its practicality.

"Jackie, I'd love to go back and redecorate...but I'm terrified. There's *no way* I'd go back there on my own".

"Well, what if I was to go back with you? We could both do the decorating together".

Freda agreed. And so it was, several days later, that both Freda and Jackie set about decorating the master bedroom in the farmhouse. Not a single incident of polt-like activity took place, and before long both Freda and Arnold had plucked up the courage to return home. They were determined to give it a try.

For the first few days and nights nothing happened. Freda later said that the atmosphere in the house was "lighter" and she was becoming more and more convinced that Jackie's "positive attitude" suggestion was working. One day, Arnold left for work and Freda found herself in the house alone.

"It was then...at that exact moment...it was then that I knew that whatever had invaded my house had gone. Don't ask me how, but I knew that it had finally gone and that it would never come back".

And it didn't. However, Mike learned a great deal from Freda and Arnold's experience when he reflected upon it later. The "time-slip" incident was certainly not typical of poltergeist symptomology, although it is part of a respected field of study within the spectrum of paranormal phenomena as a whole. More than anything else, Mike learned that no two poltergeist infestations are identical. Each one presents its own nuances and has its own, unique characteristics. This was also proving to be true of the Pallister Street infestation.

Moving on with his interview with Derek and Mandy, Mike attempted to glean yet more background information from them.

"You know when friends visit, or family...or anyone really...have they ever noticed anything strange? Has anyone commented by saying something like "hey, I just saw...?"

"Yeah", said Mandy. Most people that come in...they either

think they see things out the corner of their eyes, or feel uneasy for no apparent reason while being here".

"Are these people aware you think the house is haunted?"

"Just close family", came the reply, "but no one else".

At this point in the proceedings Darren came thundering downstairs and into the room where Mike was interviewing the couple. He asked if a decorative plate bearing the face of the murdered Beatle John Lennon - that Darren had found smashed – had been broken due to the alleged activities taking place in the house. Perhaps to his relief, the couple said no.

"Do you ever have anyone visit the house, probably female, around the age of puberty, like a younger sister, a cousin or someone like that?", asked Mike.

The couple shook their heads.

"Is there anybody that visits this house on a frequent basis that is currently undergoing any amount of stress at this particular time?"

"No, not that we can think of ".

"Do you know what, I think that these troubles here could be *me*!", said Mandy.

"Wherever I have lived I have experienced strange goings-on. My mother was a sceptic until she saw a ghost in my old house when I was a child, growing up; she said it was me, and that I was 'spooky'! So maybe she was right...and they just follow me around. Either that, or I'm extremely psychic!"

Mike pressed ahead.

"Is there a common denominator? And by that I mean do the phenomena occur only when Mandy is here, or only when Derek is here, or does it occur more when one of you is absent from the house...do you know what I mean?"

Derek was the first to answer.

"I've had experiences when Mandy is here in the house, but when she is out they are not as bad, if you know what I mean?"

"Was she at home when you saw that black shape move across the room?"

"Yes, she was upstairs asleep in bed and I was watching the TV".

"Now we never spend time alone in here", Said Mandy. "I used to live on my own in a flat, and was never frightened of being on my own - until we moved into this house. Having said that, things only started when I became pregnant with Ella. There was one night, after she had been born, when we went out for the evening to relax and have a few drinks and a meal. When we came back we found Ella's crib, or Moses basket standing on our bed on its legs! We were terrified, we know it wasn't left like that, and we even took a photograph of it as we couldn't believe what it was we were seeing; you can see it [the photograph] if you want" Said Mandy.

"That would be great", said Mike, "Darren and I would love to see that if you don't mind".

"Another thing is that on the photo you can see all the bairn's clothes on the bed...and a doll just lying on the bed...it wasn't like that when we went out; it was so eerie", Mandy added.

"Do you ever have problems with any electrical equipment in your house? I know you mentioned the fuses before, but this aside...."

Mandy answered. "Yeah, when we moved in a lot of stuff broke and wouldn't work in the new house".

"Could the gear have been broken in transit, during the move?"

"No, they all worked fine before we moved, and we are very careful people that look after our belongings ...anyway, loads of stuff refused to work; what are the chances of them all being broken on the one journey?"

Derek had a point.

"I know", said Mike, "but the questions have to be asked!"

"There were even times", added Derek, "when appliances would work when we didn't want them to...I mean, the kettle would boil up on its own about ten times a day, not so long ago. We would walk past it in the kitchen, and find it bubbling and steaming away".

"The TV has turned itself on, on occasions too – for no reason", Derek went on to say.

"Do you have any mobile phones?"

"Yes, but they don't work anymore", came the reply.

"Does it ever mess around with your phones...I mean, have you went for them and...they aren't there?"

"Oh, *all the time*".

"Uh-huh...have you ever heard noises in the house, and felt as though something has been thrown over and found nothing out of place?"

"Yes", said Mandy, "I sometimes notice things moving like Ella's coat...out the corner of my eyeswhile sitting here watching the TV".

"Going back to the mobile phones...have you ever, to your recollection, found your mobiles *upstairs* in the house after they'd been left downstairs? In other words, does 'it' ever move your mobile upstairs?"

"Yeah...all the time!"

"Fascinating...you see, these questions are not trick questions. We are not trying to catch you out. These questions are giving Darren and I a good indication of what may be going on in your house, the type of activity that is going on, so we are narrowing down and whittling away...you may be thinking, mobile phones upstairs... What are they asking *that* for? It's to give Darren and I more information to go on. Believe it or not, what you have provided us with so far has been brilliant. At this point in the evening we may now have an idea of what might be happening, so the quicker we can work out exactly what is happening, the quicker we can help you deal with it, or at least come to terms with it until it decides to depart from the house...which, if we are correct, we think it will. I am happy to say, but not in all cases that what you have...although it is intimidating and frightening...can be dealt with quite easily. I say *vast majority* of cases; there are exceptions to the rule, and Darren and I just recently dealt with one of the most vicious types of poltergeist you can get, for almost 12 months".

"So could this one be like the last one?" Mandy asked nervously.

"I don't think so, simply because cases like the one Darren and I have dealt with are very, very few and far between. The most vicious poltergeist documented at this level *before* our case was in Enfield in North London, thirty years ago. *Thirty years*! The chances of Darren and I getting another case of this magnitude are very slim indeed, so we think you have nothing to worry about there. In fact, we were discussing this very same thing on our way down here in the car, and Darren mentioned this very fact, that 'We are never going to be this lucky twice in a row'".

"I feel it might get worse," said Derek.

"It *has* been getting worse", added Mandy.

"I feel that whatever it is, it is getting stronger by the day, and I feel it is going to show itself to me...and I don't want it to", said Derek.

"If that happens, rest assured we are here to help you...like we said at the last house we investigated, *we will not cut and run* and leave you. We will stay with you until this thing has passed, and your normal family life can resume. That we promise."

"Thank you", said Mandy, "That means a lot; we don't know where else to go!"

"There will be certain things we can do to help you...methods, techniques, experiments and trials to help you rid this thing from your lives...if it does get worse. If it *is* a poltergeist, it can be dealt with. The word poltergeist probably scares you even when you think about it, but if you knew poltergeists and understood a little of their behaviour - like their patterns and the way they work - or even the modern theories that may explain them, you would not fear them as much. If you do have a poltergeist here at the house, it will be typical of the vast majority of poltergeist cases. It will be a polt - a very low level, sporadic one - that will probably go away in its own time without Darren or I having to do anything but sit it out with you".

Darren admits that the contents of the interview disturbed him. There were certain things said in response to Mike's questions that struck a chord with him. Now he knew why Mike had said, "Listen to the recording, it will knock you for six". What he heard had sent shivers down his spine. Mike had been right. He told Darren that the recording would surprise him, and it had. Echoes of the Lock Street Polt came thundering back to the forefront of Darren's mind. The mobile phones being hidden and then found again later on, the mobile phones being *moved* upstairs purposely by the entity...all echoed the phenomena at Lock Street, including the thundering bangs or "polt raps" that the couple had described as like "having an intruder" in their house". Granted, at this stage the couple didn't even know what polt raps were; and yet the phenomenon was described so ironically by Mandy as like having an "invisible intruder" in their home. *Invisible Intruder* – two words that had been incorporated into the sub-title of their as-yet unpublished book on the South Shields Poltergeist. This case had "poltergeist" written all over it, but the thought struck Darren and Mike like a runaway freight train – was this actually *the* Lock St. Poltergeist making some sort of obscene return into their lives? The authors did *not* want to see the South Shields Poltergeist resurrected.

When Mike and Darren reviewed the evidence, they were startled to see the number of parallels between the South Shields and Jarrow cases. Some were relatively general, but others were incredibly specific, as the following chart illustrates:

	Phenomena Present in Both Cases
1	Windows opening and shutting repeatedly
2	Appearance of anomalous black shapes, shadows or silhouettes
3	Feeling of uneasiness and disorientation at the top of the stairwell
4	Feeling of uneasiness and disorientation by the entrance to the kitchen
5	Sounds of footsteps "running" in the loft
6	Banging and thumping noises emanating from bedrooms
7	Light switch in hallway "blowing"
8	Experients being pushed violently from behind
9	Sensation of being held down by an invisible force whilst in bed
10	Hearing one's name spoken by an invisible entity
11	Appearance of anomalous scratches on experients
12	Finding baby's cot on top of bed in master bedroom
13	Spontaneous switching on of electrical appliances
14	Translocation of mobile phones from downstairs to upstairs
15	Spontaneous ringing of mobile phones when no call is being received
16	Sounds of "something falling or crashing" in an adjacent room, but on investigation nothing is found to be out of place.
17	Articles of clothing moving, as if being pulled or touched by invisible hands
18	Spontaneous opening and closing of recess cupboard doors
19	Household artefacts thrown around, as if by invisible hands
20	Child seems to follow movement of "invisible person" around the room.
21	Turning on and off of taps

22	Disappearance and reappearance of household objects
23	Anomalous sounds of "breathing"
24	Sensations of being touched as if by invisible hands
25	Removing bath panels

Although to all intents and purposes the South Shields and Jarrow cases were entirely disconnected from each other, the similarities between them were simply too great to ignore.

Seven
THE HOUSE ON PALLISTER STREET

More than once in previous chapters the authors have stated that, from the outside, there was nothing even faintly remarkable about the house in Pallister Street where Derek, Mandy and young Ella lived. Inside, however, it is a different matter. There are things about the dwelling that to some would seem truly disturbing, and we will scrutinise these aspects presently. However, there is another element of the investigation that needs to be discussed at this point.

Everyone should have a hobby or interest; something that allows us to leave the workaday world for a short while and indulge in something more enriching. Hobbies and interests are really nothing more than a positive form of escapism, and they can be incredibly therapeutic. Mike, for example, has a passion for restoring badly damaged photographs. Darren, when he is not out investigating ghosts, or writing about them, loves to relax by spending time with his daughter, Abbey, followed by some quality quiet time with a drop of Scotch and a good book. More often than not, these days Darren is out and about indulging in his other pastime of wildlife photography.

Derek and Mandy also have an interest. They simply love horror movies, and this becomes immediately apparent when you enter their home. A bookcase in the living room is stacked up with CDs and videos of old movies such as *Dracula* and *The Abominable Dr. Phibes*. And Gothic-style mirrors hang upon the walls. To a number of people this would raise a number of "red flags" and suggest an obvious reason for the paranormal activity taking place there. In the minds of some, particularly evangelical Christians, horror movies are all part and parcel of "the Devil's work" and are likely to attract "demonic activity". The authors disagree. Although the décor in Derek and Mandy's home is certainly unusual, they found it in no way threatening; just the opposite, in fact.

At the time Mike commented, "Putting aside the moral and theological arguments, the motivation behind Derek and Mandy's fascination with the horror genre is, I believe, entirely innocent. They simply love the ambience created by the old Hammer films that were so popular back in the 60s and 70s. As you walk from room to room, wonderful actors like Vincent Price, Peter Cushing and Lon Chaney reach out to you. To Derek and Mandy there is an innocence about it all, and if anything, a certain charm that actually offsets the brooding presence of the poltergeist. Whatever one thinks of the horror genre, I'm not convinced that their interest in old horror movies has anything to do with the paranormal phenomena they are experiencing. It's simply a coincidence"

But there are other things that characterise the house, and they, the authors believe, are not so innocent at all.

On the first visit to Pallister Street, Mike recalls feeling rather disorientated when he stood at certain locations. This feeling was at its strongest when he stepped onto the landing at the top of the stairs. His chest and stomach muscles tightened, and he felt as if he was going to fall over. The sensation subsided to a degree after a few minutes, but not completely. This was identical to the feeling that the medium Rhianne D'Morgyn had experienced, and this told Mike that whatever was causing it; it almost certainly wasn't a coincidence. Darren, too, while downstairs earlier on in the evening, commented upon the floor being lopsided, or uneven, as a feeling of disorientation came over him when he ventured into the dining room from the hallway at the bottom of the stairs.

The authors cannot rule out the possibility that there is a psychic or paranormal element to the strange sensations of disorientation that Mike, Rhianne and Darren experienced at Pallister Street. However, another explanation suggests itself more forcefully, and it is one that the authors hit upon during their very first visit.

The first thing that struck Darren and Mike was that although the disorientation seemed to pervade the entire house, in most places it was so mild that it was barely noticeable. However, in certain locations the feeling was overwhelming. The obvious question was, why? Was the paranormal phenomenon in the house – whatever it may be – only "active" in certain "hot spots" within the dwelling? Or was their another, more prosaic explanation? As soon as Derek and Mandy moved into Pallister Street, they noticed something decidedly odd about the interior; all of the walls, ceilings, door frames, window frames, skirting boards and floorboards seem to juxtapose with each other at odd angles. Few corners are a true 90°, and if one stands in a number of locations throughout the house the effect of all these "odd angles" upon the eye can be incredibly destabilising. Anyone who has visited the "Crazy House" at their local fairground will know exactly what this sensation is. The difference is that in the Crazy House down at the fair one *expects* to be disorientated and will therefore not be surprised. But one doesn't expect to be subjected to this sort of disorientation in an overtly normal terraced dwelling. To Mike and Darren, the effect of this visually disturbing phenomenon, although not paranormal in origin, should not be underestimated.

Derek pointed out another strange thing about the house on Pallister Street. Earlier, the authors mentioned an incident where a cupboard door had, twice in rapid succession, seemingly opened of its own accord. The cupboard is actually a recessed space built into the wall of the dining room, barely three feet in depth and not much more in width. The unusual feature about the cupboard is not the space itself, nor the door; rather, the mystery concerns the door *handle*. Most householders are familiar with interior door handles that are lockable from one side only. Commonly, such handles are fitted to bathrooms and toilets, enabling the user to lock the door from the inside and prevent unwelcome intrusions. It is just such a handle that is fitted to the small, recessed cupboard in the dining room at Pallister Street. The puzzle is *why*.

Obviously, fitting such a handle with the locking mechanism on the outside of the cupboard would be superfluous unless one wanted to lock someone inside the cupboard and prevent them from getting out. This is a disturbing thought, but the handle in question is fitted the other way round, with the locking mechanism on the *inside* of the cupboard. Bizarrely, this would only be of use to someone who wanted to lock themselves inside the cupboard and prevent others from *getting in*. There is, of course, a patently obvious solution to this enigma. Possibly, the previous householder had such a handle spare, and, even though the cupboard door didn't need a locking mechanism, he or she utilised the handle instead of spending money on a new one. We may never know why a handle with a locking mechanism was fitted to the cupboard. Perhaps there is an innocent explanation; or, just perhaps, there is a more sinister one.

Darren suggests the room may have been used as a "darkroom" - although it is quite small - for developing photographs. The handle on the door would pull the door shut from *inside,* keeping the light out in order to successfully develop the prints without light contamination. Mike decided to keep an open mind, recalling that two incidents of possibly paranormal provenance had been connected to the cupboard. He also felt – it was nothing more than a hunch – that something malign had connected itself to that small recess in the wall. He didn't know what it was, and to date he has not been able to verify that there was anything other than sloppy DIY involved in fitting a locking handle instead of a non-locking one. The jury, as they say, is still out.

It was at this juncture that another thought struck Mike. During the investigation at Lock Street, there had been a recessed cupboard almost identical in appearance to the one in the dining room of the house on Pallister Street. The only difference was the location, the cupboard in Lock Street being situated in the bedroom of young Robert. However, he also recalled another recessed cupboard in the kitchen at Lock Street. It wasn't so similar in appearance, but it was more similar in regards to its location. Both of the cupboards in the house at Lock Street had been subject to the work of the poltergeist; the doors would open (and sometimes close) without human assistance. It struck him as strange indeed that both entities seemed to operate in such similar ways.

Eight
CATALYST

Even before the authors had begun their investigation into the Lock Street case, they were aware of the almost universally acknowledged belief that every poltergeist infestation has a *focus*; that is, a person from which the poltergeist seems to emanate, or is in some way attached to. Many researchers believe that the majority of poltergeist *foci* are young teenage girls who are either going through – or have just emerged from - puberty. No one seems to know just why this is so, but the authors accept that in the majority of cases the notion holds good. Lock Street had been different. There was no pubescent teenager living in that house, and, according to the residents, none who even visited it on anything like a regular basis. This also forged a peculiar parallel with the case at Pallister Street. There, too, the typical pubescent, female focus was notable by her absence.

Nothing in the world of paranormal research is ever absolute. There are no exact sciences. If paranormal researchers were to be brutally honest with themselves, they'd have to admit that they are, almost all of the time, groping around in the dark. Be this as it may, we can say with some certainty that most paranormal phenomena have a catalyst; something that precipitates events or experiences that are currently beyond our ken. Naturally, then, the authors were keen to establish just what the catalyst was at the House on Pallister Street.

The first piece of evidential information that came to Darren and Mike's attention was that whatever was going on at Pallister Street, it had not begun there. The couple had experienced a number of bizarre incidents at their previous home – enough to suggest that it was there, and not at Pallister Street, that the polt –

or whatever it was – had possibly originated. It had simply followed them to their new abode. This fits in well with the belief held by many researchers that the poltergeist phenomenon, whatever its nature, is person-centred as opposed to place-centred. This in itself needs a few words of explanation. Most seasoned researchers will tell you that ghosts or apparitions are place-centred; that is, they seem to be attached to a particular location. When you move house, you'll leave any ghosts you may have encountered behind. Poltergeists are different. They seem to be attached to people rather than places. Move house, and your poltergeist will likely move with you. The authors, having established that the entity that was currently troubling the family at Pallister Street had seemingly moved with them from their previous dwelling, were thus leaning towards the idea that it was indeed a poltergeist infestation that they were dealing with.

The authors never seriously entertained the notion that the family's interest in old horror movies was the catalyst in this case, so something else had to be at the bottom of the phenomenon; but what?

The second visit to Pallister Street took place on Tuesday 25 March, 2008. This time, Mike and Darren would be joined by Mark Winter, a member of Darren's ghost-hunting group the North East Ghost Research Team. The weather was rather miserable; dull, clouded skies accompanied by a steady stream of rain. At 6.30pm, Mike caught a bus from his home and alighted at Jarrow. He then walked the short distance to Pallister Street. Again, memories flooded back of his time spent at the now-demolished school he'd attended. Apart from the fact that the school was no longer there, the area had changed little in over thirty years.

Essentially, the second visit was almost a re-run of the first. Recording equipment was set up in various rooms and Mike, not as technically minded as either Darren or Mark, sat on the sofa and talked to both Mandy and Derek. Rather than focus upon the strange phenomena that the couple had been witnessing, Mike tried to elicit more background information from them. Where had they worked? How had they met? What other interests did they share apart from a love of horror films? It was at this juncture that Derek mentioned something, almost casually, that struck Mike and Darren as truly significant.

Apart from horror movies, Derek had another hobby; he collected memorabilia associated with famous people. Memorabilia-collecting is like most other hobbies, inevitably more complex on the inside than it appears to be to the outside observer. When Mike was a kid, his cousin Robert gave him an autograph book filled with the signatures of sporting heroes, including the legendary speedway champion Ivan Mauger and the runner Brendan Foster. The autographs were not in any particular order, but to Mike they were precious. Serious collectors would not be satisfied with this, however. Those who are into collecting memorabilia in a big way usually specialise. They may collect the signatures of footballers, cricketers or rugby players. Alternatively, they may specialise in photographs of movie stars, bone china containing images of members of the Royal Family or books written by famous authors. Darren, for example, collects both old and new books on the subject of ghost-hunting that have been signed by the authors; indeed, he has a rather good collection with some of his books containing personal messages to him from the likes of Peter Underwood, Colin Wilson, Guy Lyon Playfair and SPR archivist, Dr Melvyn Willin. Darren even owns a signed 1936 first edition of '*Confessions of a Ghost Hunter*' by his main influence, Harry Price. Each to his own, as they say. For Derek's part, he specialised in collecting memorabilia associated with some of the world's most notorious criminals.

To some, this would seem an incredibly macabre pass-time. Indeed, it is, and it is something that neither author would care to indulge in themselves. However, it is important to note that Derek does not seem to have engaged in this specialised form of collecting for any dark motive. He takes no delight in the notion that there are people out there who have robbed banks or single-handedly slaughtered dozens of innocents. He has no liking for the personalities of homicidal maniacs – particularly those who have killed not one person but many. Neither Darren nor Mike had gained the slightest impression that there was any distasteful motive behind Derek's hobby. Strange though it seemed, Mike concluded that Derek had chosen his specialist field more by accident than design, and would probably have been just as happy collecting photographs of opera singers, Formula One racing drivers or pugilists. Unfortunately, though, innocence of motive is not enough in itself to protect oneself from malign influences. Some years ago, Mike accompanied members of the Dubberly Volunteer Fire Department in Louisiana on a training exercise. One grizzled firefighter, who had obviously been around the block, as they say, told Mike; "You know, when someone shouts *Fire!*, you may not be inclined to believe them – but that don't mean there ain't no fire".

And he was right, of course. Derek had innocently engaged in a hobby that may seem strange to some, but he had no dark agenda. However, there was no guarantee that his innocence of intent would protect him from any malign influences that his hobby would generate. The more Derek told the authors, the more concerned they became.

Derek's collection had started almost by accident. He'd contacted a fellow dealer who happened to mention that he had a particularly rare specimen for sale connected to a notorious American serial killer. Even better, he was able to offer it to Derek at a knock-down price. Sensing a bargain, he snapped it up, and decided to go hunting for more of the same. Later, he expanded his collection by purchasing an artefact that had allegedly been associated with a well-known American criminal. True, it wasn't much, but he felt it would enhance his collection and so he bought it. To build his collection even further, he decided to write to a number of serial killers both in the UK and the USA. If they responded, he figured, he'd not only have their autograph but an entire letter to go with it. To his surprise, a number of them wrote back. The authors were intrigued, and asked Derek what their responses had been like.

"It differed", he told Darren and Mike. "Some actually came across like really nice people – they'd ask what the weather was like in England, and so on. There was nothing in their letters that would give the faintest clue that they were mass murderers, or whatever. Others were different. From the outset, you could tell there was something creepy about them. They'd be arrogant and boastful about what they'd done, even if they didn't mention their crimes directly. Others were different again. They'd be nice at first, and then, suddenly, their tune would change. One guy was really pleasant at first, and then, out of the blue, he said that he was going to arrange to have me killed. It was scary. I never wrote back to him after that".

There was one particular incident, however, that intrigued the authors more than any other. One morning, a letter arrived. Derek inserted the tip of his forefinger under the flap and slit the envelope open, but as he reached inside to remove the letter something extremely unpleasant happened.

"It was weird. Suddenly the entire room turned icy-cold. I looked around, and it was like being at the North Pole. Everything in the room took on an icy, blue-white complexion and I had the feeling that I was surrounded by something completely evil".

The letter was, in fact, from one of Britain's most notorious serial killers. The authors asked Derek if anyone else had been present at the time.

"Yes", he responded. "My wife and my mother were there, and they experienced exactly the same thing. I'd never experienced anything like it, and I never want to again".

Later, after the strange disturbances began in their home, Derek's mother actually suggested that his collection of criminal memorabilia might have been in some way responsible. The authors were beginning to wonder if she was right. But there was a large problem looming on the horizon for the investigators. Their gut instinct was that there might well have been such a connection. Unwittingly or otherwise, Derek had established contact with a number of people who, by any rational definition, were consumed by evil and the need to destroy the lives of others. Even if one reduces the concept of contagion down to a purely psychological level, it is hard to deny that corresponding with people whose souls are saturated with such malevolence could quite easily have a detrimental effect. The difficulty that faced the authors was the way in which that negative effect had manifested itself. Had Derek simply read the letter and been disturbed by its contents, there would have been no mystery. Had he suddenly been consumed by regret for having established contact with a maniac, then there would have been no enigma. But this was not the way it happened. When Derek first opened the envelope, it was as if a torrent of pure evil had gushed forth from within - and this was before he even knew whom the letter was from. This suggests that something preternatural had occurred, for such an experience cannot be explained within the confines of modern scientific understanding. It seemed to the authors that, in some way they could not understand, the evil within the heart of one of Britain's most notorious murderers had attached itself to that letter and touched the souls of Derek and his family as soon as it was opened in their presence. Darren and Mike could not deny the *process*, but they could not figure out the *mechanism*. They believed they knew *what* had happened, but they were at a loss to explain *how*.

Mike suggested an experiment. He urged Derek to remove his collection of memorabilia from the family home in an effort to see whether their absence would make any difference to the level of paranormal activity they were experiencing. If, by removing the collection to another location, the bizarre phenomena reduced or stopped altogether, then it may hint to a connection between the two. The problem was where such a collection could be stored.

"I suppose I could ask a friend to keep it", offered Derek.

"I'm not so sure that's a good idea", responded Mike. "If your collection of memorabilia *is* generating the phenomena you're experiencing in some strange way, your friend might end up with the problem too".

Derek said that he'd give some thought to the matter.

"Maybe I can think of a friend who won't mind keeping the collection – even if he knows why I'm asking him".

During the rest of the evening, Darren and Mark made several trips upstairs to check on their cameras and other equipment. On one such occasion, they were standing just inside the door of the master bedroom when something decidedly odd happened. Without warning, a pre-recorded video tape shot out from under the couple's bed and landed at their feet. The investigators looked underneath the bed but could see nothing that would have caused something like that to happen.

"It was as if someone had been under the bed and simply thrown the tape towards our feet", Darren later recalled. "I also couldn't help but notice the title on the tape; it was *Friends*. I don't know why, but I thought there was something creepy about that".

At one point, when everyone was gathered in the dining room, a loud *thud* seemed to come from upstairs, followed by the gruff sound of a man's voice. Mike went up to investigate, but found nothing. However, as on the previous occasion, he noticed that the desktop image was clearly visible on the screen of Derek and Mandy's computer. He decided to resolve the issue once and for all. He shouted down the stairwell for Mandy, and asked her to join him. She walked up the stairs, followed by Darren and Mark. Mike explained to her that he'd like permission to look at the settings on the computer to see whether the screensaver feature was active. Mandy said she had no problem with that, and Mike asked her to watch over his shoulder as he did so. He felt uncomfortable about trawling through someone else's computer unless they were present. Sure enough, the couple's computer was configured so that the screensaver would "kick in" after exactly four minutes of inactivity. On each occasion when Mike had glanced at the computer screen, far more than four minutes had passed. So, why hadn't the screensaver engaged after the required period of inactivity? Mike then noticed that there were no programmes currently open on the computer. This jogged his memory, and he remembered that some operating systems had a "glitch" that sometimes prevented the screensaver from activating unless there were programmes open on the desktop. Mike opened up a programme at random so that the desktop wallpaper was no longer visible. Four minutes later, the screensaver was automatically activated.

Essentially the mystery seemed to be solved – except for one curious occurrence. When Mike moved the mouse and automatically disengaged the screensaver, the wallpaper that had previously covered the desktop – a photograph of the Beatles – had disappeared and been replaced by a blank, orange screen. A short discussion ensued, during which Mike apologised for "losing" Derek's photograph of the Beatles. Eventually, Mike and Darren simply shrugged their shoulders and walked downstairs, followed by the others. As Mike got to the door he turned and glanced in the direction of the computer, just in time to see the screensaver engage itself.

Hardly had the householders and the investigators got back downstairs when the voice returned; gruff, domineering and decidedly male. Again, it was frustrating not to be able to make out the exact words. The investigators all dashed upstairs to investigate. Everything looked normal, except for the chair next to the computer desk in the master bedroom. Mike could visualise the position it had been in when he'd last left the room, and was reasonably certain it had moved. Mandy, Mike recalled, had "seen" the computer chair move in one of her dreams. Hopes were raised when Darren reminded Mike that his camcorder had been running in the master bedroom all the time. Sadly, however, it turned out that the chair next to the computer desk was just out of camera shot. There was no way of establishing whether it had moved or not.

Before the investigators left, they enjoyed another cup of coffee provided by Mandy. During the ensuing conversation, Derek mentioned that both he and Mandy had been members of a local paranormal research group at one time. This also intrigued the authors, for witnesses who have a predisposition to investigating "the unknown" have to be treated rather differently from those who have no interest in the subject whatsoever. Both Mike and Darren have known occasions where just such a disposition had coloured the experients' own view of what they were witnessing to such a degree that the accuracy of their recollections could no longer be accepted without question. In this case, however, Derek and Mandy's interest in the subject seemed to be quite superficial, and a telling factor was their reluctance to offer any suggestions as to what was going on within the confines of their own home. In the authors' experience, "armchair expert" amateur researchers are usually chomping at the bit to offer a plethora of different theories about a whole host of subjects, especially if they are at the centre of the alleged paranormal activity. This was not the case with Derek and Mandy, however, and the authors concluded that their previous interest in "the unknown" should not be allowed to unduly colour any judgement they would eventually make about the case.

Mike, Darren and Mark packed up their kit-bags and put on their jackets before venturing out into the rain. Before they could make for the door, however, the entity decided to entertain them one more time. Mark jumped; "Did you hear that *bang*?"

I heard that voice again", answered Mike, "but I didn't hear any bang or thump".

"Well, I never heard the voice, but I definitely heard the *bang*!" said Darren.

This reminded Mike of something that had occurred years earlier when he'd been investigating another poltergeist case.

Again, the parallels were eerie:

When Stuart and Lauren Smith had moved into their terraced house in 1995, they were under the perfectly reasonable impression they would be the only persons residing there. They were wrong. One day, Stuart was watching TV in the living room when he noticed a peculiar odour. It was the smell of aromatic pipe tobacco. What struck him as odd was that no one in the house smoked a pipe

"It only lasted for about five seconds," he told Mike, "but it was quite strong. It was as if someone was smoking a pipe right there in the room. Then it disappeared just as quickly as it had come."

From that point, barely a day passed by without Stuart or Lauren noticing other odours in the room, such as strawberries, perfume and even the smell of roasting meat. However, not all the smells were pleasant: Sometimes the room would be filled with the cloying stench of either dog excrement or vomit.

"The smell of vomit is the worst", said Lauren. "Sometimes it's so strong you actually feel like being sick yourself. Sometimes it can last for a few seconds, other times for three or four hours. The smells even follow you from room to room. It's as if they become attached to you as a person."

Eventually, the couple were forced to consider the possibility that their house was haunted, and a number of other bizarre phenomena seemed to reinforce this idea. A pair of shoes belonging to Lauren disappeared and was never returned. One minute they were there, and the next they were gone. The same thing happened to a pair of silver earrings which vanished from the top of the TV.

Several months passed by, and then the nature of the bizarre occurrences intensified. Stuart was standing in the bathroom one afternoon when he heard the distinctive sound of the gas fire being turned on in the living room. As the weather was particularly balmy, Stuart shouted, "Lauren, why have you put the fire on?" But Lauren hadn't put the fire on. She was sitting in the living room at the time, but hadn't touched the fire. Stranger, although she was sitting adjacent to it she hadn't heard the sound of it igniting. Actually, the fire wasn't on at all.

From that day forth, virtually anyone who used the bathroom would hear the same, distinctive noise; *click, woomph. Click*, the sound of the ignition button being depressed, and *woomph*, as the gas actually ignited. Those who heard it were unanimous that what they could hear was the sound of the gas fire being ignited, and yet the fire *never went on.* What truly baffled them was that the noise could only be heard whilst standing in the bathroom.

When Mike visited the dwelling to investigate, Stuart and Lauren made both he and his colleague Craig* some tea. Then they gave the investigators a demonstration; they actually ignited the fire so that they would be able to recognise the sound should they hear it again. Mike and Craig then entered the bathroom and shut the door. After just a few seconds they heard it; *click, woomph.* Then they heard it again; *click, woomph.*

They knew from the outset that Stuart and Lauren were not hoaxing the event: You really could only hear the sound when standing in the bathroom. Mike and Craig later determined that it wasn't coming from the heating system, any other appliance or equipment in the house or from the adjacent property.

The investigators experienced this weird phenomenon several times. Once, Mike clearly heard the sound of the ignition button being depressed, but *not* the sound of the gas igniting. Craig, to Mike's amazement, said that he'd clearly heard the sound of the gas igniting but had *not* heard the sound of the ignition button being depressed! Eventually the investigators became convinced that the phenomenon had a paranormal origin of some kind, but just couldn't figure out what it was.

Lauren told Mike and Craig that the smell of vomit was "not consistent". "Sometimes it smells like someone has just thrown up their lunch", she stated, "but other times it has a milky odour, like baby sick".

Stuart said he'd also began to notice another odd smell: "It's just like the smell of a shaggy dog that has been out in the rain", he said; "Musty and damp". "Sometimes I can smell perfume", Stuart added, "but Lauren will be in the same room and detect nothing but the overpowering smell of dog excrement".

Readers should be able to see the parallel between the two cases immediately; at both locations there existed a raft of specific symptoms that manifested themselves as either aural or olfactory stimuli. However, in both cases some witnesses would experience *some* symptoms whilst others experienced *different* symptoms – all at the same time. Mike recalled an occasion at Lock Street, when some investigators heard what they described as a "piercing scream", whilst others heard what they said was a "throaty growl", or even nothing at all.

One more parallel – and many more questions. The authors felt that their experience at Lock Street had definitely given them a *better* understanding of the poltergeist phenomenon, but it was far from perfect. Some bits of the jigsaw puzzle were stubbornly refusing to fit. The relatively low level of the phenomena at Pallister Street, compared to the South Shields case, had led the authors to believe that this polt was a mere babe in arms compared to the one at Lock Street. What they didn't know was that the entity at Pallister Street was watching and waiting, patiently biding its time.

Nine
THE HAUNTED LOOM

Steve Taylor, the proprietor of Alone In The Dark Entertainment (AITDE), telephoned Mike in March 2008 and told him that he had yet another "interesting case brewing" and wondered whether he'd like to get involved. Mike asked Steve for some more details, and what Steve told him certainly piqued his interest.

Apparently, Steve had been contacted by the owner of a small store in Blyth, Northumberland, who told him that there were some "strange things happening" on the premises. The store was actually a craft shop that provided materials and equipment for a wide range of traditional crafts such as card-making, cross-stitch and scrapbooking. The proprietor had seemingly purchased two large weaving looms from a university that she'd formerly attended and installed them in a room above the shop. Since then, a series of peculiar events had taken place which led the owner to conclude that the looms themselves, as opposed to the shop premises, may have been haunted. Strange noises had been heard emanating from upstairs, including voices, and on more than one occasion passers-by had seen an old woman staring down from the upstairs window in the room where the looms were situated. Perhaps the most disturbing incident took place when Victoria Nesbitt, the proprietor, was sitting in the room where the looms had been reconstructed, going about her work. Vicky was in the habit of playing the radio, and she went about her work the presenter of the programme she had tuned in to played a series of popular songs. Suddenly, the song that was currently playing was interrupted by static, or as Vicky described it, "an electronic hissing noise". The noise disappeared as quickly as it had came, but the music did not return. Instead, there was a short period of silence which was punctuated by a female voice. It uttered one word; *Vicky*. Then there was another burst of static before the music returned, and everything went back to normal.

The strange interruption of the radio broadcast was peculiar, but what frightened Vicky was the voice which had clearly spoken her name. She ran out of the room in fear, and did not return for over two hours. On another occasion, Vicky was using the older of the two looms to weave a scarf. One morning she sat down at the loom as usual to continue her project, and was amazed to find a *second* scarf lying underneath the one she'd woven herself. To this day she has no idea how the second scarf came into existence, and, further, has not been able to work out how it could have been woven on the loom without her own scarf being removed first – which it wasn't.

The scant details provided by Steve had Mike fascinated, and he said he'd genuinely appreciate being able to visit the premises personally.

On Friday 28 March, the day of the investigation, Steve telephoned Mike and said that his car had broken down. His father was making an attempt to fix it, but he'd be a little late in arriving. Complications ensued, and Steve ended up having to drive through to Sunderland to borrow another car from a colleague. Originally, Mike and Steve had planned to arrive at Blyth mid-morning, but due to the transport problems it was early afternoon before they got there. Mike's wife, Jackie, accompanied the two investigators on their journey. Her interest in paranormal phenomena is not as intense as Mike's, but she enjoys card-making as a hobby and the idea of a visit to a new craft shop – coupled with the knowledge that Mike would, of course, have his wallet with him – made the trip nigh - irresistible.

The craft shop sat on a gable end of a street in Blyth, and was a delight for "crafters" like Mike's wife. On entering, Mike was taken with the warm atmosphere and overall pleasant ambience of the store. The shop was airy, decorated in a modern style and bore little resemblance to what lay upstairs on the first floor. To the left of the counter was a narrow stairwell that led up to the room in which the "haunted loom" was situated. Vicky ascended first, followed by Mike, Steve and Jackie. As Mike approached the landing in the middle of the stairs, he felt the muscles in his chest tighten ever so slightly – something he usually interprets as a sign of paranormal activity.

At the top of the stairwell there were two rooms. On the left was an office and storeroom, and on the right a workroom that contained the two looms and several other bits of equipment, along with a kitchen bench and kettle for making refreshments. The doorway that led into the workroom had no door, and the aperture was covered by a blanket that had to be pushed to one side to gain entrance. Vicky held the blanket back and allowed Mike to enter first. It was at this juncture that he noticed something distinctly odd; even though the room and the landing outside were only separated from each other by a thin blanket, the difference in temperature was absolutely incredible. The temperature on the landing was warm, cosy even – but inside the workroom it was as cold as a refrigerator. Mike was immediately reminded of his first journey to Lock Street in South Shields, when a sudden temperature drop had occurred in the living room. On that occasion, Mike felt as if he'd been dropped into a bath of ice water, and it actually caught his breath. This was no different. As the others trooped into the workroom one by one, they all commented on the coldness of the room.

"Wow!" said Steve, "I can't believe how different the temperature in here is compared to on the landing. It's amazing".

"It's always like this", replied Vicky. Sometimes it's colder than others, but it *never* gets warm. We just can't understand it".

Steve – who, like Darren, is more familiar with the technical side of ghost-hunting – immediately began to take readings with a digital thermometer. Then he used his EMF meter to detect fluctuations in electromagnetic frequencies. None of the readings proved to be of great interest, and were well within normal limits.

During the course of the next hour, the investigators accumulated as much information about the history of the "haunted loom" and the strange phenomena that seemed to have begun when it was re-housed to the craft shop. Mike then decided to take some audio recordings. Over the years he'd been incredibly lucky when attempting to record "EVP" – that is, electronic voice phenomena. During some investigations he'd even captured entire conversations on tape – conversations held by people who weren't visibly present in the room at the time. Over the next hour, he made three separate recordings on his digital recorder. The results proved interesting indeed.

Tape 1 was the least interesting, but did contain one enigmatic sound. At 3 minutes and 40 seconds into the recording, an anomalous noise could be heard; a distinct *woomph*. Mike is convinced that the noise hadn't been audible when the recording was in progress.

On Tape 2, at precisely 2 minutes and 10 seconds into the recording, a distinct *crack* could be heard. At 2m 32s a faint but distinct voice uttered the word "*Wow...*" The word was repeated at 4m 47s. Finally, at 7m 19s, there was another clear *crack*.

On Tape 3, after 1m 5s, a voice could be heard. However, it sounded muffled and it was impossible to make out specific words. At 1m 54s a voice could be heard saying, "*Hah!*" Finally, at 3m 08s, there was what sounded like a chair being dragged across a wooden floor.

After Mike had finished making his digital recordings, he switched off his recorder and watched intently as Steve started to make some of his own. Steve was obviously hearing noises through his headphones. Every minute or so he would suddenly stiffen and say, "Hey...can you guys hear that?" At first they couldn't, but intermittently Steve would hear things that were also audible to the others who were listening *sans* headphones. On one occasion, everyone present in the room could distinctly hear the sound of music. Mike commented later:

"It was faint, but clearly audible. To me, it sounded like a harp being played, as well as a piano. The music was melodic, but also sad. It had a haunting quality to it – if you'll excuse the pun – and seemed to echo. To be honest, I'd never heard anything like it before".

At one point, Steve spoke openly and asked, "If there's anyone present...could you make a noise of some kind just to let us know you're here...maybe a *bang* or something?"

Almost immediately there was a loud *crack*, which seemed to emanate from the vicinity of the workbench at the back of the room. Vicky jumped and looked quite scared. Whatever the cause – natural or preternatural – its timing was perfect. Steve and Mike immediately walked over to the bench and attempted to see what could have caused the noise. After an exhaustive examination of the bench and its contents, they determined that nothing they could see could have produced a noise such as the one they'd just heard – with one possible exception.

On the bench was an electric kettle with an on/off switch located adjacent to the handle. Occasionally such switches can "jump" and turn themselves off without human assistance, particularly if the mechanism is faulty or the temperature gauge isn't working properly. However, this almost always only happens when the kettle is hot, having just been freshly boiled. Mike checked the kettle; it was stone cold. He then flicked the on/off switch back and forth several times. As it switched position it made a series of dull *clicks*, but nothing like the sharp crack the witnesses had heard minutes earlier. Mike asked Vicky if she'd ever had any trouble with the kettle before, or noticed whether the on/off switch was faulty. She was certain – the kettle had *never* acted up before, and she'd never known the switch to jump spontaneously.

The final proof that a faulty switch on the kettle could not have been responsible lay in the fact that, when the investigators examined it, the switch was set to *OFF*. Had it jumped, then, the switch must have previously been set to *ON*. However, the electrical flex for the kettle was plugged into the wall socket, and the switch on the wall socket was also set to *ON*. This meant that had the kettle switch been set to *ON* also, the kettle would have begun to boil. It hadn't, which meant that the kettle switch must have been set to the *OFF* position for some time – probably since it was last used to make tea. Whichever way you looked at it, it just didn't seem possible that the strange noise, made in swift response to Steve's request, could have come from the kettle. Frustratingly, there seemed to be nowhere else it could have come from, either.

Steve openly admits to being "sensitive"; sometimes, on investigations, he "picks up things" about the history of the building and its former occupants. The thoughts just seem to pop into his head. As he stood in the room, he suddenly began to stare into space and declared, "I'm getting the name *Edward*". He then went on to say that he believed someone called Edward had formerly lived in the building, although he couldn't ascertain any further details.

Later, after Mike returned home, he received an e-mail from

Vicky:

Hi Mike,
Thank you for your visit; it was very interesting. I wanted to let you know I found a man called Edward Spencer in the 1901 census. He was born in Blyth, and was a railway driver. I have left my CCTV cameras on in the shop to see if we can see anything, but they only record for 3 hours. Let me know if you find anything interesting on the tape.
Thanks again,
Vicky.

As he read the e-mail, Jackie came into the study.

"There was a call for you earlier on when you were over at your mother's house. It was a man, but he wouldn't leave a number. He said he'd ring you later".

"Did he leave his name?"

"Yes...he was called Edward".

Mike, curious and somewhat disturbed by the coincidence, went to the phone and looked at the call log. The last call received was registered as NUMBER WITHHELD. There were several things that bothered Mike about this seemingly trivial incident.

Firstly, it seemed odd that the man had been called Edward; the very name that Steve had "picked up" during the visit to the craft shop. Secondly, it was even stranger that Jackie should have told Mike about the call at the very moment he was reading Vicky's e-mail.

But there was more. During their investigation at Lock Street, the South Shields Poltergeist had displayed a fascination – perhaps even an obsession – with telephones. It had sent messages – sometimes vile and threatening – to Marianne, the occupier of the house. It repeatedly removed mobile phones from where they'd been left and took them upstairs into the bedrooms. Also, it had caused a phone belonging to a friend of Mike to ring Mike's mobile when the man was driving past the house in Lock Street, even though he knew nothing about the authors' investigation into the South Shields case at the time.

But the most disturbing thing of all, to Mike, was the fact that "Edward" had withheld his number. Mike's phone will not accept calls from withheld numbers – but somehow "Edward" had circumvented the system. Mike had seen this sort of trickery with phones before; it had been the work of the South Shields Poltergeist.

Mike noticed a number of parallels between the Blyth case and the others he and Darren had investigated. The most obvious was the utterance of the experient's name. In the Blyth case it was that of the proprietor, Vicky. Another was the inexplicable temperature variation in adjacent rooms, and a third was the presence of clicks, bangs and other anomalous noises. With every passing day, these bizarre "coincidences" were becoming more obvious – and increasingly harder to rationalise.

Ten
FRIENDS & FAMILY

During their investigation into the South Shields Poltergeist, Darren and Mike had been made privy to numerous instances of what seemed to be contagion. Mostly, these involved members of Marc and Marianne's extended families, along with several friends and work colleagues.

Marc had told Darren and Mike of an incident that occurred at a relative's house when the investigation at Lock Street was at its height. The woman of the house had been dusting and vacuuming the living room in her home. When she'd finished she took the vacuum cleaner into the kitchen and stood it against the wall, intending to put it away later. She then returned to the living room and continued with her housework. Some time later, when she walked back into the kitchen, she was astonished to find that the contents of the vacuum cleaner's bag had been disgorged onto the floor. Baffled, she took a brush and swept the dust and detritus into a pile with the intention of depositing it in the bin when she'd finished dusting the living room. When she returned to the kitchen yet again, she was shocked to see that the neat pile of dust had been disturbed. It had been scattered across the floor, but not in a random manner. As she stared at the mess she could see that the dust and muck had been carefully arranged into a pattern. In fact, it had been arranged in such a way that it actually spelt a word; *Marc*.

On another occasion - again, at the house of one of Marc's relatives – one of the residents had on display an attractive arrangement of ornamental candles. Several small candles, each ensconced in its own decorative holder, floated in a larger dish containing water. When lit, they created an atmosphere of serenity and cosiness. Until the polt got to work, that is.

When the young woman's attention was distracted, the polt picked up several of the candles floating in the water and poured the molten wax onto the surface of the water itself, where it immediately solidified. When she noticed what had happened she was naturally bemused, but her confusion turned to alarm when she saw that the wax on the surface of the water spelt out a word; *Marc*.

Another incident of contagion involved a male relative of Marianne. He'd taken Marianne's young son, Robert, for a ride in his car and during the journey suddenly became aware of what he later described as "a presence" beside him. The authors have been unable to ascertain whether or not the man actually *saw* anything, but when the story was related to them they distinctly recall being told that he was terrified. Young Robert, apparently, was unperturbed by the incident and merely said, "Its Sammy". Sammy was an "imaginary" childhood friend of Robert's, and, as the authors found out later, the poltergeist at Lock Street had no reservations about masquerading as "Sammy" when it suited. Seemingly, that is exactly what happened in the car on that very day.

Perhaps the most disturbing incident involved a work mate of Marianne called Kara*. During the investigation at Lock Street, when several investigators were present, Marianne, perhaps unwisely, sent a text message to her colleague claiming to be from the poltergeist. Marianne did this "as a joke", but it naturally frightened Kara. The polt, seizing a golden opportunity, then sent Kara a text message of its own which was far more chilling. The ability of the polt to be so spontaneously creative in its wickedness was something that the authors saw demonstrated time and time again.

The authors noticed something else. The spelling of Marc's name – on one occasion with dust from a vacuum cleaner, and on another with molten wax – was eerily reminiscent of the way the polt had audibly recited the names of other experients in different cases.

Eleven
THE AUTHORS' EXPERIENCES

On Monday, 24th July, 2006, whilst Darren and Mike were fully immersed in their investigation of the South Shields Poltergeist, an incident occurred which demonstrated the reality of the contagion phenomenon. Marc, one of the principal experients in the case, had lost his credit card. He searched the entire house, but could not find it. Sometime later he found the card on the stairwell of the house in Lock Street. It was standing vertically on edge, upon a stair, as if held in an upright position by invisible fingers.

The following day, Marianne's travel pass disappeared. Later she found it on the stairwell – in exactly the same place that Marc had found his credit card the day before. Alongside the travel pass was a lottery scratch card that had gone missing several weeks earlier. These two incidents were the first in a cluster of occurrences which acted as a warning that the polt was becoming increasingly active.

That evening, as the entire country basked in a heat wave, Marianne's son Robert was playing contentedly in his bedroom. Marianne and Marc were also there. Suddenly, Marianne became aware of something extremely strange. Bizarre flashes of white light seemed to be dancing hither and thither around the room. Sensing that the polt may be about to engage in some of its malign tomfoolery, she removed her mobile phone from her pocket and switched on the video camera facility. Marc grabbed his mobile and did the same.

As both Marc and Marianne fumbled with their phones in an effort to activate the camera facility, Robert clambered upon the bed and lay down. He looked hot, which was not surprising considering the soaring temperature.

Not wanting to alarm Robert, Marc tried to maintain an air or normality. At the beginning of the footage, extracted later from Marianne's phone, Marc can be heard chatting. He sounded nervous, breathless. He suggests that Marianne takes Robert downstairs for something to eat. This, the authors think, was probably an attempt by Marc to remove Robert from the room so that he would not have to endure whatever it was that the polt was about to do. Robert pointed towards a cupboard door in the room and muttered something, as if in conversation with someone. At this point, the clip ends. When Mike visited later, Marianne forwarded the footage to Mike's mobile phone.

After Mike returned home he decided to download into his computer the footage that Marianne had sent to his phone. He made a fresh pot of coffee, washed, and then got to work.

In his study, Mike inserted into one of his computer's USB ports the wireless "dongle" that could pick up multimedia files remotely. Then he activated the connection between his phone and his PC and prepared to download the footage. It was at this point, as the files were transferring, that he noticed something distinctly odd. Three files, not two, were now sitting on the desktop of his PC. Files 1 and 2 contained the footage that Marianne had sent to Mike's phone. The third file was different and had an unrecognisable grey and black icon. What baffled Mike even more was that the file had no name – there was just the strange, grey and black icon.

Mike was reticent to open the file, wondering if it may have been malicious – perhaps containing a virus. Regardless, he took the risk and double-clicked on the icon with his mouse. The file opened in QuickTime, a multimedia player. The screen was perfectly white, but in the centre, in large black letters, were the words, *HA HA*. Mike immediately wondered if he could save the file onto his desktop with a name, but before he had time to even think about carrying out the operation, the media player shut down and the file disappeared from his computer's desktop completely. He could find no copy of the file on his phone, and none on his computer. It was as if it had never existed.

Had the file actually been on his phone to start with, or had it simply appeared alongside the transferred movie clips on his computer? The authors do not know.

Mike also experienced other instances of contagion; some when Darren was present, others when on his own. Despite his years of research into paranormal phenomena, Mike was still apprehensive about the possibility of his own home being subjected to contagion – not for himself, but because of his wife and others who visited the family home. On one occasion, this heightened sensitivity to the possibility of contagion led Mike to misinterpret something completely innocent.

After the North East Ghost Research Team had engaged in one of its Lock Street investigations, Mike was dropped off at his home just before sunrise. His wife, Jackie, was still at work, as she'd been required to do an "overnight shift" at her place of work. Mike made some tea and unpacked the equipment he'd taken with him on the investigation, before deciding to take a bath. As he walked up the stairwell of his home he noticed an object lying on the upper landing. It was an air freshener – the type that plugs into an electrical socket and expels regular doses of one of several heady aromas during the day. The device had been plugged into a socket in the upper hallway at the top of the stairs. What Mike couldn't understand was what it was doing lying on the floor. He picked it up and plugged it back in, but he was disturbed by what ostensibly was something of little or no importance.

During the investigation at Lock Street, Darren had taken photographs of a night-light; the type parents plug into sockets and which discharge just enough of a glow so that children can make their way to the bathroom safely from their bedroom should they need to "pay a visit" during the hours of darkness. The night-light, which was approximately the same size, shape and colour as the air freshener, had discharged itself from a socket in the upper hallway of the Lock Street house on two separate occasions. To Mike, the sight of the air freshener lying on the floor in his house was a chilling eerie reminder of the Lock Street events. He was seriously wondering whether contagion was at work.

When Jackie returned home later that day, Mike made her something to eat and then gently broached the matter. He asked her whether the air freshener had been in the socket before she'd left the house the previous day. No it hadn't, she replied. She'd been in a hurry to get to work and had suddenly realised that her mobile phone needed charging. She'd removed the air freshener from its socket and plugged in the mobile phone charger. She had fully intended to replace the air freshener in the socket before leaving the house, but had simply got distracted. The mystery was over, but Mike had learnt a valuable lesson; no matter how weird or "supernatural" things might seem, a rational explanation may be waiting just around the corner.

As mentioned earlier on, Darren had experienced his own incidents of contagion, although during the Lock Street investigation he kept them very much to himself, not even telling Mike about them. There was, in Darren's mind, a sound reason for this. The proximity of Mike's home to the house in Lock Street was an influencing factor in how the authors carried out their investigation. Darren lives in North Tyneside, several miles further away from Lock Street and on the other side of the River Tyne. Logic dictated, therefore, that the authors spent far more time at Mike's house than vice-versa, as it was much closer to Lock Street if they needed to go there. Whether it was because of the geographical distance between Darren's home and the house on Lock Street, or for some other reason, the instances of contagion that occurred seemed to take place largely at Mike's home – at least in the early part of the investigation. Even the instances at Mike's house were few, but at Darren's home they were virtually non-existent. Darren, quite naturally, was happy at this state of affairs. His partner had just given birth to the couple's first child, and Darren was deeply worried that contagion events may occur at his home when Jayne was alone there with their baby daughter. Eventually, though, things started to happen at Darren's home too.

Being a paranormal investigator had necessitated Darren spending many nights away from Jayne during his on-site research, and it was on one such occasion, after he had left his home to go to South Shields one evening, that an incident of contagion occurred.

Jayne had needed to "pay a visit", to use a polite metaphor, and popped upstairs to the bathroom. While she was up there she noticed something move out of the corner of her eye. She turned, looked and saw to her utter surprise that a round bath sponge - known colloquially as a "white puff" - was moving. It suddenly jumped from the holder it was sitting in and landed in the bath.

Darren returned from his overnight investigation, and Jayne informed him of what she had seen the previous night. Darren tried to play it down, and suggested a rational explanation. He didn't want to alarm her with the possibility that the South Shields polt had made its presence known at their own abode. However, Jayne knew there was no rational explanation for what she had seen.

But then, on 10 March 2008, Darren had felt the unnerving "presence" in the kitchen when he'd been making a sandwich. That changed things. Whereas previously he'd harboured a hope that the bath sponge incident Jayne had witnessed may just have had a mundane explanation, now he *knew* that something strange was going on. Eventually he confessed to Mike that contagion may now have become an issue at his own house, although he still decided not to tell Jayne about the incident of March 10. Quite simply, he didn't want to frighten her.

After 10 March there were no further incidents at Darren's house, but then, on April 28, Mike received an e-mail from Darren out of the blue. There was something that he wanted to get off his chest:

> *Dear Mike,*
>
> *During the past few days at home I have been very jumpy and on edge. To be honest I didn't want to say anything, because as we are writing this new book about "contagion" I thought it would sound rather cheesy - or as if I was making something up to go in the book. I AM NOT. During the last few days I have been seeing fleeting shadows at home out the corner of my eyes. One instance was upstairs on the landing and another at the bottom of the stairs near the wall mirror. The latter one I saw from the kitchen while preparing some food. Sometimes I think I see things. I turn my head quickly and nothing is there - well not until last night.*
>
> *I was in bed, but I was snoring and keeping Jayne awake. I decided to go downstairs and sleep on the sofa so that I didn't disturb her. At some point I woke up, and I saw an elderly woman standing in the middle of the floor. She was bent over and looking at me with a puzzled*

expression on her face. Her head was moving in a way that resembled a robot - turning her head, moving it up, down, left, right in a subtle, slightly jerky manner. To be honest, it looked as if she was giving me the once-over. It was fucking creepy. I looked at the clock – I suppose that's the ghost-hunter in me – and it was 12.20am. What happened next I can't be sure, but somehow I thought that I'd gone back to sleep, only to be woken up by Jayne's mobile phone. Someone was sending her a text through the night. It seemed as if ages had passed since seeing the old woman, so when the text came through and woke me up again I presumed I'd been asleep for a few more hours.

Jayne phoned me this morning on my way to work and told me about the text that she'd received.

I'd forgotten about the text coming through the night, so never mentioned it to her this morning. In any case, I certainly never mentioned seeing the old woman. The text was from her sister telling her that a new baby had arrived in the family. The girlfriend of Jayne's nephew had given birth during the night. The text had arrived at precisely 12.21am; just one minute after I'd seen that old woman! I thought I'd been asleep for few hours after seeing the woman, but it was really only a few seconds later.

Don't know if there is a link - not even sure if I was dreaming or not - but it has spooked me. Must talk more to you about it sometime soon.

Darren.

Superficially, it seemed that Darren had gone through a number of strange experiences but there was nothing about them that would directly link them to the entity that had so terrified the family at Lock Street. Seeing strange shadow-shapes out of the corner of your eye and witnessing the apparition of an old woman in your lounge would alarm most people; but Darren was a seasoned investigator for whom such experiences were nothing more than an occupational hazard. On reflection, it's likely that he was unnerved for one, simple reason; he suspected deep down that the South Shields Poltergeist really *was* back. Such suspicions were not to be taken lightly. The authors found out to their cost that the poltergeist at Lock Street was a master of disguise and deception, so Darren could have no confidence that the old woman he'd seen during the night was not really the poltergeist. Also, it could easily have been responsible for the "shadow-figures" Darren had seen on a number of occasions.

Whatever the truth, there was no denying the possibility that Darren, as well as Mike, might now have been subjected to instances of contagion. It was not a pleasant thought.

There was one instance in particular that had occurred when both Darren and Mike had been present. To the authors, it was highly indicative of contagion at work.

On Friday 25 August, 2006, when the South Shields case seemed to be reaching its zenith, Darren and Mike had been at the house at Lock Street. On this occasion it was extremely active and carried out a series of intimidating stunts in full view of three investigators and the principal experients. After Darren and Mike left the house it completely trashed one of the bedrooms, leaving it in such a state one could be forgiven for thinking that a tornado had hit the place. The authors went back to Mike's home to assess the situation.

Darren and Mike sat in front of the computer, typing up case notes and looking for anything significant. After a while they took a break and walked into the kitchen. Now it just so happened that in Mike's office, upon a bookshelf, was a hardback copy of George B. Hodgson's *The Borough of South Shields*. This volume – the definitive work on the Borough of South Tyneside's capital town – weighs almost four pounds. As the investigators walked away from Mike's office there was an almighty bang emanating from behind them. They both flinched and ducked simultaneously. When they turned round, *The Borough of South Shields* was lying in the middle of the office floor.

"D'you think we've brought back something with us?" asked Darren.

"I hope not," said Mike. "Jackie will hit the roof."

The almost humorous notion that the investigators might have "brought something back with them" to Mike's home wasn't made with any seriousness. They would later come to see how gravely they had misjudged the situation.

Twelve
TIME & TIME AGAIN

Let's imagine a hypothetical scenario. The setting is New York, the year 2012. A body is found in an apartment in a run-down area of Staten Island, and the deceased person has obviously been murdered. The victim has been brutally strangled, and the killer has left a "calling card" upon the torso – a playing card, specifically the Five of Hearts. Over the succeeding weeks, further bodies are found in the same area. Again, all the victims have been strangled and a Five of Hearts playing card has been left upon each body. Even before the murderer is found and arrested, homicide detectives will be able to determine two things with a high degree of certainty. Firstly, after autopsies have been carried out and forensic evidence analysed, they will be able to announce that the victims were indeed murdered and did not die accidentally or of natural causes. Secondly, the presence of a Five of Hearts playing card at each murder scene is highly indicative of the fact that the same individual has carried out each homicide.

Murder, sadly, is a common occurrence in our society. No one would suggest that all of the hundreds of murder victims found each day have been slain by the same individual. People commit murder for a wide variety of reasons. Of course, we know that the murderers all belong to the same species; they are all human. Beyond that, it may or may not be possible to narrow down the number of suspects to *one particular* human in any given case. Even the *modus operandi* of the murderer may not be enough. Strangulation is a common method of killing, so just because two murder victims are found strangled in the same city on the same day or even in the same week does not mean that the same

1. (*Above*) Michael J. Hallowell & Darren W. Ritson with Guy Lyon Playfair, one of the principal investigators of the Enfield Poltergeist case. (*Thunderbird Craft & Media*)

2. (*Left*) The late Maurice Grosse, who, along with Guy Lyon Playfair, investigated the notorious Enfield Poltergeist. (*Guy Lyon Playfair*)

3. (*Above*) A small, plastic nut which flew across a bedroom whilst the authors were investigating the South Shields Poltergeist case. (*Darren W. Ritson & Michael J. Hallowell*)

4. (*Below*) During the South Shields Poltergeist case, numerous household objects were moved around, including this chair, which was found in the centre of the kitchen. (*Darren W. Ritson & Michael J. Hallowell*)

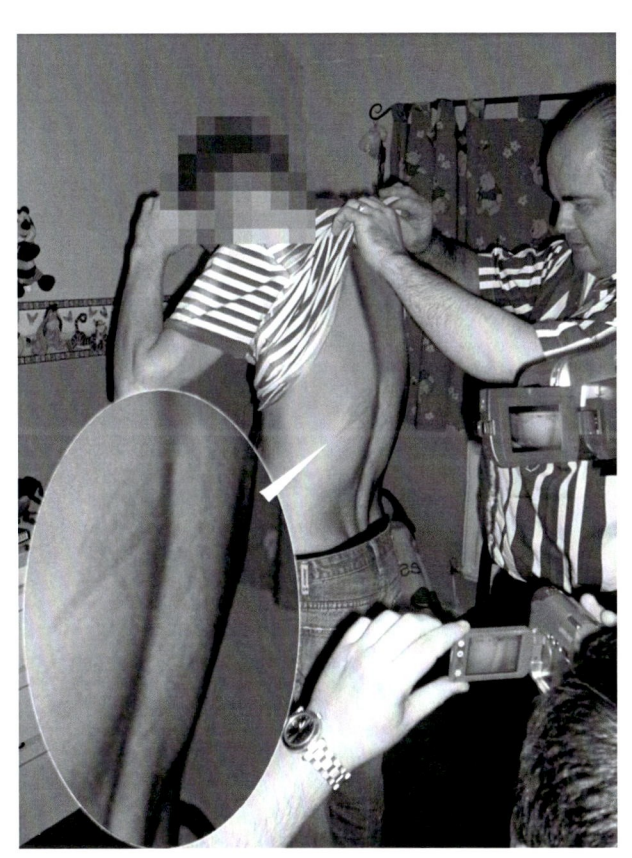

5. (*Left*) Author Michael J. Hallowell examines cuts which appeared spontaneously on the back of Marc during the South Shields Poltergeist case. (*Darren W. Ritson & Michael J. Hallowell*)

6. (*Below*) More cuts appear on Marc's body. (*Darren W. Ritson & Michael J. Hallowell*)

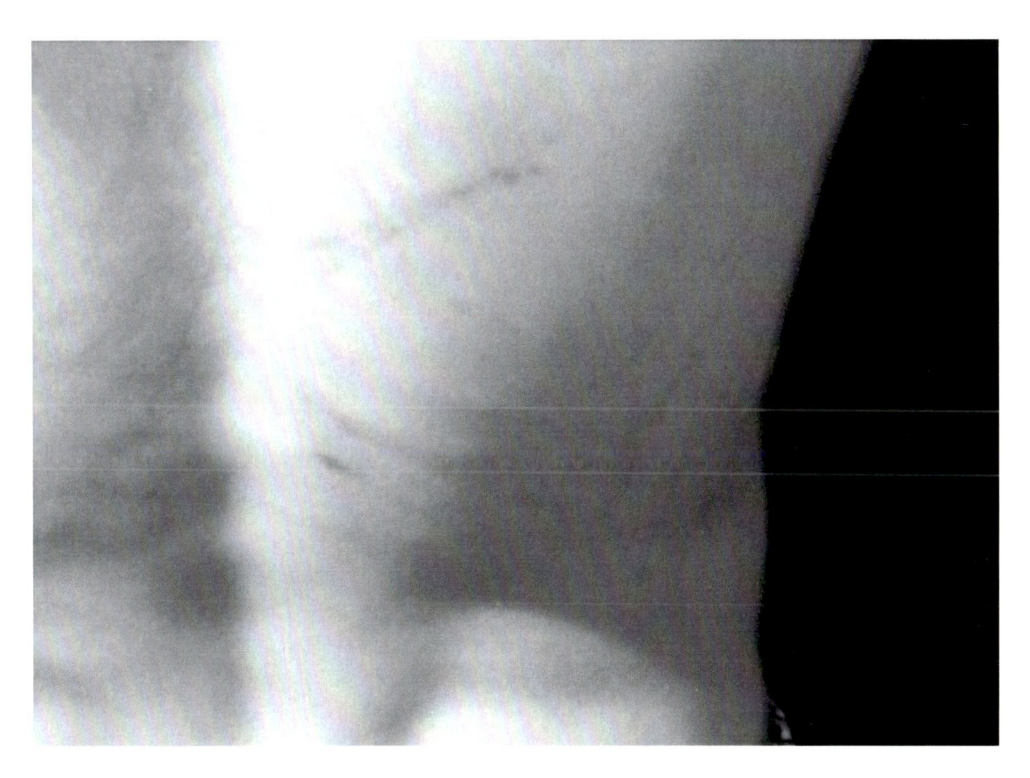

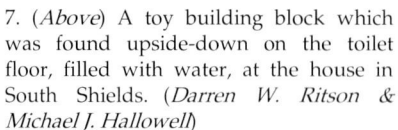

7. (*Above*) A toy building block which was found upside-down on the toilet floor, filled with water, at the house in South Shields. (*Darren W. Ritson & Michael J. Hallowell*)

8. (*Right*) A statuette known as "the African Lady", which moved without human intervention whilst standing on a shelf in the hallway of the house at South Shields. (*Darren W. Ritson & Michael J. Hallowell*)

9. (*Below*) The statuette of the African Lady after it relocated itself from the shelf in the hall to the stairs. (*Darren W. Ritson & Michael J. Hallowell*)

10. (*Left*) On numerous occasions a ceramic pig would move from the window ledge in the WC, usually to the seat of the toilet itself. (*Darren W. Ritson & Michael J. Hallowell*)

11. (*Below*) Displaced objects: The top two photographs show the plastic nut after being moved by the poltergeist on two separate occasions during the South Shields investigation. The bottom two show ice cubes that appeared spontaneously – one in the bedroom, the other in the refrigerator. (*Darren W. Ritson & Michael J. Hallowell*)

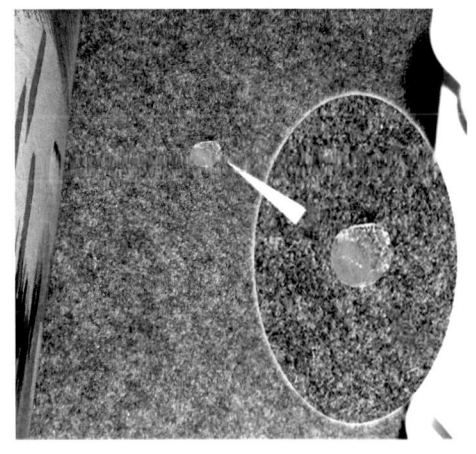

12. (*Right*) Ornamental candle holders on the window ledge at the top of the stairwell at the house in South Shields. The second photograph clearly shows that one of the objects has been moved.
(*Darren W. Ritson & Michael J. Hallowell*)

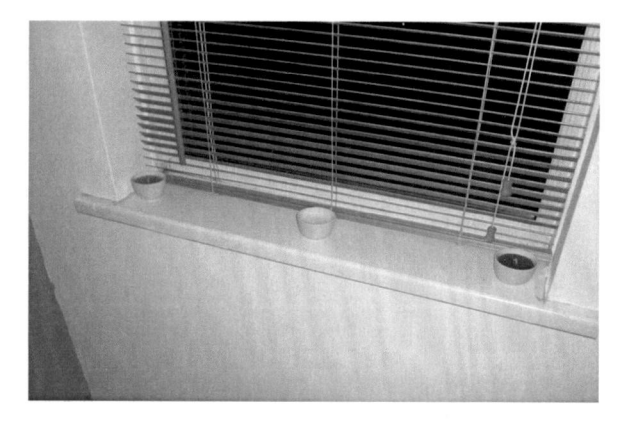

13. (*Below*) During the Enfield poltergeist infestation, the polt would often line up household objects in geometric patterns. This photograph was taken in the kitchen and shows coffee mugs and plant pots placed in two neat rows. Similar occurrences have been recorded by the authors during other investigations.
(*Maurice Grosse / Guy Lyon Playfair*)

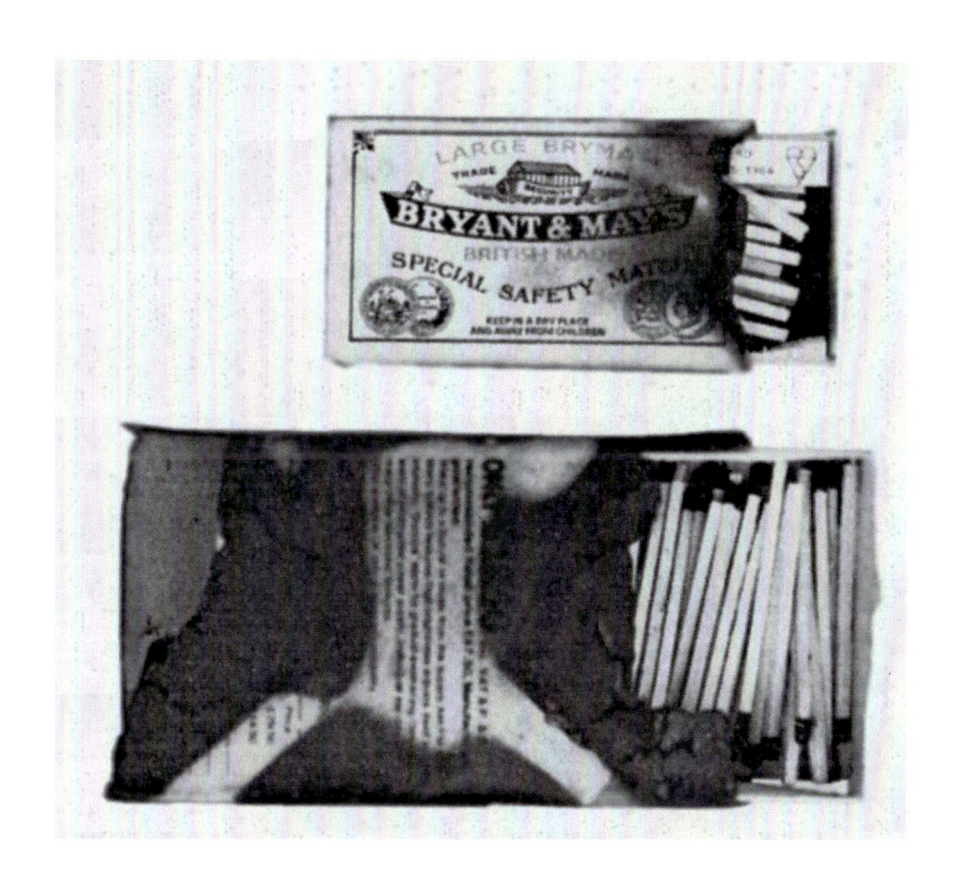

14. (*Above*) Matchboxes which spontaneously combusted during the Enfield and Holloway investigations. Curiously, although the boxes burnt, the matches themselves didn't catch fire.
(*Guy Lyon Playfair*)

15. (*Left*) The Enfield Poltergeist also liked to leave messages on walls. On this occasion it spelt out the words, "I AM FRED" with pieces of electricians' tape. (*Maurice Grosse/Guy Lyon Playfair*)

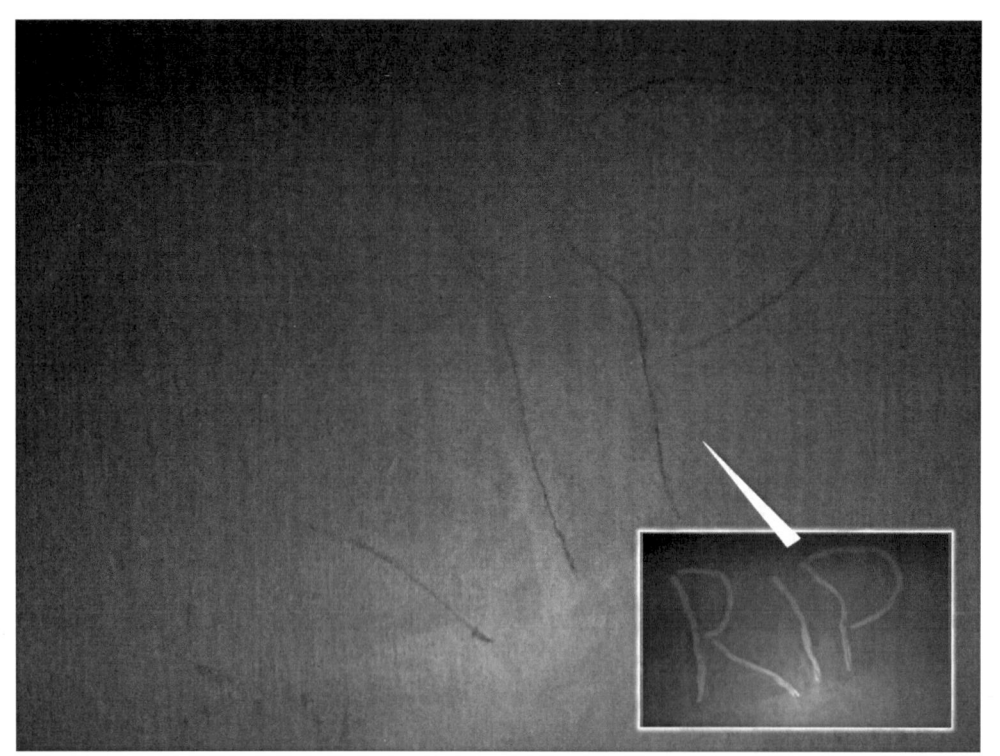

16. (*Above*) The letters "RIP" were scratched into the wall of one of the bedrooms at the house in South Shields. (*Darren W. Ritson & Michael J. Hallowell*)

17. (*Below*) A stuffed toy which appeared mysteriously by the kitchen door at the house in South Shields. (*Darren W. Ritson & Michael J. Hallowell*)

18. (*Above*) Robert's room, after being trashed during the South Shields investigation. A bizarrely-shaped urine stain can be seen on the floor at the bottom left-hand (facing) aspect of the picture. (*Darren W. Ritson & Michael J. Hallowell*)

19. (*Right*) The Enfield Poltergeist was also extremely destructive. In this picture a chest of drawers has been thrown over. (*Maurice Grosse/ Guy Lyon Playfair*)

20. (*Above*) A chair and trash can which had been placed against the door of Robert's room at South Shields. The objects had been placed against the door from the inside of the room although no one was inside at the time. (*Darren W. Ritson & Michael J. Hallowell*)

21. (*Below*) Coins thrown to the floor during the South Shields investigation. They seemed to drop from the air mysteriously and their source was never determined. (*Darren W. Ritson & Michael J. Hallowell*)

22. (*Left*) Guy Lyon Playfair examines a similar disruption involving a chair at Enfield when it was placed on top of a wardrobe. The parallel between the two incidents is obvious. (*Maurice Grosse/Guy Lyon Playfair*)

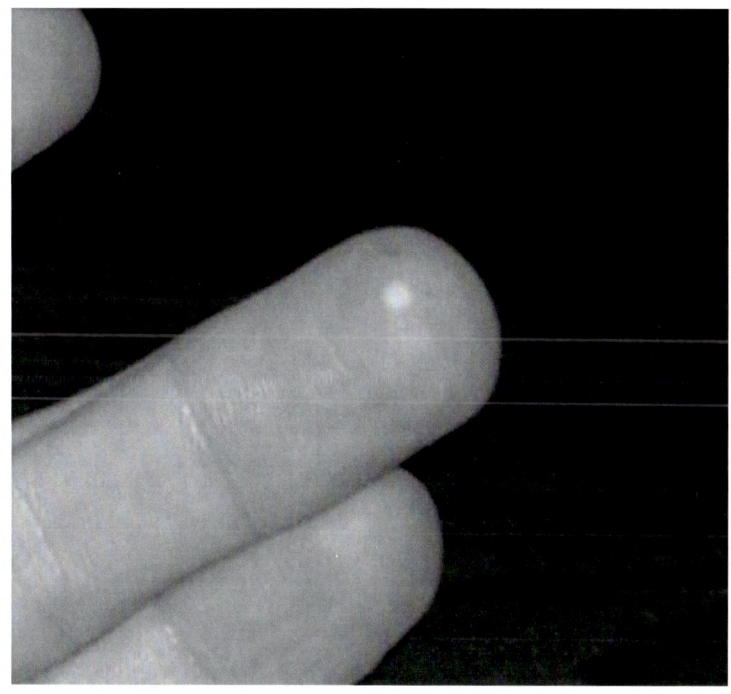

23. (*Left*) A large blister on Mike's finger caused by his attempts to beat out the flames after the sleeve of his dressing gown caught fire. (*Thunderbird Craft & Media*)

24. (*Left*) The hall and stairway of the student flat in Newcastle upon Tyne which was subjected to a protracted period of bizarre, poltergeist-like activity. (*Darren W. Ritson*)

25. (*Right*) The crucifix which was used as a "trigger object" by investigators at the Newcastle premises they investigated. In the picture, Arrow 1 points to the original location of the crucifix, whilst Arrow 2 shows where it ended up after being mysteriously thrown across the floor. (*Darren W. Ritson*)

26. (*Left*) Rhianne D'Morgyn, the experienced spirit medium who accompanied the authors on a number of their investigations. (*Rhianne D'Morgyn*)

27. (*Below*) Staff and investigators outside of the *Un Tesoro* craft shop in Blyth, home of the "haunted loom". (*Thunderbird Craft & Media*)

28. (*Above*) The old haunted loom inside the *Un Tesoro* craft shop in Blyth. *(Thunderbird Craft & Media)*

29. (*Below*) Vicky Nesbitt and the scarf which was woven by unknown hands on the haunted loom. *(Thunderbird Craft & Media)*

30. (*Left*) The poltergeist at Jarrow lifted a baby's crib onto the bed whilst the family were out. Fortunately, they had the presence of mind to photograph it.
(Copyright restricted)

31. (*Below*) The stairwell at the house in Jarrow, where numerous people reported feeling disorientated.
(Thunderbird Craft & Media)

32. (*Right*) In this 15th century oil painting, Jesus can be seen casting out an evil spirit from a possessed man.

33. (*Left*) In this 19th century painting by Jose de Goya, the 15th century saint Francis Borgia can be seen casting out a demon in the well-worn Christian tradition.

34. (*Left*) In a painting by Giotto di Bondone, St. Francis of Assisi is seen to be casting out demons, including incubi and succubi.

35. (*Below*) An incubus is about to attack a woman in this 19th century painting. The creature bears a close resemblance to those in the previous picture by Giotto di Bondone.

The authors, whose involvement with the South Shields Poltergeist case began in June 2006. (*Darren W. Ritson & Michael J. Hallowell*)

person killed them. However, when the killer leaves a unique "calling card" or "signature" at the scene of each crime, the situation changes. Leaving a Five of Hearts playing card on the body of each victim is so specific – so unique – that it strongly suggests that a serial killer is at work.

What can we learn from this? Well, we can see clearly that some actions merely allow us to narrow down suspects to a species, whilst others are so unique that they allow us to state that one individual is responsible, even if we haven't yet determined exactly who that individual is. When the homicide detective finds a body with a Five of Hearts playing card on it, he knows that he is looking for *one particular* killer as opposed to *a* killer. Basically, it's all to do with characteristics. Some traits are widely prevalent throughout an entire community or race, whilst others are specific to one person only. This feature of human behaviour would become crucially important to the authors as their investigation into the contagion phenomenon progressed.

There was one other incident of contagion that occurred at Darren's home that the authors have not yet detailed. Shortly after Darren and Jayne's daughter was born, the child was given a cuddly toy as a present – a stuffed bear. When Abbey would drift off to sleep, the bear would be at the bottom of her cot. One evening, Darren went in to Abbey's room and found to his surprise that the bear was now "tucked up" under the blankets with his daughter. The question was, how had it got there? Abbey was not yet able to walk or crawl; how could she have retrieved the bear from the bottom of her cot and placed it under the blankets beside her? More, how could she then have tucked the blankets around herself, cocoon-like, without help? She simply wasn't old enough to accomplish this. Darren asked Jayne if she had placed the bear next to Abbey under the blankets, but Jayne answered firmly in the negative.

There were two occasions when the polt at Lock Street did something similar with the toddler Robert. On one occasion it removed him from his bed and placed him on the floor with a quilt wrapped very tightly around him. On another occasion it placed him in a wardrobe in the next room. It would also take Robert's toys and place them in bed. On one occasion, it took a stuffed toy duck and placed it next to him under the blankets – exactly the same as had happened at Darren's home. Darren happened to be talking to his colleague and fellow ghost-hunter Darren Olley, and mentioned the incident with the bear that had occurred all those months ago. Darren Olley had also played an integral part in the investigation of the South Shields Poltergeist, and had visited the house at Lock Street on a number of occasions. Perhaps this makes his reaction to Darren's recollection all the more intriguing.

"It's funny you should say that. My girlfriend and I had a similar experience when we lived in Gosforth. The flat we lived in had a spare room with a wardrobe in it. The wardrobe was on the right just as you walked in the door, and on top of it there were some stuffed toys – you know, teddies. There was also a stuffed toy donkey that used to sing 'Happy Birthday' which had been sitting on top of the wardrobe for several months. One day, when Lez my girlfriend walked into the room, it started to sing and dance. She nearly had kittens. This had never happened before, and has never happened again".

When Darren related his friend's account to Mike it set bells ringing in his head. At Lock Street, the polt would often place cuddly toys on top of a wardrobe; one specific wardrobe, actually – *the one in the bedroom which stood against the wall on the right-hand side as you entered.* It seemed an extraordinary coincidence to Mike that both incidents involved cuddly toys on top of wardrobes – wardrobes which were in exactly the same position as each other in two separate houses. Another coincidence struck Darren. At South Shields, a stuffed *Tigger* toy was found on the top of the wardrobe. At Darren Olley's flat, the donkey that had burst into life was actually *Eeyore*, and the teddy bear that was moved in Abbey's cot at Darren's Ritson's house had been none other the *Pooh Bear*! Three characters – all from the same series of children's books written by A. A. Milne.

Later in the day, Darren sent an e-mail to Darren Olley and asked him when the incident had occurred. He couldn't quite remember, so Darren Olley in turn e-mailed his girlfriend Lez and asked her. Lez e-mailed Darren Olley back and stated that they had lived in the flat in Gosforth between May 2006 and March 2007 – plum in the middle of the time period when the South Shields Poltergeist investigation was at its height. Darren and Mike now strongly suspected that Darren Olley and his girlfriend Lez had both been subjected to contagion.

As if this wasn't enough, both Darren Olley and his girlfriend had experienced another strange occurrence in the flat. One day, Lez had needed her passport and had looked for it in the place where she thought she'd left it – a drawer. It wasn't there, and consequently Lez was forced to carry out a thorough search of her entire home. The search was fruitless, and so she once again checked the drawer where she thought she'd left her passport. Still no luck. Frustrated, she checked the drawer a third time. As Darren Olley watched her searching, he too became frustrated and said, "Lez, where did you actually put it?"

In response, Lez opened the drawer once again and replied, "Darren, I put it in *here*!"

Both Darren and Lez stared down into the drawer, and saw, to their astonishment, that the passport was there in plain view on top of the rest of the drawer's contents.

"I saw Lez search that drawer on several occasions", Darren Olley commented later, "and I can tell you that it definitely *wasn't* in there".

This also made both authors recall a specific incident at Lock Street. On the afternoon of Thursday, 21 September 2006, Marc suddenly realised that his employers' ID card was missing. Concerned, he began to search for it systematically. On two occasions, Marianne checked a drawer in the kitchen. On the first occasion she took a cursory peek inside, but on the second she ransacked the drawer completely until she was absolutely satisfied that Marc's ID was not inside. Unbeknownst to Marianne, Marc had also searched the drawer thoroughly too. After thirty minutes of fruitless searching, the ID card appeared: in the drawer, sitting on top of all its other contents. The parallels between what had happened at Lock Street and what was happening in other cases that the authors were either investigating or being made aware of were uncanny.

From the time when the authors began to investigate the South Shields Poltergeist, they had become aware of a series of strange "coincidences". In themselves they were nothing startling, and, in fact, Darren and Mike had often joked about them. The first incident of its kind came just before Darren found out about the infestation at Lock Street.

One evening, Darren had telephoned Mike and they were discussing a number of different "paranormal" subjects, including the poltergeist phenomenon. Darren said, "Wouldn't it be great, Mike, if we got a really *big* case to investigate...something like Enfield? Mike agreed, and responded, "It would be. Who knows? One day we might".

As the conversation continued, a thought struck Mike: "You know, I also think it would be a great idea if we were to write a book together".

Darren paused for a moment and then said, "Are you serious?"

"Absolutely".

"What would we write about?"

"I don't know – something will turn up" said Mike.

Days later, Darren was told about the infestation at South Shields. It not only turned out to be their "big case", but they also wrote an extremely successful book about it.

But there was another strange parallel that the authors had noticed. During the Enfield case, back in 1977, Maurice Gross had been the first investigator to take up the challenge of investigating it. Guy Playfair had then joined Maurice in his endeavours. Darren once commented to Mike, "You know, that's exactly what happened at South Shields. I got the case and then you came in on it".

To the authors, this was nothing more than an amusing coincidence. Or at least, it seemed that way at the time.

Another similarity was the fact that just before the Enfield case broke, Maurice had become a member of the Society for Psychical Research (SPR). Just before the South Shields case broke, Darren had joined the SPR also. Unlike Enfield, however, the South Shields case was not an investigation formally looked into by the SPR, although the authors lectured about it at one of the society's meetings in December 2007, and Guy Playfair was heavily consulted by the investigators as their research proceeded. Their investigation into the South Shields Poltergeist case was later given an extremely positive review in *the Journal of the Society for Psychical Research*.[1]

In 2003, New Dominion Pictures, in conjunction with the Discovery Channel, produced a series of dramatised documentaries called *A Haunting*. Each hour-long programme featured a particularly traumatic true-life haunting, some of which contained classic signs of poltergeist infestation. At this time of writing the programme is now in its fourth season, well-produced and hugely popular. Two episodes in the series, both produced in 2006, proved to be of immense interest to the authors. As the South Shields Poltergeist first reared its head in the latter part of 2005, and the infestation lasted for almost a year, we can safely say that the filming of the programmes in question overlapped in whole or in part the South Shields investigation.

The series was first shown in the UK in 2008, thus reducing almost to zero the possibility that the principal experients had seen the two episodes concerned. This is important, as cynics will inevitably suggest that the family at Lock Street copied incidents contained within the documentaries. There is no doubt that such criticisms *will* be levelled, for the parallels between *A Haunting* and what occurred at Lock Street are nothing short of mind-blowing.

Episode 9 of series 2 was entitled *Demon Child,* and concerned a family from Western Kentucky. The child at the centre of the drama, given the pseudonym Cody to protect his real identity, starts to display disturbing character traits at the age of 7, including the use of foul language in front of his "nanny" or child-minder. Cody then claims to have an invisible or "imaginary" childhood friend called Man. Man claims to be 7 years old and dead.

Slowly but surely, Man exercises an ever-increasing influence over Cody whose behaviour is spiralling out of control. Cody's mother begins to suspect that Man is not really the spirit of a young child at all, but something far, far darker. A Native American shaman is brought in to help the family, and he shows the family how to perform cleansing rituals with the aid of incense made from sage and sweetgrass. The entity eventually manifests itself before Cody's mother, appearing first as a young boy. However, she soon realises that it is no child as the entity metamorphoses into a large, anthropomorphic creature with a hideous countenance.

The poltergeist – for that is what the authors concluded the entity was – had simply been masquerading as the innocent spirit of a young boy who had died under tragic circumstances. Those who have read *The South Shields Poltergeist – One Family's Fight Against an Invisible Intruder*, will realise immediately how close the parallels between the two accounts are, for the Lock Street polt *also* masqueraded as an "imaginary" childhood friend, called Sammy. As with the Western Kentucky case, Sammy turned out to be a full-blown poltergeist in disguise which ended up terrorising an innocent family.

As the authors watched the programme, they were struck with other bizarre similarities. Both Robert and Cody liked to play with a toy fire truck, for instance. On one occasion, Robert's stepfather, Marc, found the toy in a cupboard soaking wet. The South Shields Poltergeist once urinated on the floor in Robert's room. The mother in the West Kentucky case found her son's closet soaked in urine, although to be fair Cody did seem to have admitted responsibility for it. Man, he said, had encouraged him to do it. The polt at Lock Street also seemed to have a fascination with stuffed "cuddly" toys, including a teddy bear. In the West Kentucky case, Cody's father found his son cutting up a teddy bear with a pair of scissors. Man had told him it would be fun. Also in the West Kentucky case, the polt would arrange the child's stuffed toys theatrically in the middle of the bedroom. The South Shields polt did exactly the same thing. The polt that invaded Darren's home during an episode of contagion messed around with his daughter's teddy bear, and the entity that infiltrated Darren Olley's flat also had a fascination with cuddly toys. The West Kentucky polt repeatedly threw a teddy bear across the lounge.

But perhaps the strangest coincidence involved a scene in the dramatised documentary when Cody can be seen playing in his room. On the floor, just under the bedroom window, is a play mat which contained roads upon which toy cars could be driven. Mike had a similar play mat when he was a child. When Mike first noticed the play mat it rang a bell with him, so to speak, and he was sure that he'd seen an identical mat in Robert's room at Lock Street. Mike looked through the dozens of photographs they'd taken in the Lock Street house but he couldn't see any such item.

On the afternoon of 29 April, 2008, Mike e-mailed Darren and asked if he too had any such recollection:

> *Hi mate,*
> *I know this sounds like a stupid question, but can you remember whether Robert had one of those play mats*

> containing roads and stuff for toy cars? I'm sure he had, but I can't see it on any of the photographs.
> Mike

Darren replied within a few minutes:

> Yes he did mate. It's on the full version of the picture of me examining the warped table.
> Darren

On one occasion, the Lock Street polt had turned its attention to a plastic table in Robert's room. When Mike found it, it looked as if it had been melted; the legs were bent and the surface of the table warped beyond recognition. Later, Mike had taken a photograph of Darren examining the table. There, underneath Darren's feet, can be seen an identical play mat to the one featured in *Demon Child*. When Mike had looked through the photographs before contacting Darren, he'd glanced at the one of Darren examining the table but hadn't noticed the play mat on the floor. After Darren's reply arrived he looked at the picture again. Not only was it an identical play mat, but it was also positioned *in exactly the same location on the floor* – directly under the bedroom window. Mike found it very difficult indeed to believe that this ostensibly meaningless parallel was simply a coincidence. Whether the "real" Cody had had such a mat in his room the authors didn't know. Perhaps it had simply been added to the dramatised reconstruction. To Mike it didn't matter – the parallel was there in any case, in all its stunning simplicity.

Another coincidence – if such it was – involved the employment of a Native American shaman who showed the family how to "smudge" with sage and sweetgrass in an effort to rid their home of the entity. *The South Shields Poltergeist – One Family's Fight Against an Invisible Intruder* details how Mike – who has Native American heritage – used almost identical smudging rituals in an effort to combat the entity at Lock Street. The herbs he used were also identical; sage and sweetgrass.

The next episode in the series was called *Sallie's House*, and detailed the experiences of a family who had just moved into a house in Atchison, Texas. The couple's son suddenly starts to communicate with an "imaginary" playmate called Sallie. Sallie, at first, seems to be the spirit of a young girl. However, mediums who visited the house soon identify the presence of an older, "very powerful" spirit who was really pulling the strings, so to speak.

During the Atchison infestation, the polt would make eerie, threatening noises over the baby monitor which led from the child's room. The polt at Lock Street did exactly the same thing. The Atchison polt would slam doors and trap the occupants inside rooms. The Lock Street polt did exactly the same thing. The Atchison polt would sometimes appear as a woman looking out of the upstairs window. The South Shields polt did this on one occasion, as did the entity at the craft shop in Blyth and the West Kentucky polt. The West Kentucky entity would pull books from shelves and throw them on to the floor. The South Shields polt did exactly the same thing. The authors could go on listing many more coincidences, but it isn't necessary. The point is that in all the cases detailed by Darren and Mike – both in the UK and abroad – there are uncanny parallels that undeniably demonstrate an intimate link between them.

In the West Kentucky case, the entity eventually showed itself to Cody's mother in its true form. In the dramatised documentary, the entity is shown with blue, deformed skin. During the Lock Street investigation, Mike interviewed young Robert, a toddler at the time, and asked him what "Sammy" was like:

What does Sammy look like?
He has blue skin.
Really?
Yes. His skin has bubbles on it.

The truly disturbing common denominator between all these cases is that the poltergeist – whatever one conceives it to be – repeatedly masquerades as something innocent to hide its dark, terrible nature. Slowly and systematically it will insert its psychic hooks into the principal experients and then, when it is too late, reveal itself as it truly is.

NOTES
1.   Alan Murdie, *Journal* of the Society for Psychical Research, Vol. 73.2, No. 899, April 2010.

Thirteen
"I'm Sick of the Bastard!"

On 15 February 2008, Darren was informed of a poltergeist-like experience that had the hallmarks of a *bone-fide* and very interesting case. Darren feels it warrants inclusion in this volume because the experient is known to the author and is considered by him to be an utterly reliable source. It must also be stressed that this particular narrative is a first-hand account and, as it had occurred fairly recently, the details were still fresh in the mind of the principal witness.

Darren stumbled across the story purely by chance whilst chatting to a neighbour, Doreen*, at the bus stop one morning. Darren – neither shy nor reticent by any standards – took the opportunity to tell Doreen about the book *The South Shields Poltergeist* which he'd co-authored with Mike and which was due for release in little over a month. He warned her that what she would read in the forthcoming tome, should she buy it, would undoubtedly be questioned since the phenomena detailed within it were of such a bizarre nature.

Darren proceeded to give Doreen several examples of some experiences detailed in the book. As she listened to him talk about this extremely peculiar case, she turned to him with a stern look on her face before announcing, seriously and solemnly, "I was forced out of my last house by a ghost, only for the damned thing to follow me. I'm sick of the bastard!"

Darren, by now intrigued, asked Doreen to tell him more.

Darren's neighbour had been living in a house in North Tyneside with a friend, and had experienced some things that, to seasoned investigators, would certainly hint at the presence of a poltergeist. After moving into the house everything was fine;

nothing of a paranormal nature had occurred, and she was happy, content and at ease with her surroundings. Then, out of the blue, the disturbances began. Doors opened and closed on their own, a chair in the living room slid across the floor one day, and three tins of peas were removed from the kitchen cupboard and placed one on top of another in her bath!

This reminded Mike of a case he investigated in 2003 and subsequently wrote up in his *WraithScape* column. It involved a man from the Cleadon Park area of South Shields who, on two separate occasions, found four bottles of fresh milk standing in his bath. Someone playing a prank? A likely explanation, until you analyse the facts.

The man lived alone. No one else had a key to his flat. Plus, on the second occasion, he had used the bath just ten minutes earlier. Again, he was the only person at home. The upshot was that this otherwise rather tough individual became too frightened to stay in his house.

It was, he said, "really scary. If someone gets in my face I would normally just hit them – that's my way, the way I was brought up – but I couldn't fight this; it was invisible".

It is hard to overestimate the negative effect that such experiences have on those who witness them. When bizarre events – events of which we can make no sense whatsoever – invade our lives and instil fear in us, that fear is exacerbated because we are dealing with an enemy that we can neither see nor touch. If someone wants to burgle your house you can take action to stop them by purchasing an alarm, but how do you stop an entity which seemingly stalks your house whilst you are in it and fills your bath with milk bottles – or tins of peas - when your back is turned?

Sometimes people treat these experiences lightly and make fun of them, and that was true in this case.

"My mates were laughing at me, and saying things like, 'I hope you can train it to put the tea bags and hot water in as well', or 'Does it put the empties on the doorstep?' It was alright for them to laugh; they didn't have to live with it".

Let the authors tell readers something for a fact; the gigglers and leg-pullers may think they're being smart, but they'd be laughing on the other side of their faces if they were to go through the same thing.

Nevertheless, people talk more openly about the paranormal now. It's no longer seen as cranky to believe in ghosts, or UFOs, for example, but more incongruous phenomena are things that few will admit to experiencing. The reason, of course, is simple. There are some things which are just too strange to be believed, and, should we admit to them, we will inevitably be labelled as delusional or downright liars.

In the case of Darren's neighbour, Doreen, *knocks* and *bumps* were also heard, as was a gruff voice that called out Doreen's name. Later, Mike would recall how the owner of the craft shop in Blyth had had her name called out by the entity also, albeit over a transistor radio. Back in 2001, when Mike was researching his book *Ales & Spirits,* which detailed the ghost stories attached to many haunted pubs, he investigated a number of chilling encounters that had taken place at a public house in Jarrow. The then pub manager, Alan, related his own experience.

It seems that on one occasion he had said goodnight to the rest of the staff and secured the building, after which he found himself entirely alone on the premises. Without any sense of unease, and feeling perfectly relaxed, he carried out a number of small tasks which would prepare the pub for business the following morning. It was roughly 2am by the time he had concluded his work, and he was just about to retire to his flat upstairs. As he traversed the short corridor next to the lounge and the bar, he suddenly heard a voice. When Mike interviewed Alan he related that the voice was deep – "almost husky" – but certainly female. It simply said, "Alan".

"It was really close…just behind my ear. It was loud and clear. I jumped round expecting to see someone, but the place was deserted. I admit I was shocked. It's easy to joke about this sort of thing, but I know what I heard".

In July 2006, Darren took part in an investigation at a location in Durham City, which must remain anonymous at the request of the building's key-holders. With Darren were a number of other investigators from a local paranormal research team of which Darren was one of the co-founders. During the course of the investigation, a number of anomalous voices were recorded under controlled conditions. These voices were not heard at the time, but could be heard with crystal clarity when the tapes were replayed later. The voices did not belong to any of the investigators present. One voice was that of a female with a distinct brogue. Darren and others are convinced that the accent sounds distinctly "Irish", whilst Mike and others strongly disagree and think that the brogue is distinctly that of South Yorkshire provenance. Regardless, however, the mysterious voice can be heard to plead, chillingly, "Can you help me?"

After this recording was made, Darren later returned to the room with another researcher, Suzanne, to carry on with the investigation. What happened next is taken from Darren's own account, written up in his book *Ghost Hunter – True Life Encounters from the North East* :

"We settled down in the office and proceeded with the investigation. Just on the off-chance, I decided to leave my audio-dictation machine running whilst in there, and in retrospect I'm glad I did as yet another anomalous voice recording was made".

"It was not until the day after the investigation, when I played the tapes back, that I heard something that I had recorded. Suzanne and I were in the office upstairs, and were 'calling out' to the woman who had previously asked, 'Can you help me?"

"Unbeknown to us at the time, another voice had been recorded, only this time it was that of a man. The disturbing thing about this recording was that he said nothing but my name, 'Darren'. To hear such a weird recording of what some researchers would presume to be that of a ghost or spirit is one thing, but to hear one call out your name is something else".

Later, Darren recalled a number of peculiarities about the incident that made it even stranger. Firstly, Darren has no recollection of actually hearing the voice at the time, and yet he *must* have heard it, for on the recording he can clearly be heard responding to it by saying, "Hold on". The conversation between Darren and the entity, short though it is, sounds completely natural; someone calls out Darren's name, and Darren responds to the person by saying "Hold on", essentially asking them to wait a moment.

The second peculiarity is that the other investigator present, Suzanne, did not hear the anomalous voice, and neither did she hear Darren's reply. Had she heard it, she would have undoubtedly asked who Darren was responding to.

Perhaps the strangest aspect of the incident concerns the fact that the disembodied voice sounds uncannily like Darren's own. These enigmas may give us a hint regarding the nature of the disembodied voice. Had Darren *subconsciously* heard the voice, thereby explaining why Suzanne didn't? Perhaps he also *responded* to it subconsciously, not actually uttering the words, "Hold on", but merely thinking them? Of course, this only deepens the mystery, for if neither the entity or Darren physically uttered the words, how on earth were they picked up on tape? The only other explanation is that Darren deliberately uttered his own name and then responded to it, essentially having a conversation with himself. However, this doesn't explain why Suzanne, who can be heard talking in the background, didn't hear either Darren utter his own name or his response to his own utterance.

At the time the recording was made, all the investigators except for Darren and Suzanne were in another part of the building and therefore could not have been responsible. Had it been another investigator shouting Darren's name, then both Darren and Suzanne would have responded to their call. However, on the tape the voice, although clear and distinct, is not loud. It is also obvious that the entity that uttered Darren's name was in close proximity to the recording device. The more one studies the tape, and the circumstances in which it was made, the more baffling it becomes.

In the case of Darren's neighbour, Doreen, household objects began to move around on their own, personal possessions seemed to disappear for weeks-on-end and then suddenly re-appear in exactly the same place where they had been seen last. One particular article, a music CD, was placed on the mantelpiece for just a moment while Doreen tended to another matter. When she turned around to retrieve the CD it had gone. It mysteriously reappeared on the mantelpiece one week later.

Other phenomena occurred too. Picture frames that were placed upon the walls came thundering down the stairwell after they had been pulled from the wall. No one, of course, was upstairs at the time. On occasions the frames actually jumped off the wall when more than one person was in the room to witness it.

One of the more alarming incidents of this case was when two apparitional children were seen inside the house. While a friend of Doreen's was sleeping on the settee one night, she was awoken by the sound of what she described as a "plastic bag rustling". Stirring from her slumbers, the friend noticed that with every passing second the sound became more pronounced. By now she was wide awake, but still lying down; yet the rustling continued. Darren felt that this was significant, and indicated that this particular symptom could not have been caused by what is known as the *hypnopompic state*.

The hypnopompic sleep state is experienced when an individual is waking up from a deep sleep. It is a transitional state of semi-consciousness and has been described by parapsychologists as a time when subjects are more likely to experience visual or auditory hallucinations. Many allegedly paranormal encounters are experienced during this time. We have all heard stories about people waking up during the night and seeing someone at the end of the bed, or hearing footsteps in the room as they lie there in total darkness. This hypnopompic state is said to be responsible for misinterpreting mundane events as paranormal phenomena. The same principle applies when the individual is drifting off to sleep in what is called is called the hypnagogic state. The authors have no problem accepting this, as they believe that on occasions they too have experienced bizarre symptoms of these sleep states themselves. On one occasion, Darren thought he heard a voice calling out to him as he was dropping off to sleep and jumped up with a start. On another occasion he distinctly felt someone sit on the end of the bed, but upon looking there was no one there.

Mike has had similar experiences. Often, just as he is dropping off to sleep or waking up, he'll think he hears the phone ringing or someone knocking at the door. The noises for the most part are illusory, although on several occasions he has experienced anomalous noises that, although superficially similar, were almost certainly of paranormal provenance.

Creepy though such instances are, the authors do not believe that their houses have ghosts, and therefore they believe that these experiences were probably symptoms of these two sleep states. Having said that, strange things have occurred at their abodes as the reader will have noted, but only when they were actively involved with dealing with poltergeist cases elsewhere.

As stated earlier, however, Darren believes that this is *not* the case with Doreen's friend, as she clearly specified to Darren when they met that she had woken fully by that point and yet the rustling sound still continued.

After hearing the bizarre noise, she then turned around and was stunned to see two children in the room with her. When she called out to ask what on earth was going on, they simply disappeared. The rustling sound ceased immediately at this point too. Doreen then informed Darren that her best friend henceforth refused to stay over at her house because it was "too spooky". Eventually the phenomena became so intense and frequent that Doreen decided it was time to leave. By then Darren was totally absorbed by the story, and arranged a time when he could fully interview Doreen and attempt to ascertain more details. It did indeed sound like a good case to follow up. Whether it was a poltergeist at work or just a normal haunting – if you can define hauntings as "normal" – it did not matter at the time.

Darren thinks, "When investigating things of this nature one has to be careful not to get certain phenomena mixed up or confused with others, leading an investigator to wrongly diagnose what is occurring in the infected house. If a doctor did this he may well be struck off the medical register. There is no official code of practice and no governing body supervising ghost and poltergeist investigators; therefore, misinterpretation and faulty diagnoses are sadly all too commonplace".

The authors have heard countless stories of well-meaning amateurs, accompanied by their "team medium", entering a household and seemingly discovering not one ghost but an abundance of them; one on the stairwell, one in the kitchen, two children in the living room, a dog, a cat and a goldfish called "jaws". The householders end up more frightened after the investigators have visited than they were before they came. Often, they'll never see the investigators again.

This actually happened at the house on Lock Street, and the family in question were at one point informed that no less than six ghosts resided in their abode. In Darren's opinion this was – and he begs the reader to overlook his robust language - "a load of shite". Darren believes that there may be reputable psychics out there that may be able to help; one just needs to be careful which ones you choose. The authors eventually come to believe that they'd gotten to the bottom of the Lock Street case after months of hard work, dedication and determination - and found that there certainly weren't "countless spirits" at work at all. Darren and Mike stayed with the family - saw it through with them - until the polt eventually departed from their home, hopefully for good.

Darren thinks that there is a fine line between true polt activity and a spirit that is merely mischievous. He has investigated literally hundreds of hauntings in private houses, pubs, castles, social clubs, museums, restaurants, community centres and theatres across the UK, and has experienced some quite frightening phenomena during the course of his research. One simply has to be able to determine "what causes what" when it comes to paranormal phenomena. Darren recalls one investigation where a trigger object - a crucifix - was left in a locked-off room for a couple of hours. The crucifix was placed on a sheet of paper and a line carefully drawn around it to mark its original position. On returning to the room the investigators noticed that the cross had been moved a distance of one inch from its original resting place.

"Oh my God!" said one of the investigators, "This can only be described as major poltergeist activity!"

"*Major* poltergeist activity?", asked Darren. Later he reflected, "The cross had only moved an inch, for goodness sake! Yes, we had a result, as the cross had indeed been moved by something – but not necessarily a poltergeist".

Darren went on to explain to the investigators, "Look, if you experienced *true* 'major poltergeist activity' you would damn well know about it. Furniture moves across the room, cupboards topple over with a crash, objects are hurled at you, you may hear thunderous bangs coming from nowhere, you may even get dragged out of your bed at night and thrown around the room. *That* could be described as 'major poltergeist activity'!"

Later, Darren added, "Granted, they [the poltergeists] *can* displace objects such as when the crucifix was moved on that particular occasion, but I *don't* think that was a poltergeist at work. For starters, polts need a focus or catalyst. They need to draw their energy from someone to do the things that they do, and that is why most polts operate in normal, everyday households where the foci live, work or visit. As far as we know, polts don't switch from focus to focus, and there was no one attached to the pub at that time who we could even tentatively identify as a focus or host. The truth is that other types of paranormal phenomena can cause polt-like symptoms, so we need to be careful in our analysis. "Personally, I think the chances are that the crucifix was moved by a spirit or a ghost that was simply intrigued by it, and that is what we set out to do; achieve some interaction between ourselves and the spirit world. Too many people these days put the mischievous work of restless ghosts down to 'poltergeist activity', and we have to be wary of that".

On another investigation, Darren and a few members of the team witnessed a chair moving in an old room within the bowels of a castle. On another occasion a coin was thrown across an empty room - which sent shivers down the spines of those present. Poltergeist activity? Not necessarily; perhaps just a playful spirit that enjoyed toying around. Darren comments:

"You see, poltergeist-like activity is not necessarily from a poltergeist, hence the term poltergeist-*like*. It could merely be a ghost messing on with your belongings, maybe trying to tell you something or get your attention. Poltergeists often appear to have a pattern, an agenda, and seem to operate by a set of rules - but not in all cases, as we found out at Lock Street. The typical polt will normally adhere to these patterns and agendas, and it is these predictable aspects that emerge in cases over time. They provide knowledgeable and clued-up investigators with inklings regarding its nature, or at least lets them know what might be going on".

Darren arranged a time when he could speak to Doreen regarding her experiences, and on the following Sunday he carried out his interview. Darren was invited into his neighbour's domicile and settled down at the dining room table with a tape recorder, notebook and pen. Doreen, for her part, provided tea and packet of ginger nuts and twenty *Lambert & Butler* cigarettes.

"So, can you tell me how long your house was...infected?" Darren asked.

"Infected? What do you mean?"

"It's just a term we use; What I'm asking is how long did the occurrences go on for?"

"Oh, about three months", Doreen said.

At this point Darren began to think that it could well have been a poltergeist at work. The three months during which the occurrences took place suggest a short visit from a polt. This fact, combined with the actual phenomena that were detailed to Darren a few days earlier, also indicated that a polt was at work. So far, then, all the evidence seemed to point in the polt direction.

"Was anyone in their early teens living at the house?"

"No".

"Was there anyone in their early teens that visited the house regularly?"

"Yes…….my niece", Doreen said.

"Tell me about her".

"What can I say? She is fourteen years old, a canny lass and gets on well with most people - except one or two at her school, bless her; she's having a hard time of it at the moment".

Darren, at this point, realised that another piece of the metaphorical jigsaw has just fallen into place.

"What was going on with her at school then…and is it still going on?"

"Why do you ask that?", Doreen asked bluntly. "What's *that* got to do with *this*?"

At that point Darren sensed that an uncomfortable situation was arising and presumed the rest of the dialogue was going to be difficult. He pondered for a second or two and then vouched forth just why he had asked the question. After delicately explaining the theories behind the polt phenomenon, and explaining how her niece's troubles could in some way be directly or indirectly responsible for the disturbances in her former home, Doreen sat back and laughed.

"Fuck! She's not coming back to *this* house then!"

Doreen now understood what Darren was trying to explain to her, and she then told him exactly what was going on with her niece at school. The authors have decided not to include the details of the teenager's troubles in this book due to their personal nature. However, as the penny dropped, her face went white.

"She comes to this friggin' house a few times a week; do you think that is why things happen here as well?"

"What happens in this house then?" Darren asked.

"Well, not much really; the odd thing here and there...it's not as bad as what it was in the other house".

Darren thought for a minute or two, and then asked another key question: "Is your niece *still* having trouble at school then?"

"Not as much as she used to; things are getting a bit better".

Darren realised that as the trouble at the school was slowly subsiding, and her niece was coming to terms with what was happening, the paranormal activity at Doreen's new house was slowly tapering off too.

"Right", said Darren, "I'm going to lay my cards on the table then, and make a prediction. When all her troubles are over and things return to normal, I guarantee you that your 'ghost' will go away – for good. I'm confident this will be the case; in fact, there is no need to continue with what we are doing today. Help your niece through her bad time - and just watch!"

This recorded interview took place on Sunday 17 February 2008, and at this time of writing, Darren understands that all the troubles at the teenager's school and home have ceased. Doreen's niece is now well over her ordeal and is getting on with her life as a normal youngster. When Darren spoke to Doreen she commented that all was well, and thanked him for his time and his help. However, she had a question that she wanted him to address: "You know, it's all over now and nothing odd has occurred for months; but remember my friend - the one I lived with at the other house and who saw the two apparitions and heard the rustling?"

"Yes?"

"Well, if all this was down to my niece and the trouble she was having........."

"Yup?"

"Then how the hell could it follow my friend to *her mother's* house? My niece had never been there!"

As Darren pondered over Doreen's words, a singular word flashed through his mind; *contagion*.

NOTES
1. Darren W. Ritson, *Ghost Hunter: True-Life Encounters from the North-East*, GHP, 2006.

Fourteen
ECHOES OF LOCK STREET

In early 2008, Darren was approached by a young woman named Gemma Gorner who thought she was living in a haunted flat in the centre of Newcastle. She told him that she had gleaned his contact details from the curator of Newcastle Keep - Paul McDonald - after a visit there one day with a friend. She had noticed Darren's previously-published books which happened to be on sale there, and told Paul that she, too, "had a ghost". Paul then gave Gemma Darren's work number so she could contact him, and for this he deserves the authors' thanks.

Whilst on his lunch break at work one day, Darren's telephone rang. He picked it up and found himself talking to Gemma. She was more than happy to explain to him about the ghost in her house. Although there had indeed been a number of strange occurrences reported by Gemma and her housemates, Darren felt a visit was not yet justified. The usual array of phenomena had been witnessed, such as objects seemingly being moved around, footsteps being heard inside the property when no one else was around and a barrage of strange noises. In all honesty, Darren thought that as she lived with four of her student acquaintances, maybe a lot of the reported phenomena were actually down to themselves without them even knowing it. With five student girls under one roof, the alleged phenomena could easily have been a case of misattribution.

On May 30, 2008 Darren was again contacted by Gemma and informed that the "ghost" (whom they had named *Tom*) was still making his presence known; only this time it had became a little more intense. Darren was told that noises were quite often heard while Gemma was "in on her own". When Darren asked her to tell him more about what exactly she had heard he admitted it sounded very similar to a poltergeist case that the authors had investigated in the summer of 2006. Darren was informed that one day, while Gemma was home, a loud noise was heard. She told Darren:

"It sounded like a large spoon or something metallic being thrown down the corridor, only when I went to see what it could be I found no explanation for it".

Another incident occurred that was documented on her mobile phone's video-clip facility, again while she was in the flat on her own.

"I woke up one night to the sound of a banging noise in my room; one minute it was in my room, the next it was coming from out in the corridor. It was really terrifying and I knew no one would believe me so I grabbed my mobile phone and recorded the noises. I successfully taped them but on the recording they are not as clear as they were on the actual night".

By far the most impressive report of her unwelcome visitor came when Darren asked her if she or any of her flatmates had seen anything move around with their own eyes.

"You know, there was one thing I meant to tell you about, and you have just reminded me of it. My flatmate Rosie went in to her room one night and saw on her table top a bottle of water standing on its edge, leaning over 45 degrees and spinning around. Round and round it went! She couldn't believe her eyes and was rooted to the spot".

Darren could hardly believe it. He then had to ask Gemma if she was winding him up, and she said "No". He really did believe her. This led Darren to accept that Gemma and her flatmates may have been experiencing a low-level poltergeist infestation. Darren subsequently informed Mike and explained the whole situation regarding the "bottle balancing" episode in Rosie's room. Well, you could have knocked Mike down with a feather. Darren knew exactly how Mike would react to this phenomenon being reported, and he also knew exactly what Mike was now thinking. The true significance of what Rosie saw will become apparent later on.

Darren subsequently, and almost immediately, arranged a time to visit Gemma in her home. On Monday June 2, 2008 the authors arrived at the flat at about 12.30pm. After enjoying sandwiches whilst sitting on one of the public benches in the Bigg Market soaking up the glorious sunshine, Gemma met Darren and Mike downstairs and took them up to her top-floor flat where one of her friends, Liz Mills, was sitting waiting. Another flatmate, Jo Risolino, was at the shop getting in some supplies for the visit. In next-to-no-time she arrived back and, after a cup of tea was prepared, the girls delighted the authors with more stories of their ghostly goings-on.

Jo started first. She told the authors that one night she woke up and saw a dark shadow in her room and, to her horror, realised it was standing over her bed. This actually happened the night before the visit and she experienced what she described as, "...a creeping, ice-cold rush that began at my toes and crept right over my body; then, as quick as it came, it went".

Gemma then went on to tell Darren and Mike that she had recently heard footsteps walking along the narrow corridor while she was in her bedroom; they then ceased after they reached a certain point. Then they were told that Rosie, although not in attendance on our visit that day, had witnessed her TV being turned on in her room when no one else was around. Liz Mills had experienced little or nothing at all.

During the afternoon the authors spent there, they utilised their time carefully and carried out a number of tests and experiments, but little did they know how successful they were to be. They recorded taps and knocks coming from within Gemma's room, and it sounded like something was clattering about in there.

At one point in the afternoon, the flatmates and the authors went into the hallway that led from the flat to the stairwell outside. Both Darren and Mike switched on their digital sound recorders and placed them on a shelf, after which they found somewhere to sit. Darren and the girls positioned themselves on the stairwell, whilst Mike sat down on the floor. The lights were switched off, and the hallway was plunged into inky darkness.
After several minutes, Mike's eyes adjusted to the blackness. The only light he could detect was a thin column shining through the gap in between the door which led into the lounge and the frame which surrounded it. At some point Mike slightly adjusted his position on the floor and noticed something odd; If he moved his head slightly to the left, the shaft of light shining through the gap

in between the door and the door frame seemed to break into two horizontally. Then, if he moved his head back again, the two shafts of light joined back together to form one. Puzzled, Mike stood up and tried to figure out what was causing this anomaly. It seemed to him that something three-dimensional was in front of the door, and that the movement of his head - changing the angle of his vision - caused whatever was in front of the door to obscure the light and seem to cut it in two.

At this point Mike felt rather uncomfortable, and developed an overpowering feeling that something was standing in front of the door even though he couldn't actually see it due to the almost complete absence of light. Slowly he walked forwards along the hallway towards the door, and as he did so the shape of the object became faintly but tangibly clear. It was anthropomorphic, completely black and three-dimensional. When Mike came within two feet of the entity he paused and stared straight ahead. He then called out to Darren and the girls and told them what he could see. Slowly but deliberately he stretched his right hand forward, fully expecting it to make contact with whatever it was in front of him.

At that point everyone there that day heard a long drawn-out sigh which made the women distinctly afraid. They, too - all five, including Mike - could see the six- foot tall, three-dimensional, black shadow while they were sitting in the darkened hallway. This was Liz's first experience of the paranormal activity at her home and, deep down, it was obvious to the authors that she truly didn't like it.

As the deep sigh echoed throughout the hallway, Darren shouted, "Mike...was that you?"

Mike, not realising that Darren was talking about the sighing sound, replied, "Was that me *what*?"

"The sighing sound we just heard – was that you?"

It was obvious that Darren thought the sound may have had a perfectly logical explanation – that Mike may have sighed, perhaps without even realising it. However, Mike had *not* sighed. But then it happened again, and immediately one of the women sitting on the stairs jumped forward with a start.

"*I* heard it – and it came from just behind my head!"

As the girls became increasingly frightened and rapidly began to lose their composure, Mike continued to stare at the thing in front of him, his arm still outstretched. Darren tried to calm the flatmates down and reassured them that they were perfectly safe. The *thing*, the *entity*, then dissolved into the ether leaving nothing behind but two startled investigators and three terrified flatmates wrapped in a mantle of darkness. All five then entered the lounge and the welcoming light.

Mike had seen this entity – or something very like it – once before. At Lock Street both he and Marianne had witnessed a similar creature stride across the hallway from the bathroom into one of the bedrooms. It had paused momentarily, stared at Mike and then carried on. The "shadow man" at Newcastle hadn't walked anywhere; it had just stared. This, however, had not made Mike feel any easier in its presence. Both Mike and Darren were aware of what seemed like a strange coincidence; two entities of identical appearance – or was it the same one? - had appeared in two different and seemingly unrelated cases. Mike had seen it the first time. Now both Darren and Mike had witnessed it together.

A date for a full investigation was then planned in which they would put the flat under surveillance with CCTV, video cameras and all the latest mod-cons for a protracted period of time in the hope that they could catch Tom, or whomever the ghost may be, on tape.

On the night of June 14, 2008, Darren and a group of dedicated paranormal investigators – G.H.O.S.T - arrived at the Bigg Market flat to carry out the full investigation. Mark Winter (from the North East Ghost Research Team) and Darren arrived at about 10.30pm and were soon met by Drew Bartley, Fiona Vipond, and Jim and Paul Collins. Mike Hallowell was unavailable for the investigation. At 10.50pm, Fiona Vipond and Paul Collins carried out the initial baseline tests in the apartment and discovered nothing odd whatsoever. Squeaky floorboards were discovered in certain areas of the flat and draughts/ winds from outside were virtually non-existent. The average room temperature was between 20 – 22 ° Celsius. Trigger objects were placed down in their respective locations and motion sensors were situated in both the upper corridor and lower hallway. Last but not least, the CCTV and laptop were set up and the researchers were then ready to commence with the investigation.

After the baseline tests had been carried out, but prior to the first vigil starting, the ghost – it seemed – was already beginning to make itself known. A huge, white light came into view at one end of the upper-floor corridor and moved in the direction of Drew Bartley with great speed. It then shot over his right shoulder and he had to move to miss it. Not long after this, Drew, Fiona, Jim and Paul noticed that the toilet door handle was being moved up and down and subsequently reported it to Darren. The team then split up into three groups to cover the flat.

In the first group were Fiona, Gemma Gorner, and her two friends, Rebecca and Karen. They investigated the upper corridors. In group two there were Drew, Mark and Jim; they investigated the entrance hall and corridor. Paul and Darren stationed themselves in the living room.

Throughout Darren's first vigil in the living room area the investigators called out to see if anything would occur, but without result. Darren then tried some voice-recording experiments, with this attempt also yielding no results. The only strange occurrence for the duration of this vigil was when Darren was filming with his video camera and, for no apparent reason, it turned itself off in his hands. Drew, Mark and Jim, while investigating the entrance foyer, experienced something odd when they found that the door, which had previously been closed, had now been opened. Again, no explanation was forthcoming as to how that could have happened, as the door was closed with the latch clicking into place. Two of the girl's upstairs (Gemma and Karen) experienced a phenomenon that would end up repeating itself later in the investigation in the form of whistling – and it was *inside* the room where they were located.

During the first break, Gemma's flatmate Liz Mills had returned home and joined in with the overnight investigation. The researchers then re-located themselves in their new positions but they didn't stay in them for long. Things began to turn truly bizarre when Drew, Mark and Jim were in the upper corridor. Paul and Darren were investigating the entrance hall and corridor area at the time, and they could clearly hear the team upstairs. Their vigils were broken up when they heard Drew call out and ask if the alleged spirit could make itself known. A distinct whistle was then heard by all upstairs – and also by Paul and Darren downstairs. Darren then actually called out to Drew and asked if the whistle came from any of the investigators. He was told it had not.

After asking for more phenomena, the investigators heard knocking down in the entrance foyer, which was rather odd to say the least. Then, suddenly, a remarkable series of crashes and bumps was heard coming from the upper corridor.

"Did you hear that?" Drew called out.

"Yes I did, what the hell was it?" Darren yelled up the stairs.

"I don't know yet; I'm checking it out", replied Drew, as he made his way to the scene.

Suddenly, from out of the darkness came a number of choice expletives too crude to mention. It turned out that the crucifix trigger object had been thrown from its original position on the floor at the end of the corridor, had travelled about four feet across the floor and landed just short of the strategically-placed beam barriers.

By this time, Paul and Darren had ran upstairs to find out what was going on and saw the dislocated trigger object lying far from its original position. Jim then hurried past them along the corridor and was absolutely terrified. Drew rewound the video camera footage so the investigators could all watch it. The noise could clearly be heard as the three investigators stood at the *other* end of the corridor from where the object was placed. One can clearly see Jim and Mark on the footage, and it shows them both to be at the other end of the corridor at the time. Drew was with them too, as he was filming there. No one was near the trigger object, then, when it was launched with some force down the corridor.

The investigators then went downstairs and met up with the girls. They knew something odd was going on as they too had heard the object as it was thrown, but had decided to stay in their current vigil location. During the next break, cups of tea and coffee were drunk in abundance while the investigators excitedly discussed what had just taken place. Darren then took it upon himself to return to the corridor with his EVP recorder and carry out some more tests. Mark, Fiona, and flatmate Liz Mills accompanied him. He proceeded to switch on his device and began recording. Darren then asked a number of questions, leaving enough time for any spirit that may have been present to reply – and they were not disappointed. After posing about ten questions or so, they were rewarded with two replies to two of the questions:

"How old are you?"

On the tape, a distant but clear voice can be heard saying, "Forty-eight".

"Do you know that you are dead?"

"Yes."

Intriguing results to say the least. The EVP recording was immediately transferred onto a laptop computer and analysed. The rest of the night was spent thrashing out the paranormal events that had taken place there until a séance was held in the area where all the excitement had occurred. The séance lasted over forty-five minutes, and during it Darren was pushed by something from within the darkness. It moved him back a little, and it didn't feel to the author as if it was particularly welcoming. Minor temperature drops and the occasional breeze were also felt by some of the circle members, and then the activity seemed to dry right up.

This investigation proved to be a good one for all concerned, with some astonishing activity both witnessed and documented. The girls had for some time been reporting comparable incidences at their Newcastle flat, and were now convinced more than ever that they were not imagining it. The investigation there seemed to suggest that something distinctly otherworldly was occurring and warranted further investigation. However, since the writing of the investigation report based on Darren's findings it has came to light that the girls have since moved out of the premises.

A number of disturbing occurrences that were witnessed at the Newcastle residence intrigued the authors very much. A lot of the phenomena documented during the authors' visits (Darren twice, Mike once), were typical of a low- level polt at work; objects being thrown around, a nasty sense of presence in the bedrooms, unexplained thumps and strange whistling noises. But during the whole investigation there was one particular incident which, metaphorically, grabbed Darren firmly by the balls.

When he was informed about it for the first time he almost went white; hardly able to believe what he had just heard. It was the time when Rosie saw the bottle of mineral water in her bedroom spinning crazily at a 45-degree angle.

What the Newcastle experients did not know was that during the investigation at Lock Street, South Shields, Mike Hallowell had actually recorded this *exact* phenomenon on camera. A half-full bottle of water can be clearly seen balancing on its edge of its own volition, although it was not spinning around as in the Newcastle case; but nonetheless the same thing *had* occurred in that investigation. Darren and Mike had to ask themselves a very simple question; what were the chances of two separate poltergeists both deciding, seemingly on a whim, to entertain their human hosts by balancing a plastic bottle of mineral water on a table, at pretty much the same angle, and effectively defying the laws of physics?

The authors knew that these were exactly the type of meaningless things that poltergeists did, but the similarities between the two incidents simply couldn't be put down to coincidence. Also, the appearance of the "shadow man" in both cases drew Mike and Darren to the tentative conclusion that the Newcastle and South Shields events were, in some way they couldn't yet figure out, linked. But why? How?

Fifteen
THE INCUBUS

After the authors' investigation into the South Shields Poltergeist had drawn to a close – at least insofar as its manifestation at Lock Street was concerned – Darren wondered whether they would ever get such an opportunity again. Cases of that degree of intensity are incredibly rare, and Darren felt it unlikely that the gods would smile upon them twice. Mike was a little more optimistic.

"You know, when our book about the South Shields Poltergeist is eventually published its going to cause something of a stir. My bet is that a lot of people who are experiencing polt infestation are going to get to hear about us by reading the book. If they're desperate for help, we could very well be the first one's they'll call. My guess is that we may not just get *one* more good case, but a boatload of them".

On Monday 28 April, 2008, Steve Taylor from Alone In The Dark Entertainment rang Mike at his office. A new case – possibly involving a poltergeist – had come to his attention and he wanted to know if Mike would like to investigate.

According to Steve, an elderly woman who lived in Ashington, Northumberland, had suddenly found herself under attack from a rather malign entity which had entered her home without invitation. The woman, a widow, had seemingly been involved with spiritualism for many years and had gained something of a reputation as a medium. To her, the concept of spiritual beings making their presence felt from time-to-time was a perfectly normal and natural one. Initially she'd been unperturbed at the realisation that a "spirit" was in her home, but then it had started behaving in ways that left her deeply disturbed. The only other information that Steve had was that the woman had occasionally allowed her home to be used for "open circle" meetings by local spiritualist believers. If Mike wanted to follow up on the case, Steve said he'd arrange a visit and try to accrue further background information. Mike asked Steve if he had any particular time in mind for the trip.

"The thing is Mike, this woman seems desperate. My feeling is that we need to go as soon as possible".

"Well, I can't make it tomorrow or Wednesday – how about Thursday sometime?"

Steve said he'd ring the woman to confirm the visit and get back to Mike. The following day Steve rang Mike again.

"Hi bud – I've checked with the woman at Ashington and she says that Thursday is fine. I'll pick you up around 1pm, if that's okay".

Mike said that was perfect, and asked Steve if the woman had been able to tell him anything else that may be of use.

"Well, she did give me a few more details. Apparently, the entity – whatever it is – is getting very 'up close and personal' with her. It's creepy, to be honest. Sometimes she wakes up and she'll feel it running its fingers through her hair. Other times it will start to caress her thigh. It seems predatory, and you don't have to be a genius to work out that there are some distinctly sexual undertones present. Personally, I'm wondering whether it's a poltergeist at all. I'm starting to think it could be an incubus".

The mention of the word incubus sent a cold shiver down Mike's spine. More than any other psychic foe, by reputation the incubus was often believed to be the most to be dreaded.

The word *incubus* is Latin, and drawn from *in*, which literally means "above" or "on top of", and *cubo*, which means "I lie upon", "a burden" or "a weight". This in itself highlights the predatory disposition of the entity, which, according to legend, is said to be a sexually driven monster which preys upon women. The female equivalent of the incubus is the succubus, who allegedly preys upon men in a similar manner.

Supposedly, the incubi are demons of tremendous power and great age. They were even feared by the ancient Sumerians and Babylonians, who believed that they could also control storms, lightning and thunder.

According to tradition, incubi constantly attempt to engage in sexual activity with women. Their reasons for this are two-fold. Firstly, they do so because they enjoy it, and secondly because engaging in sexual intercourse with human females is the means by which they procreate. During the act of intercourse, the incubus will draw or "suck out" energy from its victim – energy upon which it feeds to perpetuate its own existence.

There are two prevalent theories about the nature of both the incubus and the succubus. In some traditions they are said to be two separate genders, male and female, in exactly the same way that humans are similarly divided. In other traditions, however, the concept is a little more complex. One Mediaeval view was that both incubi and succubi are genderless, and are merely two different presentations of the same entity. In other words, the entity will appear as either male or female depending on the type of sexual activity it wishes to engage in. Some scholars suggested that the demon would first appear as a succubus – normally in the guise of a voluptuous female – and have intercourse with its male victim when he was asleep. As soon as the victim ejaculated, the demon would then metamorphose into its male form, as an incubus, and select a female victim. During intercourse with the woman, the demon would ejaculate the sperm it had "collected" from the male victim and the woman would become pregnant. The child, although human in appearance, would actually be a demon in disguise which would then go on to promulgate the species in exactly the same manner as its parents. Even though the sperm used in this bizarre form of conception was taken from a human male and the mother was a human female, the resultant offspring was almost always believed to be demonic. However, sometimes the resultant offspring would not be fully demonic but actually half-demon and half-human. Such hybrids were known as *combions* or *cambions,* and were believed to possess enormous supernatural powers.

Allegedly, there are a number of different ways in which an incubus can be identified. When the demon engages in sexual intercourse with a human female victim, its penis is said to feel either incredibly cold or uncomfortably hot. In appearance, the incubus is said to take the form of a hideous dwarf with misaligned and deformed features. Some say that before it materialises in fleshly form it appears as a small but intense light that will dart through the air at great speed like a firefly, or as a metallic sphere. In yet other traditions it is said to appear as a swan, a dog, a goose, a dragon or even a large fish.

Dealing with an incubus is not easy, and over the millennia numerous defence strategies have been employed with varying degrees of success. In the Christian tradition, predictably, exorcism has been the preferred option. The Roman Catholic Church has said that attending confession may also be helpful, along with making the sign of the cross, which demons are said to dislike intensely. Unfortunately, even thinking Christians have admitted that such tactics are basically useless. Testimony exists that incubi actually have no fear of exorcisms, couldn't give two hoots about the sign of the cross and, on occasion, have actually drank holy water and spat upon the Bible in front of their victims.

One of the most frightening beliefs regarding incubi is that, as previously stated, they "suck out" the life force from their victims. If an incubus is allowed to do this repeatedly, so it is said, the victim will endure a rapid decline in health and, eventually, die if the demon is not prevented from engaging in its rapacious behaviour.

Mike found the concept of the incubus disturbing too, but for different reasons. During the authors' investigation into the South Shields Poltergeist, they had seen first-hand how devious the poltergeist could be; presenting itself as an old woman, a sweet young child, a middle-aged man and in numerous other ways. Darren and Mike were in no doubt that this ability to switch guises was done for one reason and one reason only – to fool and confuse its victims. The incubus, Mike noted, did exactly the same thing. But there was another parallel that was even more striking. The poltergeist feeds on human fear, or - to employ a rather overused term popular with some paranormal researchers - "energy". The incubus was said to feed in almost exactly the same manner, by "sucking out" the life force or energy from its victim.

In one Mediaeval legend, the incubus was said to be able to resist exorcism completely, but needed to "rest" for several days after an exorcism had been attempted. In poltergeist cases it is well known that exorcisms, although usually unsuccessful, do sometimes result in a short hiatus before the entity resumes its business of frightening the householders. Again, a strange parallel can be seen between both the poltergeist and the incubus phenomena.

The parallels between the poltergeist and the incubus led Mike to a rather disquieting conclusion; could both phenomena actually be one and the same? In fact, the only meaningful difference between the two that Mike could see was that in cases of incubus attack there was a sexual component present that was normally absent in cases of poltergeist infestation. But then he discussed this point with Darren, who made an interesting observation: "Maybe there *is* a sort of sexual component in some poltergeist cases. In most instances of polt infestation - the 'normal' ones - the focus is often a young girl around the age of puberty or the beginning of her menstrual cycle. These are both indicators that the young lady in question is reaching a point in her life where her sexual urges will begin and eventually culminate in her reaching full sexual maturity".

This was true, and often at this point in a young girl's life she may be mixed-up, confused, and going through physical and emotional transformations – hormonal changes, for example. Perhaps the polt, or an incubus, sees this as a golden opportunity to make its attack; striking while the iron is hot, so to speak, and when "the enemy" is at its most vulnerable.

All in all, the parallels between the polt and incubus phenomena were just too strong to ignore.

On Thursday 1 May, at 1pm, Steve Taylor called to pick up Mike and his wife Jackie for the journey to Ashington. The weather was balmy, and as the trio meandered towards their destination the conversation inevitably turned towards the disturbances at the house they were going to visit. To be honest, no one had a clue what they might be facing.

As Steve, Jackie and Mike pulled into the picturesque square of houses, they could see the medium Rhianne D'Morgyn standing outside waiting for them. Beside her was the owner, an elderly lady, and Rhianne's partner, Tim*. Within the space of a minute, a troop of intrigued investigators was ascending the stairwell of Minnie's* home. By all outward appearances, it was delightful; parchment-coloured walls were adorned with country-style paintings and ornaments, and cream carpets added to the carefully orchestrated cottage effect that Minnie had created. It was hard to believe that something sinister could be lurking therein.

Minnie's living room was airy and well furnished. Gently flickering candles were dotted hither and thither, adding to the ambience. Introductions were made, and then Minnie trotted off into the kitchen to make tea. Another friend, a neighbour of Minnie's called Vanessa*, had also popped in to chat to her friend's guests. Mike looked around and attempted to connect with the surroundings. Something wasn't right, but he decided not to say anything until Minnie had returned. Rhianne, he noticed, was also looking rather unsettled and glanced over her shoulder several times.

Minnie's story was as follows: She'd spent many years within the spiritualist movement, although she was no longer able to attend church regularly. Nevertheless, she managed to enjoy something akin to a full spiritual life from within the confines of her own home. Others of a spiritual disposition, including Vanessa, had taken part in "open circle" services and similar activities there.

And then, unfortunately, "it" had arrived.

At first, there was just the usual "sense of presence"; the irresistible feeling that someone or something unseen was in Minnie's flat, watching her. Initially this didn't bother her at all; her practice of spiritualism had made her quite accustomed to such sensations which she accepted as perfectly natural. But then, on one occasion in the early hours of the morning, Minnie had woken with a start. Someone was running their fingers through her hair. Alarmed, she got out of bed and after several seconds it stopped. However, the same thing happened again several nights later. Minnie was annoyed at this unwelcome intrusion and actually took to wearing a woollen hat whilst she was sleeping. Somehow, this seemed to have prevented the entity from touching her head and she once again found herself able to sleep peacefully. Then, on the third occasion, she awoke to find that "it" was rubbing its hand up and down the inside of her thigh. This was, of course, a step too far. Whatever was taking such an interest in Minnie had taken liberties, and now she wanted it out of her home.

At first Minnie tried several techniques common within

spiritualism in an effort to remove her uninvited guest, including "shutting herself down" spiritually and asking "the spirit" to go. Nothing worked. Not to be outdone, Minnie then tried other methods, even going so far as to "close her chakras". For the uninitiated, chakras are (at least for those who countenance their existence) spiritual centres of gravity within the human body that ingest / digest / export "energies" or the "life-force" of an individual. To leave one's chakras permanently "open" can, it is said, invite in unwelcome spiritual forces. Therefore, after engaging in spiritual activity of some kind, some people will engage in a form of meditative ritual that "closes down" these spiritual centres within the body, thereby protecting them from unwanted influence. Whatever the truth about chakras, it didn't work. "It" was still there, and it continued to torment Minnie.

"I've tried everything to get rid of it...*everything*. Look, let me show you something".

Minnie dashed off down the hallway and returned moments later with, of all things, a multi-coloured feathered duster that looked like the sort of thing Ken Dodd would delight at waving in front of an audience. Minnie twirled the duster around in the air.

"How mad does this look? I've even tried wafting this through the air to change the energies in the room, hoping that it would get uncomfortable and go. It didn't work. I must look a right plonker wearing my 'protective hat' and wafting this thing around!"

Minnie, of course, wasn't a plonker. She was simply someone who was trying everything she could to rid herself of an invisible paramour, and if wearing a hat in bed and wafting a feather duster through the air did the trick, then who are the authors, or indeed anyone else, to criticise?

Both Rhianne and Steve said that they felt "drawn" to an area of the room near the stairwell. Steve picked up images in his mind; one of a young girl running quickly, and another of a soldier with head injuries propped up against a wall. Who the young girl was or might have been was never discovered, but the soldier may have been connected with an old military armoury that used to be located on the same site where Minnie's house now stood. Mike was picking up nothing at all, but still felt uncomfortable. He had a growing feeling that something truly *was* in Minnie's flat.

"Does it frighten you, Minnie?" Mike asked.

"Oh, no", replied Minnie instantly. "I don't think it's a *bad* spirit. I'm sick of it and I just want rid of it".

This puzzled Mike. The entity, whatever it was, had invaded Minnie's home and had touched her in ways that, had it been a human, would have promptly got it arrested. How could she say that it wasn't a "bad spirit"? Minnie, Mike thought, had perhaps concluded that the spirit was merely lonely and, despite the rather intimate nature of its advances, had really meant no harm; in effect, that it was *sad* rather than *bad*. As the conversation continued, Rhianne leant over and whispered in Mike's ear, "Mike, I know you're harbouring thoughts that this could perhaps be an incubus, and I..."

Rhianne never got the chance to finish her sentence. Minnie stood up, and asked Steve to accompany her to the window.

"Can you see in the garden, down there? There's a *vortex* there, and there are ley-lines running from it in all directions. One of them runs through this house, in fact, right here".

Minnie traced a line through the air with her finger, indicating where the invisible ley-line was supposed to run. Mike was intrigued.

"How do you know there's a 'vortex' there, Minnie? And how do you know where the ley-lines run?"

Vanessa interjected and said that she'd been told they were there by a neighbour.

"And how did your neighbour know they were there?"

Neither Vanessa nor Minnie seemed to be sure.

Mike is not against the concept of either spiritual vortices or ley-lines, but feels that they are vastly overused and overrated concepts. During his career he has heard dozens of people state, with absolute confidence, that vortices and ley-lines exist here, there and just about everywhere. And yet, when one pokes under the surface, their existence is almost always based upon little more than the fact that a neighbour, psychic or spiritual adept of some kind "detected" them. There seemed little doubt that Minnie and Vanessa were both convinced, but why? Was it simply because their neighbour had said so? A little more probing allowed Mike to determine that there was actually a lot more to it than that.

"Have you ever seen elemental spirits in your garden – you know, pixies, gnomes, elves...that sort of thing?"

To those of an inherently cynical nature, people who believe in elves, pixies, gnomes and faeries will likely be viewed as nutcases. However, thousands of people worldwide *do* claim to see such entities, and there is, Mike thinks, evidence that they are genuinely experiencing something of a paranormal nature. What disturbed him was Minnie's answer.

"Oh, yes...there are elves out there – and a gnome".

"Do they ever touch you?"

At this point it was Vanessa, and not Minnie, who answered in the affirmative:

"Yes. They often grab *my* legs when *I'm* out there".

Minnie then added, "I hope it hasn't come in from the garden...you know, there are some *awful* things out there..."

Mike didn't doubt it for a minute. What disturbed him was that incubi often disguise themselves as elemental spirits in much the same way that poltergeists disguise themselves as discarnate human spirits. The gnawing feeling that something dark and brooding had indeed infiltrated Minnie's flat was even stronger now. Then Minnie dropped a minor bombshell. She had, she said, taken to using "a board".

In some spiritual and New Age circles it is common to employ a device known as a *board* in an effort to communicate with other realms or dimensions. Such boards come in different types, the most common being the well-know ouija board – commonly but mistakenly pronounced *wee-jee board* by many enthusiasts. Essentially, spirit communication boards consist of a circle of letters, numbers and icons. Perhaps by employing an upturned glass or other artefact as a pointer, upon which the users place their fingers, the "spirits" will be asked to move the artefact towards the letters and numerals in sequence to spell out whatever messages they may want to give out to those present.

Using spirit communication boards is, it must be said, an extremely risky business. For years Mike refused to countenance their use under any circumstances whatsoever, because he knew of too many cases where users had "opened up a doorway" and attracted the attention of entities that were, to put it bluntly, quite evil. One chap from Leeds told Mike that he had went through "six months of hell" after his brother and some friends used a ouija board when he was in the room. He hadn't actually taken part in the exercise, but "something had latched on" to him, he said, and had almost driven him out of his mind.

In March 2001, Mike wrote the following in his WraithScape column after hearing further reports of how the use of communication boards had backfired:

> *A reader recently told me of a rather chilling experience she had several years ago. Several friends of hers had met in a pub one evening for a night out. Around 10 o'clock the landlord, on request from several regular drinkers, turned up the volume of the piped music to what she called "a ridiculous level"*
>
> *"We couldn't hear ourselves speak", she added, "but he refused to turn it down. After we finished our drinks we immediately left and went back to Jennifer's flat for coffee.*
>
> *"Whilst the kettle was boiling Jen went into her bedroom and brought out an ouija board, suggesting that we try to contact some spirits. We did – and I can tell you that I'll never use an ouija board again. I don't want to go into what happened, but I nearly ended up in a psychiatric hospital because of it".*
>
> *And Maureen isn't the only one to have had such an experience. A local postman from South Shields told me of an incident involving his mother-in-law back in the 1960s:*
>
> *"My mother-in-law, who now lives in Kent, used to work as a cleaner at Chatham dockyards during the 60s. One day, several of the cleaners decided to mess around with an ouija board during their break.*
>
> *"They gathered in a small room where they used to drink their tea. It was known as the 'bait room'. Sure enough, the glass started to move as if by its own accord and then toppled over. She said it was obvious that something strange was happening".*
>
> *"After a while they put the board away and went back to work, but Lilian was concerned. The others laughed and told her not to be silly.*
>
> *"And then, the very next day, it started. Not long after they heard four sharp knocks on the window – knock, knock, knock...knock. Startled, they looked around to see*

where the noise had come from. Then it happened again, and they realised that someone was tapping loudly on the window.

"The knocking continued, and they could see exactly where the sound was coming from. It was definitely someone knocking on the glass".

Could it not have been someone playing tricks, I asked, maybe someone knocking on the window from the outside?

"Well, that's the strange thing, you see", said her son-in-law. "The room was on the third floor. You couldn't reach the windows from outside at all. No drainpipes, outside stairwells or anything..."

There is an ongoing debate about what exactly happens when people experiment with an ouija board. The traditional view is that the experimenters are making contact with the spirits of the dead. A more scientific explanation is that the "messages" received are actually produced subconsciously by the experimenters themselves.

Personally I don't think it matters. The point is that whatever causes the phenomenon it can have nasty consequences, and therefore shouldn't be dabbled with.

One colleague of mine put it this way: "When you use an ouija board you are opening up a portal to another dimension which you can neither control nor fully understand. Opening that doorway is easy, but you may find that it is not so easily shut again. Personally, I wouldn't go near an ouija board if you paid me a fortune".

And nor would I. I think I'll stick to good old Monopoly. That way you can at least pretend you've got a fortune and it won't give you nightmares...

This was how Mike felt about dabbling with spirit communication boards back in 2001, and he has only slightly modified his view. He now believes that communication with entities that are *not* evil is possible, but should not be attempted under any circumstances. In 2007, Mike took part in a demonstration involving a spirit communication board, and the medium conducting it said she "had a man present" who wanted to talk to someone sitting around the table. When asked to identify who the person was, the glass in the centre of the table, upon which all the "sitters" had rested their index finger lightly, moved towards Mike. The spirit person identified himself as Mike's great-grandfather, and, spelled out numerous facts and dates that could only have been known by Mike himself. Then, Mike's grandfather "came through" for good measure and also said things that no one apart from Mike himself – and his deceased grandfather, of course – could have known. Mike does not believe the spirits *were* those of his great-grandfather and grandfather, but they certainly detailed things that no one else around the table could possibly have been aware of. The question was, could Minnie's use of a spirit communication board have opened up a doorway which allowed the malign entity in her home to have gained access? Rhianne D'Morgyn pointed out something which certainly made it a distinct possibility.

"There is so much energy in this room...it's like a mish-mash...I can tell you've even invited the angels in to protect you. And there are so many other energies whirling around, all confused..."

Mike knew exactly what Rhianne meant. Minnie's lounge, despite its superficial appearance of cosiness, seemed to be charged with an essence of some kind. The nearest thing he could liken it to was static electricity, but it was different. To be honest, he found this "charged" atmosphere rather disorientating, and Vanessa had commented that at times she had felt positively dizzy when she'd entered Minnie's home. The explanation for this strange phenomenon was not hard to establish.

There are many sincere people who have a passion for delving into the world of spiritual experience. Some follow one spiritual path only, and are known as *purists*; they may be a Roman Catholic, Hindu, Muslim or Mormon, but they will spend their entire lives within the confines of one religious tradition and never feel the need to go outside of it. Regardless of what one thinks of their chosen religious path, the truth is that most purists have a degree of contentment and find that their chosen *way* gives their life meaning and enriches it. However, not all those who enjoy spiritual experiences and have an inherent spiritual disposition are purists. Some, better known as *eclectics*, find following one religious tradition only to be extremely claustrophobic. To satisfy their spiritual needs they will, instead of following an established religious or spiritual path, effectively create their own *way* by mixing together aspects of many others. Being an eclectic allows you to embrace *aspects* of many other religious traditions without having to accept them all as part of a "package deal". If you like something about Wicca, you can take it on board and work with it. If, however, there's something you don't like about it then you can simply ignore it and replace it with, say, something from Judaism or Druidry that suits you better. Eclectics often end up creating their own unique spiritual path that is effectively a mixture of ideas, concepts, rituals and beliefs drawn from many disparate sources.

On the surface, eclecticism would seem to provide a great deal of freedom to those who embrace it. You can learn from every religious tradition, and yet you are beholden to none. Whilst this might work for some, it is a pathway fraught with difficulties. Most of the world's great religious traditions are internally harmonious, and their individual facets "hang together", having been carefully blended over the course of millennia. However, once you start taking bits and pieces from many different traditions and attempt to forge them into something new, the results can be calamitous because they may very well refuse to harmonise with each other at all. The result is a sort of *ersatz* spiritual path that is really just a horrible conglomeration of rituals and ideas that have very little in common, and those who practice them effectively end up being a Jack of all trades and, predictably, a master of none. To be honest, many eclectics simply use eclecticism as an excuse for creating their own spiritual version of a "cut-and-shut" motor car, which looks fine from the outside but inside is an absolute mess and actually dangerous to drive. The authors know of "spiritual teachers" who have invented such exotic conglomerations as "Ancient Egyptian Reiki", "Nordic Buddhism" and "Celtic Voodoo". They have yet to see such a recipe that has even one iota of merit.

Readers should not assume, however, that the above is meant to be a cruel criticism of those who follow such eclectic pathways. Eclectics are most often sincere people who are simply searching for meaning in their lives, and, without realising the pitfalls, have embarked upon a tour of the world's spiritual and religious traditions to see what they can find. Sadly, because their understanding of *any one* tradition is often superficial, they may find themselves "dabbling" in it when they aren't really qualified.

Spiritually and psychically, it is the equivalent of handing a chain saw to a three year-old boy and expecting him to use it without hurting himself.

From both Mike and Rhianne's perspective, Minnie was certainly eclectic. She was a follower of spiritualism, and yet she wore around her neck a Christian crucifix. She invited angels into her home for protection, and yet also embraced many pagan concepts such as a belief in elemental spirits. She was, as Steve later commented, "a textbook New Age believer". She was undoubtedly sincere, and yet her knowledge of any and all religious traditions seemed to be entirely superficial. Mike's suspicion was that by dabbling with spirit communication boards and other aspects of spirituality beyond her competency, she could well have opened herself up to attack by negative spiritual forces that she could not combat and, regrettably, could not get rid of once they had attached themselves to her. Even Vanessa commented that she "hadn't felt comfortable" about using the spirit communication board, and there was probably a very good reason for that. This, of course, put Mike on the horns of a dilemma. There was certainly something present in Minnie's flat, and Mike had the awful feeling that it was possibly an incubus. But what could or should he tell the woman? He didn't want to frighten her, and yet he most certainly wanted to help her. He decided to give her some advice, without spelling out the awful truth about his conclusions.

Mike advised Minnie to desist from any form of spiritual activity for a while; no spirit board communication, no incense, no rituals and no trying to "change the energies" with her feather duster.

"Every time you engage in something like that, you are effectively opening up a line of communication with this entity and inviting it to stay. The only way to deal with it is to stop doing anything at all that will encourage it. As far as is humanly possible you should ignore it. Hopefully, it will get bored and go away".

Minnie thanked her visitors for their help and kindly insisted that they accept a donation towards their travelling expenses. Mike, Steve, Jackie, Rhianne and Ron then departed. Mike, for his part, was not entirely confident that Minnie would be able to desist from engaging in any form of spiritual activity for a protracted period of time. The notion that the entity may have decided to turn its attention to Minnie's visitors never entered his head, but it wouldn't be long before he would begin to wonder. Within the space of a day, something truly frightening would happen that catapulted the concept of contagion into the forefront of his mind.

Thursday May 1, the day on which the visit to Minnie's home had taken place, was also the day on which the entire country would be encouraged to vote in the local council elections. It proved to be an absolute disaster for the Labour Party, which lost over 400 local council seats. To add insult to injury, the gregarious Conservative MP Boris Johnson was elected as the Mayor of London, displacing "Red Ken" Livingstone by a healthy margin. The full focus of the media trained upon a triumphant Leader of the Opposition, David Cameron – the Conservatives had won almost all the seats that Labour had lost – and a bewildered Prime Minister Gordon Brown who could simply watch and do nothing as the political sky fell in and effectively buried him. Mike, intrigued by the events, got up early on the morning of May 2 to catch up with the shenanigans on *Sky News*.

It was slightly chilly when Mike got out of bed, so he donned an ancient towel dressing gown that was full of holes, but one of his most comfortable pieces of clothing. He then went downstairs into the kitchen, switched on the kettle and made himself a cup of tea. All thoughts of the previous day's visit had left him, and his only interest at that point was to follow the election results on the TV. He picked up his mug, walked into the lounge and turned on the news. For maybe five minutes he sat comfortably on the sofa as a stream of ecstatic Conservatives and nigh-suicidal Labour supporters were paraded on the screen to offer their thoughts. It was fantastic entertainment.

At precisely 6.10am, Mike detected the distinct smell of burning. It came suddenly and without build-up. One moment it was absent, the next the overpowering odour of smoke filled his nostrils. Alarmed, he sat up and glanced around in an effort to see where it was coming from. It didn't take him long to find out. Wisps of smoke were emanating from the cuff of the right-hand sleeve of his dressing gown. These were followed by delicate tendrils of flame, at which juncture his wrist suddenly became extremely hot. The sleeve of his dressing gown was on fire.

Instinctively, Mike began to pat the ignited area furiously with his left hand. As he did so the smoke increased, but the flames, thank goodness, went out. The fire was quickly extinguished.

To this day, Mike has absolutely no idea how his dressing gown caught fire. He replayed in his mind a dozen times every action since he'd walked down the stairs, and at no time had he been near a naked flame. What's more, even if he had accidentally set his dressing gown on fire, how on earth did a good five minutes at least go by before he smelt smoke and noticed the flames?

A thought struck Mike, and it wasn't an encouraging one. As far as he could see, there was absolutely no rational explanation for his dressing gown catching fire. This led him to consider a far darker possibility. One of the most extreme symptoms of poltergeist infestation, and normally one of the last to manifest themselves, is the phenomenon of *fire-starting*. Those who have gone through the trauma of intense poltergeistry will sometimes testify that fires will break out spontaneously in their homes. Fortunately, such fires are normally small and, mercifully, will extinguish themselves spontaneously. The polt at Lock Street never did get around to full-blown fire-starting, but it came perilously close to it. Marianne once found a candle in her bed that was still warm, although not lit. The wax was still soft, indicating that it *had* been lit shortly before she found it. On another occasion, Mike, Marianne and Marc witnessed a build-up of fine smoke in the kitchen. It had no odour, but it distinctly looked like smoke. If the entity at Minnie's house had been a poltergeist – or worse, as Mike suspected, an incubus – there was a possibility that it had, through a process of contagion, attached itself to Mike and precipitated the fire itself. After sitting for several minutes and getting his thoughts into order, Mike photographed the burnt cuff of his dressing gown sleeve. He then noticed a white blister on the third finger of his left hand which he believes was caused when he attempted to beat out the flames. The only other physical damage that he could notice was the absence of some hairs on his arm where the cuff of the sleeve had been resting when the fire started. They seemed to have been burnt off, but the skin itself was untouched. Mike photographed the blister and then made another cup of tea before sending an e-mail to Darren. He needed to speak to him urgently. He decided against ringing his friend, as the night before Darren had taken part in an overnight investigation at a public house that was reputedly haunted. Darren wouldn't have arrived home till dawn, and would therefore still be in bed resting.

But there was more to come. Mike also decided to telephone Rhianne and see what she thought about this latest incident. What happened next was intriguing.

Rhianne answered her mobile phone and told Mike that she couldn't speak as she was just about to start driving her car. She'd ring him later, she said, after she'd arrived at Tim's flat. After some time had passed, Mike's phone rang. It was Rhianne, returning his call.

Mike first asked Rhianne what her thoughts had been about the previous day's visit. They chatted for a while, and then the conversation was shattered by an incredibly loud, rhythmic beeping noise. It was the smoke alarm in Tim's kitchen. Rhianne was preparing a meal, and something had begun to burn.

"Oh, no!" Rhianne shouted. "I'm cooking and I've set something on fire! I'll ring you back!"

Minutes later she called Mike for a second time. Order had been restored, the smoke alarm was now silent and the only damage that had been done was to the repast that she'd been preparing for Tim. Now, it seemed, he'd be receiving burnt offerings instead of a more conventional meal when he got back from his business.

Mike told the medium about the incident with the dressing gown. Rhianne sounded shocked – not just because of the incident itself, but because of the "coincidental" activation of the smoke alarm at precisely the moment when Mike had been about to tell her that his dressing gown had caught alight. The activation of the smoke alarm had a natural explanation, of course: as Rhianne had become engrossed in the first conversation with Mike, she'd forgotten about the meal she was cooking for Tim. Inevitably, then, it had started to burn and the smoke alarm had activated. And yet it still seemed strange that the activation of the smoke alarm had occurred just when Mike was about to tell her that an item of his clothing had spontaneously burst into flames.

After mulling over the incident between them, the conversation then took a more general tone and Rhianne expressed her feeling that, in the world of paranormal research and alternative spirituality, some people were too eager to believe anything simply because they'd read it in a book or seen it on TV. Mike agreed, and related to Rhianne an anecdotal tale which perfectly illustrated the point.

Several years previously, Mike had listened to a lecture by a colleague on the subject of some mysterious crystal skulls that had been discovered in South America, and during the talk the speaker had stated that one skull was no less than 3,468, 242 years old. Mike was intrigued as to how the speaker had been able to state such a precise age with unbridled confidence. Later, at the bar where both were ordering a drink, he asked her. The woman stared at Mike as if he was an idiot and promptly said, "I *know* it's that old because I read it in a *book* about crystal skulls. So, *that's* how I know it's true!"

"Oh, well...if you read it in a book then it *must* be true...", he replied with no small degree of sarcasm.

After Mike had finished reciting the tale to Rhianne there was a pregnant pause in the conversation, before the medium whispered, "My God...my spine has turned to ice. This is creepy!"

Mike, puzzled, asked her why.

"Because right now I'm reading a book called *The Crystal Skull!*"

The title of the publication that the lecturer had referred to all those years ago and the book that Rhianne was currently reading were almost identical. Mike knew that this just could not be "coincidental".

Later that afternoon, after Darren had woken from his lie-in, he rang Mike and was astonished to hear about the incident with the dressing gown. He, too, felt that the notion of contagion could not lightly be dismissed. Whatever it was, Mike sincerely hoped that there wouldn't be an encore.

***

May 3. It had been a long afternoon. Darren's daughter, Abbey, had been to her 2nd birthday party at a local soft play centre where she and a dozen of her little cousins and friends had played riotously for an hour or so before tucking in to a table-full of party food as well as her birthday cake. For the previous hour Darren and his partner Jayne had been running round like headless chickens looking after all the children and making sure they all had a wonderful time at the party. The event went without a hitch and all concerned had a great time.

Darren arrived home with Jayne and Abbey and subsequently took a quick bath. Running around looking after children is seriously hard work. Jayne remained downstairs and waited for Darren to take over looking after Abbey. Jayne was headed out to a friend's house to celebrate a birthday, so Darren was left holding the reins, so to speak. At 7.30pm, Jayne left the house and at 8.00pm Darren put his daughter to bed. She was tired after her exciting day and slept.....well, like a baby. At 11.30pm Darren decided to turn in, but rather than go to bed he decided to get comfortable on the sofa and nod off there, at least until he knew Jayne had arrived home safe and well.

At 1.00am, Darren woke up and realised that Jayne had not yet returned. He paid a visit to the loo and checked up on his sleeping daughter before returning back downstairs. He lay back on the settee and dozed back off. The next thing he knew was that Jayne was opening the front door; she had arrived home. Darren looked at the clock and it read 01.15am. Just as Jayne entered the living room the telephone began to ring. As Jayne picked up the phone to say hello, it went dead.

"Who the hell is that ringing at this time of the morning?" said Darren.

Almost immediately Jayne rang 1471 to see who had just made the call. As Darren lay there, waiting to see who it was, Jayne began to recite the number of the last person that rang; one by one, the digits of Mike's telephone number were read out.

"What the hell is Mike phoning at *this* time for?", Darren bellowed.

"Probably trying to ring someone else", Jayne said.

"Give me the phone please", Darren said.

Darren then also rang 1471 to check for himself that it had been Mike. Sure enough, Mike's number was repeated by the automated voice at the other end of the line.

"Wonder what he wanted?" Darren thought to himself.

Nothing more was thought about it until the next day, when Darren visited Mike at his home. Darren had forgotten the incident when Mike just happened to mention that he had been on the phone to a guy in the United States for a few hours through the night.

"Hey, that reminds me", Darren said. "Why did you phone me up in the middle of the night Mike?"

"Eh?" said Mike, "What do you mean?"

"You phoned me through the night".

"No I didn't".

"Yes you did", Darren said

"What time?"

"It was about 01.15 – 01.20am; I know this because it was just as Jayne was coming in".

"Darren, I *never* rang you through the night!", Mike said sternly. "Look, I rang this chap in the USA after he sent me an e-mail asking me to do so, he sent the e-mail at 12.30am and it was only a few minutes after when I rang him back. I was on the phone for around two hours. Jackie went to bed around 12.25 that night so when I received this e-mail I thought it was a good time to call him".

"So, what you are saying is that if my phone rang at 01.15am it must have been another number?"

"Must have been" said Mike, "It wasn't me".

"Look, I know your number; it was *your* phone, *your* number – there is no mistaking it", Darren said.

The upshot of this is that Darren was adamant that Mike rang him and Mike was adamant that he hadn't. If Mike was telling the truth – and deep down Darren really had no doubt that he was - then how could his phone have rung Darren? In fact, Mike showed Darren the call log on his phone and – sure enough – it detailed the lengthy call that Mike had made to the USA that evening. He had been on a call to the USA from 12.30am until around 02.30am. Darren had been interrupted from his sleep at around 01.15am on the morning of 4th May 2008, but by whom, or what? The thought then struck both Darren and Mike's that it could have been the polt up to its old tricks. They both knew what that particular entity was capable of.

Sixteen
"Get off Me!"

On Saturday 4 April, 2009, Mike received a call from a good friend of his who had also been an acquaintance of Darren for many years. Tony* is an electrician, and has been married to his wife Linda*, a nurse, for seven years. The couple have four children, and currently reside in Middlesbrough.

Tony is an extremely laid-back person who never takes life too seriously, and, as his friends all testify, has an infectious sense of humour. Normally, that is; but on the day he telephoned Mike he sounded uncharacteristically tense.

During the previous few days, the couple had noticed some odd things happening in their home. Occasionally they would see what appeared to be fleeting shadows out of the corner of their eye, and on a number of occasions household artefacts had gone missing, only to reappear later in rather odd places. At some point Tony, because of his professional background, decided to use an EMF meter to see if he could detect any anomalous readings. He was aware that strong discharges of electromagnetic energy could cause hallucinations and other physiological effects. He focussed on the main bedroom, and did indeed find that his EMF meter fluctuated wildly in certain spots. Tony wanted to know if Mike had heard of similar cases in which people had hallucinated under the same conditions. Mike said that, as far as he was concerned, the possibility that electromagnetic fields were causing the problem couldn't be ruled out, but there were other explanations that also needed to be considered. Tony said that he would keep Mike abreast of any further developments.

Two days later, Tony again telephoned Mike and said that Linda had gone through a rather weird experience the night before. Neither Tony nor Linda was sure exactly what to do about it. Tony gave Linda the phone and asked her to relate directly to Mike exactly what had happened.

At around 2am, Linda had woken up and gone to check on her youngest child, a baby girl named Melinda*, who had was only several months old. When she returned to the bedroom she was astonished to see someone lying in the bed where, just minutes previously, she herself had been asleep.

"The figure", she said, was "human-shaped, but it didn't look like an ordinary person. It was sort of solid, but looked as if it was made from smoke. It was really weird. You could make out dark patches on its face where its features were supposed to be, but they weren't really clear or distinct".

Mike asked Linda how long the apparition had been in view:

"I think it must have been for half a minute or so, I can't remember exactly".

Mike also asked Linda whether the figure had disappeared instantly or slowly faded away:

"I don't know, because I was startled and turned my head away. When I looked back, it was gone. The thing is, I wasn't scared at all. In fact, I felt extremely calm. The figure in the bed even looked calm, as if it was totally at peace, serene even".

The following evening, Linda had yet another strange experience. Once again she woke up in the small hours of the morning and was startled to see a woman standing by her bed, looking down at her. The only light entering the room was a dim glow shining in from the hallway, and the figure appeared similar to a silhouette. Nevertheless, she Linda could make out some features. The woman had blonde hair with a fringe and pale blue eyes. Linda sensed, somehow, that the woman was 35 years of age, or at least had been when she died.

Then the apparition spoke to her:

"My mother doesn't know what happened to me", she said.

As the figure addressed Linda, she noticed that there were now two other apparitions standing behind the first. The woman in front of her – if such it was – disappeared, and one of the two remaining figures, an elderly woman, stepped forward. This spirit, Linda noted, had been 87 years of age when she had died.

"I don't know how I knew that", said Linda, "but somehow I just did. Her age seemed to just pop into my mind".

"I can't find my husband", the woman said.

As the second apparition disappeared, the third, a male teenager who Linda estimated to be around 18 years old, said, "I never had time to say goodbye". He then disappeared like the first two. All three apparitions were, Linda said, dressed in "modern" contemporary clothing and did not appear to have hailed from some bygone era. As on the previous occasion, Linda wasn't frightened by her experience and wondered if she might possess latent mediumistic abilities that were somehow being activated by something in the house. Mike said he'd mull over her experiences and see if he could draw any conclusions about them. If he could, then he'd ring the couple back.

On Saturday 11 April, Tony rang Mike yet again. Linda had had another strange experience, but this one, unlike the previous two, was extremely disturbing.

Once more, Linda had woken during the night and gone to check on the baby. She returned to bed, climbed in and prepared to drop off to sleep. At some point, whilst still awake, she turned over and was lying face down in the bed. It was then that she felt what seemed to be a hand pressing down on the left side of her head, effectively pinning her to the bed. Panicking, she tried desperately to free herself but found to her horror that she was now completely paralysed. Worse, she could now sense what felt like another hand sliding in between her thighs, caressing her. She struggled, and tried to shout, but could not. Then, after what seemed like an age, the invisible attacker left her and she could once again move freely.

Linda came to the phone and told Mike exactly what had happened, filling in several details that Tony had omitted. Her story was punctuated repeatedly by heartrending sobs as she struggled not to burst into tears completely. Things were obviously getting out of hand, now, and Mike arranged to visit the couple on Tuesday April 14.

Tony met Mike and his wife Jackie at Middlesbrough train station early in the morning before catching a service bus to the estate where the couple live. Tony and Linda's home is in a terraced street not far from the town centre. The dwellings are all over a century old, but possess what aesthetes often refer to as "character".

On entering, both Mike and Jackie noticed how welcoming the

house felt. It was warm and just seemed to radiate friendliness. Linda made tea and then proceeded to explain in more detail just what had been transpiring over the previous weeks.

"Really, it began when we first moved in here a few months ago…actually within a day or two", said Linda.

At this juncture Mike interrupted and said, "Oh, I thought these things had only been going on for the past couple of weeks".

"Well, they've been *worse* for the last two weeks, particularly since we put the clocks back an hour for Daylight Saving Time on March 29". Linda said. "But really there were things happening before that; we just tried to dismiss them".

Linda had, without being asked, written down a list of the incidents she could recall. The significance of this action cannot be underestimated, and was to help the authors immensely later as they tried to determine exactly what sort of phenomenon the couple were dealing with. Following is a list of the phenomena presenting themselves in the couple's home as recorded by Linda:

- *Touch-activated "talking cup" began talking when no one was near it.*
- *Banging often heard from Holly's room when no one is up there.*
- *Objects often fall from kitchen benches without being touched.*
- *Sudden temperature changes. Darius's bedroom cold.*
- *Heard crying on three separate occasions. Tony and I heard it once. I heard it twice outside bathroom door.*
- *My friend saw a boy aged about 6 – 7 in the downstairs passage.*
- *Darius's baby-walker has played music by itself.*
- *Smell of urine and excrement in living room at times. Also smell of women's perfume.*
- *Feelings of being watched.*
- *Holly often feels as if she is being followed.*
- *Holly has three scratch marks on her stomach after being in the upstairs shower.*
- *Often sense presence of a little girl, normally by the living room door, mostly when I'm on my own.*

- *Have seen numerous shadows, all around the house.*
- *Tony saw someone in the corner of our room.*
- *Lights often flickering, sometimes constantly, despite new fuse boxes being fitted.*
- *Holly and I both heard drumming noises coming from Darius's room during the night.*
- *When I was in Holly's room, the top drawer of her chest of drawers suddenly opened.*
- *Computer has started acting erratically.*
- *Things are going missing, and then appearing somewhere else.*
- *Weird draughts, really strong, seem to be coming into the living room from the passage.*
- *Tony wakes up with scratches all over his torso. Looked as if they had been made with a child's hands.*
- *Something poked me in the back when I was in bed.*
- *I saw apparition lying in bed between me and Tony.*
- *Totally paralysed in bed. Something on top of me.*
- *Temperature in our room going hot and cold all through the night.*
- *Clicks in our room. I asked out and we heard a louder click.*
- *Walked into Darius's room and it was all foggy.*
- *Cat sometimes goes crazy. It has been jumping up at the fireplace a lot recently.*
- *Tony and me have both noticed a strong smell on a number of occasions. It's like earth. Tony has noticed this more than me.*

There were a few things that Linda had written down that Mike needed to explore. What was the "talking cup" for instance? Linda explained that Tony had a large, ceramic tea mug with the face of a modern rock-star moulded onto the front. When lifted up, a tiny sensor on the base of the mug activated a digital recording of the rock star saying something extremely witty. To activate the recording one has to move the mug by, for example, picking it up. However, the mug had started playing the recording without being moved at all. Mike and Darren had seen this sort of trickery before, where a poltergeist had manipulated talking toys and novelty items to wrack up the tension in the household. It had been at South Shields.

The baby-walker incident also caught Mike's attention. Linda explained that there was a toy on the front that Darius could play with. By manipulating or banging the toy with his hand the toddler could make the toy play tunes or musical sounds. Like the "talking cup", the baby-walker had suddenly started playing music spontaneously, without being touched at all.

Linda had written in her notes that the family's computer had "started acting erratically". He asked the couple exactly how it was malfunctioning. Tony explained.

"Well, sometimes bizarre things happen with it that we just can't explain. Take the other day, for instance. I booted up the computer, but the monitor wouldn't come on. The power light was activated, so I knew the electricity was getting through, but it just refused to work. I repeatedly turned everything off and then back on again, but it took fifteen minutes before the monitor began to work normally."

Mike asked Linda and Tony what it was about some of the incidents that made them think something paranormal was going on. After all, we can all put something down and forget where, and in every household electrical appliances – particularly children's toys, computers and novelty items – will malfunction. The couple accepted that when examined in isolation some of the incidents didn't look that odd, but it was the *collective* value of them that spoke differently.

"It's like...well everything started happening *together*", said Tony. "We went from nothing strange happening at all to loads of stuff within a short space of time".

"Could it not be that you're looking for strange occurrences now the idea is in your head?" asked Mike.

"How can that be?" said Linda. "It's not just the little things, like objects going missing and toys playing up, but the big stuff. Holly and Tony have both been scratched. Two of my friends have seen apparitions in the passageway. Tony has, and so have I. Everything – *all* of the weird stuff – has started happening *all at once*".

To be honest, Mike found it hard to fault Linda's logic. Something was precipitating a regular stream of seemingly paranormal occurrences. If there was a single, guiding intelligence behind the activity, then it certainly had a wide repertoire of party tricks under its belt.

Mike asked Linda and Tony if he could leave his digital sound recorder running in the master bedroom for a while to see if he could pick up any anomalous sounds. Then he and Tony talked for a while, whilst Linda and Jackie chatted in the kitchen.

Twenty minutes later, Mike retrieved his recorder and played it back. There were no anomalous sounds at all to be heard, save one; about two thirds of the way through the recording, there was what sounded like a rustling noise followed by a gentle click. It definitely sounded as if the noise had been made in close proximity to the recorder. There was another puzzle about the recording, however, that was more difficult to explain. When Mike had activated the recorder, he said, "Right, that's recording..." Tony and he then stood talking for several minutes about the anomalous EMF readings before going downstairs. Just as they left the room, Mike said, for the benefit of the recording, "Right...shutting the door".

When Mike played the recording back, both he and Tony were astonished to hear that there was no gap at all in between Mike saying, "Right, that's recording..." and, "Right...shutting the door". What happened to the five-minute conversation in between those two short utterances? Both Mike and Tony are adamant that they had a lengthy conversation in between those two points – in that very room - and yet, the recording seemed to have been *edited* to remove it.

Later that morning, Tony and Mike took a walk to a nearby street which had been famous in the 1970s because of a poltergeist infestation which had occurred there. Mike wanted to take some photographs. Just before they left, Linda asked if Mike would leave his digital recorder behind. Would he mind if Jackie and her used it to see if they could capture anything strange? Mike said that was fine.

All in all, Mike and Tony were out of the house for approximately thirty minutes. When they returned, Tony's parents and grandfather were there. After introductions were made, Mike asked Linda if Jackie and she had managed to record anything anomalous.

"Actually", said Linda, the recorder is still running up in the bedroom".

Jackie went up to the bedroom and, as she expected, the

recorder was where she had left it. The red recording light was still glowing. She picked it up, switched it off and promptly went back downstairs where she handed it to Mike.

Mike was intrigued as to whether, unlike the first time, the girls had actually managed to capture any substantive anomalous noises. Mike switched the recorder back on, and was immediately puzzled by the digital display on the screen. The last recording was numbered "*6*". When Mike had arrived at the house with Jackie earlier, there had been three recordings already stored on the machine which were entirely unconnected with the case. The first attempt Mike made to record anomalous sounds in the bedroom was, then, stored as "*4*". This meant that the last recording made by Linda and Jackie should have been stored as "*5*". But it wasn't. It was stored a "*6*". Superficially, this seemed to indicate that the girls had made not one recording when Tony and Mike were out of the house, but *two*. However, both Linda and Jackie were insistent that only one recording had been made.

Linda told Mike, "Jackie turned the recorder on, pressed the *record* button and left it. We were only in the room for seconds, and the machine was definitely recording when we left". Mike pressed the *play* button to activate recording *5*, and everyone in the room listened, expecting to hear the beginning of a recording that should have lasted nearly 45 minutes. However, after just twelve seconds the tape ended. Both Jackie and Linda looked at each other in astonishment. Jackie was the first to react:

"Eh? Where's the *rest?*"

Mike looked at the recording time on the screen. It was exactly twelve seconds long, no more and no less. All that can be heard at the beginning of the recording is a faint click as the switch is depressed and the recorder begins to work, followed by a faint shuffling noise as Jackie went to leave the room with Linda. Then, after twelve seconds, there is a louder rustling noise. Someone had seemingly picked up the recorder. Just as it ends, all that can be heard is the faint click as the *stop* switch is depressed. Someone had stopped the recording just twelve seconds after the machine had been activated, and it had *not* been Jackie or Linda.

But there was another mystery. If the only recording made by Jackie and Linda was *5*, what on earth was the recording now stored on the machine identified as *6*? His curiosity piqued, Mike pressed the play button once again. There was a faint click, followed by a short rustling noise as if someone was touching the recorder. Footsteps could be heard, faint at first, as Jackie entered the room and picked the machine up. Again one can hear a short rustling sound followed by a click as she turned it off. The entire recording lasts 10 seconds.

Piecing together the length and content of the recordings, plus the sequence of events, it is possible to work out exactly what had transpired:

> *11.22hrs:* Tony and Mike leave the house.
> *11.26:13secs:* Jackie and Linda place the recorder in the master bedroom and turn it on. The *record* button is depressed and the red recording light begins to glow.
> *11:26:25secs:* Someone or something turns off the recorder.
> *11.55hrs:* Tony and Mike return to the house.
> *12.02:41secs:* Someone or something activates the digital recorder.
> *12:02:51secs:* Jackie enters the room, picks up the recorder and deactivates it.

Whichever way you looked at it, it really seemed as if something or someone had deactivated the recorder just as Jackie and Linda left the room, and then activated it again just before Jackie entered the room to retrieve it. This meant that instead of having one continuous recording over almost 45 minutes, there were simply two extremely short recordings of the "beginning" and the "end" of that time period with no recording of the period in between. It was, Mike commented, like skipping from the opening titles of a movie to the credits without seeing anything in between the two.

On returning home from Middlesbrough, Mike telephoned Darren to tell him about Tony and Linda's experience. Darren picked up the receiver, and in the background Mike could hear music playing loudly.

"Just a minute, mate", said Darren, "I need to turn the music down so I can hear you".

As Darren walked away from the phone to turn the volume down on his music centre a little, Mike noticed that his friend was listening to a track by the band *Kiss*. The track was none other than *Unholy*, from the band's *Revenge* album, the lyrics of which seemed to be chillingly appropriate. As Mike listened, a shiver ran down his spine.

When Darren returned to the phone, Mike asked him how long it had been since he had played that particular album.

"I'm not sure, maybe a few months. Why?"

"I think you'll figure that out for yourself when I tell you what I have to tell you".

"I haven't said anything to you about this before, simply because I didn't have permission to. Now I have, so I can tell you about it".

Mike went on to relate to Darren exactly what had happened to Linda. Darren was stunned to hear about what had happened to their mutual friend, but then said, "Mike, I still don't see what that has to do with me listening to this CD".

"It's the lyrics Darren, Listen to them again. I heard the first two lines before you turned the volume down. They're singing about an *incubus*, for Christ sake. I've got a horrible feeling that it may be an incubus that's targeting Linda".

"Oh shit. How weird is that? I've only got that CD back this morning from a friend I lent it to ages ago. I started to play the damn thing just before the phone rang".

The authors don't want to read *too* much into some of the parallels and seeming "coincidences" between the Middlesbrough case and others they have investigated. However, there is no doubt that they are there; the "accompanying apparitions", other polt-like phenomena, such as household objects disappearing...and then, to top it all, the fact that a song by one of the world's most popular bands, in which the lyrics discuss the incubus phenomenon, was playing at *exactly* the same time that Mike rang Darren to tell him about a possible incubus case. Once again, the entity had *seemingly* demonstrated an uncanny ability to perfectly time its actions in a way that now left the authors in no doubt whatsoever that, like the other cases, this one was also part of a much wider circle of malign influence. What else were they supposed to think?

Later, Linda rang Mike and for almost an hour talked about her feelings regarding what had happened. Both she and Tony were happy for Darren and Mike to spend a night in their home to see if they could determine exactly what was going on there.

The authors were certain that something was going on; the question was, what?

Linda later told Mike of another experience which had disturbed her greatly. Next door to the family lived an elderly couple who had resided in the street for over thirty years. They were, said Linda, friendly and helpful. Linda tactfully asked the woman in the house whether the previous tenants had mentioned anything strange about the house.

"No, not really. They were just a young couple, like yourselves. They seemed quite nice, actually...except for one thing, that is. Sometimes...at night...well, you could hear her *shouting*. It was really upsetting. You could hear her scream, 'Get off me! Stop it! Leave me alone!" To be honest, the only conclusion we could come to was that her husband was raping her..."

Linda hadn't told the woman about her own encounter, where something invisible had pinned her head to the bed and touched her intimately on her thighs. However, Linda wondered, quite reasonably, whether the woman had really been "raped" by her husband at all. What if, she wondered, it was the *thing* that had attacked her, perhaps when her husband wasn't there?

Several nights later, two friends of Tony and Linda, Graeme* and Kerry*, paid them a visit. The couple told their friends about the strange goings-on in their home, and at some point the suggestion was made that they should try and make some audio recordings similar to those made by Mike. Tony had a digital sound recorder, and agreed to the proposition. After the device was switched on, in the living room, Graeme proceeded to ask a series of questions aimed at anyone (or anything) that might have been invisibly present. The first few questions weren't answered, but then Graeme asked out loud, "Did you die here?" Although nothing was heard at the time, when the recording was played back something strange could be heard. The following day, Tony phoned Mike and told him about the experience:

"Mike, if I e-mail you the recording as a WAV file, could you listen to it and tell me what you think?"

Mike agreed, and within a few minutes Tony's e-mail arrived. Prior to asking the question, "Did you die here?" Graeme had asked, "How old are you?" Immediately after this juncture a faint voice could be heard in the background. The sound was barely audible, but to Mike it sounded like a young male saying something like, "I am sixteen", or "I am seventeen". Mike listened to the rest of the recording, but heard nothing that sounded even remotely anomalous. He called Tony back:

"Well, I've listened to the tape, and I can hear that voice but its so faint you can barely make it out. It's intriguing, but to be honest it could be anything".

"Really? On my recording the voice is completely clear!"

Naturally this puzzled Mike, who decided to make sure that they were both talking about the same sound.

"You know when Graeme asks, 'How old are you?' After that you can hear a faint voice saying something like, "I am sixteen" or "I am seventeen"? Is that the noise you're talking about?"

"Mike, I don't recall hearing *anything* after Graeme asked the question, 'How old are you?' *I'm* talking about the sounds that came *after* that. Listen to the recording again".

Mike, who was sitting in front of his PC at the time, moved the mouse and clicked the *play* button on the screen whilst holding the phone to his ear with his other hand. Once again he could hear Graeme ask, "Did you die here?" Then he heard what sounded like either Linda or Kerry saying, "I heard that, did you?" This was followed by Graeme saying, "Aye!" The recording ended shortly thereafter.

"There, Mike!" said Tony. "Did you hear that?"

"Erm...not really pal. All I can hear is one of the girls asking if the others in the room had heard something. Then I heard Graeme answering. Apart from that there was nothing".

"But that's just it. The woman's voice you can hear – it wasn't Linda *or* Kerry. Neither of them said a word!"

Mike's immediate reaction was that one of the two women must have spoken and simply forgotten. Tony, however, was adamant:

"Mike, I know Linda's voice and Graeme knows Kerry's. Whoever that is speaking on the recording...well, it isn't them. Besides, all four of us know that no one except Graeme spoke".

"But Tony, Graeme *must* have heard the woman's voice, because when she said, 'I heard that, did you?' he answered her. I distinctly heard him say, 'Aye!'"

"I know, and that's puzzling, but listen to the voice several more times. To be honest, I don't think she's saying 'I heard that, did you?' at all. At first I did, but after listening to it over and over to me it sounds as if she's saying something else completely."

"Like what?"

"Well, it sounds as if she's saying that she *smothered* someone".

"Eh?"

"Honest – listen to the recording *again* Mike, and then ring me back".

Mike decided to try something. After listening to the tape another three times, and each time becoming more convinced than ever that the woman really was saying, "I heard that, did you?", he loaded up the recording with some audio-analysing software and slowed it down to half of its original speed. This time, the words were crystal clear. Tony was right, the disembodied voice was *not* saying, "I heard that, did you?" at all.

As the slowed-down recording played out, once again Mike heard Graeme say, "Did you die here?" Then, responding immediately, the anomalous voice says, "I did smother Jim!"

There was no doubt about it; someone was actually talking about *smothering* a person called "Jim".

Mike then spotted something else. When Graeme uttered the word, "Aye!" he did so *over the top* of the anomalous voice just as the name "Jim" was mentioned. Whatever Graeme was responding to, then, it hadn't been the anomalous voice. Mike needed to know exactly what Graeme was responding to, and the only way to do that was to give him a call. Before he did that, however, he decided to ask Tony and Linda's permission. He dialled Tony's number first, but got no reply. He left a short voicemail, and then listened to the tape again. At this point another puzzle manifested itself. Shortly after Graeme can be heard saying, "Aye!", he then says, "Right, stop the recording for one second...what did you hear?" Linda then replies, "A sigh". Graeme then responds, "Whispering? Okay..."

Graeme, it seems, had become aware that either Linda and/or Kerry had heard something. However, at no point on the tape can either of the women be heard saying so. How, then, had Graeme determined that something audible – at least to the women – had caught their attention? There were only two possibilities that Mike could come up with at the time. The first was that either Kerry or Linda had given Graeme a *visual* clue that they'd heard something, perhaps by tapping their ear. This was possible, as they may have refrained from speaking simply so that they didn't ruin the rest of the recording. The other possibility was rather mundane. If the enigmatic voice *had* actually been one of the women, and they *had* actually said, "I heard that, did you?" then Graeme's response, "Aye!" followed by, "Right, stop the recording for one second...what did you hear?" would make perfect sense.

Tempting though it was to run with this explanation, there were two major difficulties. The first was that, as previously stated, Graeme's first response was uttered *before* the anomalous voice had finished speaking. The second problem – and the major one – is that a close analysis of the sound proves conclusively that the speaker was not saying, "I heard that, did you?" at all.

Coming up with a plausible explanation for the contents of the tape and how those present – living or dead – were interacting with each other was becoming increasingly difficult. All Mike could do was listen to the tape again. And again, and again, and again. It took some time, but eventually Mike managed to create a hypothetical scenario which, he believes, is the only one that takes all the facts into consideration and still makes sense. To understand just exactly how things probably transpired, we need to look at a line-by-line rendition of the conversation on the recording:

> Graeme: *Do you have an age? How old are you?*
> Faint male voice: *I am sixteen [or seventeen].*
> Graeme: *Did you die here?*
> Anomalous female voice: *I did smother Jim.*
> Graeme: *Aye!*
> Graeme: *Right, stop the recording for one second...what did you hear?*
> Linda: *A sigh.*

Before Mike could even begin to reconstruct what had happened, though, he still needed to ascertain exactly what Graeme had been responding to when he'd exclaimed, "Aye!" He tried ringing Tony again, and this time was successful. Tony said he had no problems at all with Mike contacting Graeme. With Tony and Linda's blessing, he rang Graeme immediately.

Mike outlined as best he could what had transpired, and then said, "Graeme, there's only one problem that still bugs me; when the mystery voice says, "I did smother Jim", what were you responding to when you said, 'Aye!'?

"That's just it, Mike. That wasn't me speaking. I never said, 'Aye!' at all."

"Who was it, then?"

"No one; at least no one we could see in the room".

Mike thanked Graeme for his help and then went back to the metaphorical drawing board. Now he had another mystery to sort out; who had uttered the retort, "Aye!"? Within seconds a potential answer struck him, When the enigmatic female voice said, "I did smother Jim", the retort "Aye!" may well have been uttered by the late departed Jim himself.

This left only one puzzle. Graeme fully accepted that he had said, "Right, stop the recording for one second...what did you hear?" The question was why he had said that at all. As stated earlier, there were no audible cues from either Linda or Kerry that they had heard anything, which only seemed to leave the possibility that they had given off a visual cue that, obviously, couldn't be heard on the tape. Both Tony and Graeme acknowledged that this had indeed been the case. Just before Graeme asked them what they had heard, both women heard what they described as a faint but distinct sighing noise. Simultaneously they had both turned and looked at each other, eyes agog and jaws hanging open. Graeme had seen this, and realised that they'd heard something. *This*, then, was what had prompted him to say, "Right, stop the recording for one second... what did you hear?"

There had been, it seems, six people in the lounge that day; Tony and Linda, Graeme and Kerry and, just possibly, a rather cantankerous old woman and the man, Jim, that she had tried to smother.

At this time of writing, the authors' investigation into the case is continuing.

Seventeen
STANDBY—THE POLT POWER SOURCE?

Over the last few years the green campaign has stepped up a notch in its efforts to clean up both the planet and its environment. Brown or green wheelie bins have been introduced for garden waste, and recycling boxes have been distributed nationwide to householders so they can place their old tin cans, plastic bags and paper etc, in them for recycling.

September 2008 saw the launch of a new TV advertising campaign advising the British public to become even "greener". In fact, there are (at this time of writing) a number of TV commercials imploring viewers to do simple little things to help, such as turning off unused lights at home. Other commercials suggest turning off TV's that aren't being watched, radios or hi-fi systems that are not being used - ultimately to save electricity and money, to reduce carbon emissions, and of course, reduce your own "carbon footprint".

Essentially, a carbon footprint is the measure of human activity that has a detrimental effect upon the environment. Greenhouse gasses that are produced from our everyday actions can be counted up in measurements. These units of carbon dioxide (CO_2) can be measured individually, or as part of a group or unit, in order to determine just how much carbon dioxide is being expelled into the atmosphere from any given source, or indeed all of them. Once you know what your "carbon footprint" is, you can take steps to reduce your carbon emissions, thus helping to prevent or at least slow down the global warming process.

This latest TV advert is essentially no different from others. But there is one particular aspect of the campaign that is new on the "keep things green" front, so to speak. When Darren saw this TV ad for the first time, metaphorical bells began to ring, and he was suddenly struck with a rather intriguing thought. This particular ad mentioned the usual things such as dimming lights, half-filling kettles, saving water etc, but the aspect of it that made Darren sit up and pay attention was when it mentioned the detrimental effects of *leaving electrical appliances on standby*.

In recent years, theories have originated in regards to poltergeist activity and the mechanics behind it. These new ideas include the idea that the poltergeist might use the dormant electrical energy that is so often stored in TVs and music systems when left on "standby". If electrical energy latent in appliances in standby-mode is utilised in this way by hungry polts, turning the appliances off completely may indeed cut off one of their much-needed sources of energy or "food". The authors found this to be a relevant factor in the South Shields case back in 2006. At the Lock Street house, many new electrical appliances had been brought into the home at the same time that Marc had moved in, such as TVs, DVD players and a music system for the master bedroom. They were all left on "standby" during the night – and obviously during the daytime - when not in use. Upon the advice of the authors, (after a recommendation from Stephen Swales, a close colleague), the experients tried this potential remedy. The polt activity then seemed to cease abruptly. Could a lack of this "dormant electricity" or "polt power source", play a real part in bringing a poltergeist infestation to an end? The authors think so.

At Lock Street, the polt seemed to feed upon the principal experients' *fear* (another theory as to how polts persist in their endeavours), but after being subjected to so much terror and alarm in their home, believe it or not they simply became accustomed to it. Over time, they literally became *bored* with it to a degree rather than frightened. Subsequently, then, the polt lost its primary food source - their fear. It now needed something else to feed upon, and it wasn't long before it discovered the latent electrical power in appliances that were in "stand-by mode". This new food source sustained its ability to engage in destruction, but not for long. Once the householders at Lock Street began to turn off their appliances at night, the polt simply couldn't feed at all. This is when the authors believed they may have brought "it" to its knees.

Darren's point is that the people of Great Britain do indeed need to take heed of this new advert by turning off lights in rooms that are not being used, turning off radios that are not being listened to, and most importantly, *not* leaving one's appliances on standby (overnight or otherwise). Granted, we may be reducing our carbon emissions which is of course a good thing, but one *may* also be saving oneself from months of unnecessary trouble and torment at the hands of an uninvited, invisible intruder commonly known as the poltergeist.

In Darren's view, what needs to be monitored is the number of genuine cases that are reported to well-respected research associations such as the Incorporated Society for Psychical Research (SPR), ASSAP, or the Ghost Club of Great Britain *after* the TV adverts have been shown. Pre - September 2008 (Sept 2007 – Sept 2008) nationwide statistics for poltergeist infestations may have reached, for example 250 in that year. If the following year's statistics show a decrease in reported poltergeist cases, and the following year the reduction in cases still persists, it *could* mean that turning off electrical appliances may well be a key factor in dealing with, or maybe even reducing the possibility of, an infestation. It would be a great step forward in poltergeist research if such a discovery were to be made, but only time will tell.

Of course, we will have to wait a number of years to see if genuine reports of poltergeists increase or decrease. If the masses decide to "unplug or switch off", rather than leave their electrical appliances "on stand-by", then, who knows, maybe polt cases will drop. Steps will be taken by the authors a few years from now to contact such organisations like the SPR to find out just how many cases have been reported in the years following this green TV ad campaign. It may come to nothing; however it might prove an interesting exercise yielding positive results. Whatever the outcome, the authors believe that creative thinking, testing, hypothesising and probing possibilities like these will, one day, ultimately lead us closer to solving the enigma that is the poltergeist.

Eighteen
"My Name is Legion—For We Are Many"

To set the scene for the exposition of the authors' hypothesis regarding the poltergeist phenomenon, it will first be necessary to provide the reader with an admittedly controversial theory that may well offend those of a religious disposition, specifically orthodox Christians. We don't wish to cause offence unnecessarily, but the authors are of the opinion that people in ancient times, and some who came later, may well have had a better understanding of the poltergeist enigma than we might imagine.

It is a truism to state that the population of 1st Century AD Judea believed in the possession of people by evil spirits. The New Testament is awash with incidents in which invisible, malign entities take over innocent victims and use them for their own wicked purposes. Jesus, as we know, made quite a name for himself by expelling such demons and freeing the victims from their clutches. A close examination of the poltergeist phenomenon throws up many parallels with the concept of spirit possession. They are similar, but not the same. Cases of spirit possession usually involve radical changes in the personality of the possessed person. Those who play host to a poltergeist do not usually exhibit such changes, and may continue to behave perfectly normally. However, the two phenomena are similar in that they both involve a "host" or "focus" who, consciously or otherwise, has within them a force or power that operates independently and has a great degree of autonomy. In both phenomena, the attendant symptoms are almost always negative, counter-productive and destructive.

In Judaeo-Christian theology, demons are believed to be evil spirits who are subject to the whims of a master, commonly called Satan or the Devil. Muslims, it must be said, hold a somewhat different view. Further, some believe that demons do not exist as sentient, autonomous entities, but are merely fragmentary aspects of a higher, Satanic personality. Conversely, some Christians believe the same about angels; that they are not independent entities but merely "aspects of God". A similar belief exists in ostensibly polytheistic societies or cultures, where many different "deities" are believed to be simply one, great deity presenting in different forms.

Is there any evidence to suggest that this idea – that spiritual entities may be more a part of a greater whole and less fully autonomous entities – affected the thinking of those who lived in Jesus' day? Indeed there is, and it can be found in one of the gospel accounts themselves.

In the Gospel of Luke , there is an account of a man who, it seems, was acting rather bizarrely. He had taken to wearing no clothes, and had forsaken his former abode and began to reside in a local graveyard. Jesus happens to bump into the man, who was believed to be "possessed by devils", and at this point the possessed individual speaks to him. However, it is clear from the outset that it is not the man as such who is doing the talking, but the entities which allegedly possessed him:

"What have I got to do with you, Jesus, you Son of God Most High? I plead with you, do not torment me!" the devil says.

Jesus, it seems, had attempted to carry out an impromptu exorcism and had commanded the evil spirits to come out of the man; something which they were clearly reluctant to do. In addition to living naked amongst the tombs, the man had also developed incredible superhuman strength. On several occasions he had been chained, but apparently shattered his bonds with ease. Desperate to rid their community of the possessed person, locals had driven him into the desert.

Just before the exorcism was complete, Jesus asked, "What is your name?" This is intriguing, for although the man was said to be possessed by *many* devils the son of Mary addressed them *in the singular*, as if he was talking to one personage only.

The devil (or devils) replied, "My name is Legion, for we are many".

Jesus, as we know, then cast out the offending entities and sent them into a herd of swine, which then all raced over the edge of a nearby cliff into the water below.

The fascinating thing about this account is that it alternates between the singular and the plural repeatedly. Was the man possessed by many demons, or just one? One interpretation would be to say that he was possessed both by one and by many at the same time. Let us imagine that evil spirits are not fully autonomous entities or spirits, but are essentially parts of a greater whole - an arch-spirit, if you will, and call him Satan if you like – who merely presents himself to victims as a single individual or in a multiplicity of aspects depending on how the mood takes him. If this is the case, then it is technically correct to speak of such an entity in both the singular and the plural, for it is truly both.

In cases of spirit possession, victims often manifest strikingly similar symptoms; levitation, use of foul language (often in Latin, Aramaic or some other defunct language), evacuation of huge amounts of excreta from the bowels, speaking in strange accents...all of which could reasonably be presented as evidence that the same guiding hand is behind each and every possession. Indeed, the cases of possession are often so similar that we may be confident enough to suggest that the same personality is at work, much as we may say the same about the serial killer who leaves a particular playing card on the bodies of his victims.

At this point we can now ask what may metaphorically be deemed the $64,000 dollar question; can we apply this same hypothesis to the poltergeist phenomenon? Could it be that there is, in reality, only *one* poltergeist – the arch-poltergeist, if you like – who, like demons, devils and deities, presents itself as one or many depending on how he/she/it feels? It is only a hypothesis, but it is one that Darren feels may well be correct, both because of his own personal experience, and the testimony of many other poltergeist incidents.

NOTES
1.   Luke 8: 26-33.

Nineteen
ENFIELD & OTHER CASES: CONTAGION & PARALLELS

One of the strangest aspects of the poltergeist phenomenon, and one which impacts heavily upon the theme of this book, is the bizarre parallels that often occur between separate cases of poltergeist infestation. Some of these parallels will be obvious to even the amateur researcher; objects being moved without human intervention, disembodied footsteps and loud rapping noises are but three examples. However, there are other, more peculiar parallels that, as previously stated, would seem to imply that the same entity is responsible for all of the phenomena - even in cases that are temporally and geographically disparate.

Before going into detail regarding what conclusion the authors reached about this peculiarity, it is necessary to spell out exactly what sort of symptoms and signs they are referring to. Overleaf is a chart which draws attention to some - although certainly not all - of the parallels between the numerous cases that the authors have either encountered or investigated. In the "Location or Case" columns, the following key is used: En: Enfield. SS: South Shields. Ja: Jarrow. As: Ashington. Ne: Newcastle. Bl: Blyth. Go: Gosforth. Ho: Howdon. WB: West Boldon. NT: North Tyneside.

Readers will note that there are some cases detailed earlier in the book that are not recorded. Some of these cases also contain extraordinary parallels with cases detailed in the chart, but they were not investigated personally by the authors. Readers will also notice that by far the greatest number of parallels can be found between the Enfield and South Shields cases, but the temptation should be resisted to read too much into this. In both

		Location or Case
No	Presenting Symptom of Poltergeistry	En SS Ja As Ne Bl Go Ho WB
1	Presentation of contagion or contagion-like phenomena	✓ ✓ ✓ ✓ ✓ ✓ ✓ ✓ ✓
2	Books flying off shelves	✓ ✓ ✓ ✓
3	Knocking or rapping noises	✓ ✓ ✓ ✓ ✓
4	Polt-fascination with plastic building blocks	✓ ✓
5	Phenomena involving glass marbles	✓ ✓
6	Drawers opening of their own accord	✓ ✓
7	Doors opening or closing of their own accord	✓ ✓ ✓ ✓
8	Objects passing through solid matter	✓ ✓
9	Sudden, icy breezes	✓ ✓ ✓ ✓
10	Stacking of objects	✓ ✓ ✓ ✓
11	Physical attacks upon experients	✓ ✓ ✓ ✓
12	Hearing of voices	✓ ✓ ✓ ✓
13	Seeing apparitions	✓ ✓ ✓ ✓ ✓
14	Appearance of shadows or shadow-like shapes	✓ ✓ ✓ ✓ ✓ ✓
15	Movement or interaction with children's toys	✓ ✓ ✓ ✓
16	Movement of mobile phones from downstairs to upstairs	✓ ✓ ✓
17	Involuntary movement or relocation of sleeping children	✓ ✓
18	Movement of furniture	✓ ✓ ✓
19	Polt-fascination with fish or fish tanks	✓ ✓
20	Intervention of clergy or other religious leaders	✓ ✓ ✓ ✓
21	Phenomena related to mineral water bottles	✓ ✓
22	"Shaking bed" or "moving bed" phenomenon	✓ ✓ ✓ ✓

		Location or Case								
No	Presenting Symptom of Poltergeistry	En	SS	Ja	As	Ne	Bl	Go	Ho	WB
23	Aggressive us of projectiles	✓	✓	✓	✓					
24	Inexplicable power drainage from electrical equipment	✓	✓	✓		✓	✓			
25	Lithobolia, or "stone-throwing" phenomena	✓	✓							
26	Possible masquerading of the poltergeist as a child	✓	✓	✓						
27	Fascination of the polt with technological or mechanical objects	✓	✓	✓		✓	✓	✓	✓	✓
28	Precise "timing" of phenomena, indicating sentience on the part of the part of the poltergeist	✓	✓	✓	✓	✓	✓			✓
29	Polt-fascination with "red chairs"	✓	✓							
30	Witnessing the spontaneous materialisation of objects	✓	✓				✓			
31	Polt-related phenomena outside of "Ground Zero", or the home of the experients	✓	✓	✓	✓			✓	✓	✓
32	Inability of experients to open doors	✓	✓	✓						
33	"Florescent light" phenomenon (not "orbs")	✓	✓		✓					
34	"Mischievous" movement of chairs as experients are sitting or attempting to sit down	✓	✓							
35	Throwing of/fascination with miniature or toy vehicles	✓	✓							
36	Spontaneous appearance of water pools	✓	✓							
37	Spontaneous appearance of urine		✓							
38	Movement of kitchen tables	✓	✓							
39	Poltergeists verifying their authenticity/existence to investigators	✓	✓							
40	Children subjected to trance-like states	✓	✓	✓						
41	"Burning sensations" felt before attacks		✓							

Enfield & Other Cases

		Location or Case								
No	Presenting Symptom of Poltergeistry	En	SS	Ja	As	Ne	Bl	Go	Ho	WB
42	Pulling of bedclothes from bed	✓	✓	✓	✓					
43	Polt-fascination with footwear	✓	✓							
44	Soft toys thrown at experients whilst they lie in bed	✓	✓							
45	Polt-fascination with crayons, pencils, writing implements	✓	✓	✓						
46	Complete "trashing" of rooms	✓	✓							
47	"Throwing" of knives	✓	✓							
48	Door-knocks by invisible entities	✓	✓							
49	Leaving of written messages by poltergeists	✓	✓							
50	Spontaneous fire-starting	✓	✓							✓
51	Polt-fascination with wardrobes	✓	✓	✓	✓			✓		
52	Polt-fascination with refrigerators	✓	✓			✓				
53	Lavatory-related phenomena	✓	✓	✓					✓	
54	Coin or monetary-related phenomena	✓	✓			✓				
55	Experients being thrown or lifted out of bed	✓	✓							
56	"Doppelganger" phenomenon	✓	✓	✓						
57	Possibility of a "collective polt"	✓	✓	✓		✓		✓	✓	✓
58	Use of foul language by poltergeists	✓	✓							
59	Use of taunting euphemisms by poltergeists	✓	✓							
60	Threats to investigators by poltergeists	✓	✓							
61	Sexual undertones present			✓	✓					
62	Use of personal names by the poltergeist	✓		✓	✓		✓		✓	
63	Removing bath panels			✓	✓					
64	Spontaneous removal and replacement of documents from drawers			✓	✓		✓		✓	

the Enfield and South Shields cases, a detailed case study was written up in book form, thus making it much easier for parallels to be spotted and noted.

Often, it is not the *number* of parallels that is the important thing, but rather the quality of them. As readers will see, there are occasions when a parallel can be drawn between only two cases, but it is so specific that any reasonable person would be forced to conclude that a link - whatever one may perceive it to be - is present.

There are a number of quite startling parallels that need to be drawn to the reader's attention. In both the Enfield and South Shields cases, the poltergeist seemed to have an unusual fascination with children's plastic building blocks. The authors are aware of other cases in which this same fascination was evident.

In one US case, detailed earlier, a children's toy "play mat" was involved. The authors have already pointed out the precise, undeniable parallels present with the case they investigated at South Shields.

During their research whilst writing this volume, the authors contacted their friend and colleague Guy Lyon Playfair, one of the two principal investigators of the Enfield case and asked him whether either he or the late Maurice Grosse had experienced anything that could be classed as contagion-like phenomena. Guy e-mailed Darren and related the following:

> *Dear Darren,*
>
> *Maurice had all kinds of strange experiences and of course I can't prove they were polt-related, but they did seem to escalate post-Enfield.*
>
> *The best one I remember which Maurice told me about soon afterwards, was when his wife's ring went missing overnight from the bedside little china pot where she always kept it. Weeks of search of the whole house and grounds failed to find it. Reluctantly, Maurice wrote to his insurance company for a claim form. The next morning the ring was back in its pot.*
>
> *My own experience is:*
>
> *After listening to a rather silly BBC Radio 4 play, obviously based on the Enfield case, I heard a loud ping*

and found that one of the tops of the knobs on my electric cooker had come off, travelled 2-3 feet and banged into a bottle on the floor. There was absolutely no conceivable way that could have been normal. The tops are quite hard to get off. The cooker was on, but on very low heat, and I have used it daily since 1975 (and still do). It has never malfunctioned in any way. Here, there was a clear connection to Enfield.

The radio play was obviously based on the Enfield case - but set in South London and involving 2 teenage boys instead of girls and investigated by a woman. I listened to it without much interest, mainly to see if the author violated my copyright, which he took care not to do. When it was over, I thought to myself "what a waste of time", and soon afterwards there was this loud ping. You're welcome to quote that.

Yrs Guy".

Guy Playfair and the late Maurice Grosse are recognised as two of the most knowledgeable researchers regarding the poltergeist phenomenon, and if they experienced phenomena that they believed to be contagion-like, we must take their arguments seriously.

On 4 May, 2008, Mike had a lengthy discussion with Darren about the whole matter of contagion and afterwards both Darren and Mike took a break from working on the book manuscript so Mike could take care of a personal project he had been working on. In 1918, his great-grandfather Thomas Trewick was serving with the British Army in France and was stationed in the town of Forceville. His battalion was moved to a nearby town to stall a German advance, when, with two colleagues, he clambered down into what had been a German trench. Almost immediately, a shell landed inside the trench and all three men were killed.

Mike was particularly interested in his great-grandfather's war service, and had been working on a website dedicated to the man. At that juncture he did not know the exact date when Tom Trewick had been killed, although there was a story prevalent in the family that the tragedy had occurred on Armistice Day, November 11, 1918. Mike had an old, battered photograph of his great-grandfather and took it out of his file to examine. He flipped it over, and noticed for the first time that a small piece of paper had been glued over the back. Written on the reverse of the picture were the words, "TOM TREWICK, KILLED 1918". However, Mike could see that there was something else written underneath the piece of paper. For the next twenty minutes, Mike carefully scraped away at the now-brittle paper until the writing underneath was exposed. It was, quite simply, the exact date on which Pte. Trewick had been killed. The date was May 4 - the very day that Mike was actually examining the photograph, and the very day that he had not only discussed the subject of polt-contagion with Darren but had been writing about it in the manuscript of this book.

The fact that the date was the very same as the one on which his great-grandfather was killed was extraordinary, but can this be robustly connected to the poltergeist phenomenon and classed as contagion? Directly no; but the authors and other researchers have reported experiencing quite extraordinary "coincidences" of this nature when dealing with polt cases. There may be no direct connection - in the same way that there was no direct connection between the Enfield case and Maurice Grosse's wife "losing" her ring. However, the insistence of such phenomena in manifesting themselves when investigations are going on leaves one having to admit that there may indeed be such a connection.

In the South Shields, Ashington and Jarrow cases, the experients all reported feeling a "sense of depression" which overtook them when they felt the "presence" of the poltergeist. This is not uncommon. This is not a physically observable parallel, of course, and more of a subjective observation, but it is still worth mentioning.

When the authors were working on this book, Mike had occasion to ring their agent, Natalie Lisbona. Just before the phone conversation, Natalie opened a cupboard in her kitchen and subsequently had a rather unnerving experience. Inside the cupboard was a packet of dried lentils. Without warning, the packet shot out of the cupboard and careened across the floor. What made the experience all the weirder was that, just before entering the kitchen, Natalie had been reviewing some footage which the authors had taken during their investigation into the South Shields poltergeist case.

Around the same time, Natalie also had another strange

experience. Whilst lying in bed with her husband, the couple repeatedly heard the sound of someone placing a key in their front door and trying to open the lock. Every time they opened the door there was no one there. The mystery was never solved. Again, it seemed that the poltergeist phenomenon, whatever one thinks it to be, has an ability to transcend fixed geographical locations and "infect" those who are only indirectly involved with the case at hand.

One of the most disturbing aspects of the poltergeist phenomenon - although, to be honest, it isn't a common one - is the presence of sexual undertones. This was certainly true at Ashington, and it was also true at Jarrow and Middlesbrough. During an interview with Mandy, Mike said, "Mandy, you mentioned earlier on that you felt something touch you on the leg; again, that is something that is frightening, but have you ever felt any other of your body parts being touched – say, for example, something like fingers running through your hair?" Mandy replied, "Erm…Just when I walked in from the kitchen one time, and I thought Derek touched my behind in a saucy-but-fun way - but he said it wasn't him".

To some, this incident may seem trivial, but in reality it speaks volumes about the essence or nature of the poltergeist. Whether such incidents are common or not, there can be no doubt that, at least on occasions, the polt can display sexually provocative behaviour. Earlier in this book, the authors discussed the possibly-related incubus/succubus phenomenon. However, as in all the cases they have investigated the victims of such behaviour are female, the question must be asked whether the poltergeist is a particularly male phenomenon who may present itself in female form, but is essentially masculine in nature.

In 1981, a screenplay written by Frank deFelitta was turned into a movie. The film, *The Entity*, detailed the experiences of one Carla Moran, who claimed that she was repeatedly physically (including sexually) assaulted by a demonic entity. The movie is alleged by some to be based upon a true-life story. Whether this is true or not we do not know, but it certainly wouldn't surprise the authors. The sad truth is that when people *do* claim to have genuinely experienced such encounters they are usually disbelieved. Cynics, it seems, just don't possess the broadness of mind to grasp that these things really do happen.

Imagine that you are a woman at home alone. Then imagine that a demented psychopath is trying to break down your front door, and you strongly suspect that his sole intention is to rape you and possibly kill you. You pick up the phone and dial the police. What you want, of course, is for officers to respond immediately and both protect you and arrest the felon. But supposing you don't actually get what you want. Suppose, for one terrible moment, the police refuse to respond to your call and tell you that, quite frankly, they don't believe your story.

"We don't get any rapes happening around here", you are told. Imagine your horror and disbelief at such a reaction. You know you are telling the truth, but the only people who can help you refuse to act because they simply don't believe what you are telling them. What you thought was your worst nightmare has now just become even more terrifying. It's a horrible thought, isn't it? And yet, all over the globe, there are women who are genuinely afraid of being raped and brutalised - not just by flesh-and-blood males, but by psychic entities with far more potential for doing harm. Very few are believed, and hence they have nowhere to turn. The authors understand that there are troubled - or even mischievous - individuals out there who are for one reason or another only too ready to lie and make up such stories. But they aren't *all* lying. Some are telling the truth. In a classic case of throwing the baby out with the bath water, sceptics will often argue that if one such person is lying then they all must be. Even if one takes the sexual element out of the equation, being attacked and/or terrorised by a poltergeist – whatever it may be - is a terrible thing.

Are such people lying? Sometimes, yes. Unfortunately, nowadays, too many people use the "my house is haunted" excuse in an attempt to get re-housed when they are unhappy with their rented homes for whatever reason; noisy neighbours, bad surroundings or living conditions - or simply because they just want to move. Pleas for help from genuine victims of hauntings to be re-housed have worked in the past so why not lie about a ghost or poltergeist and get re-housed hassle free? In genuine circumstances like the Maud Street case in Lemington, Newcastle-upon-Tyne, in 1974, the principal victim was affected so badly she had to be hospitalised. There was, as far as we know, no sexual aspect to this poltergeist infestation, but the victim was clearly traumatised.

When bare-faced liars claim the same thing has happened to them it is an insult to genuine victims of hauntings and poltergeist phenomena. Bogus claims are a serious headache for investigators. Time after time the so-called victims are proven to be untruthful, and when a genuine case does come along no one will believe it.

This happened to the authors after they had investigated the South Shields poltergeist case in 2006. After the book that details the whole affair was released; some folk suggested that the family members in question were merely publicity-seeking liars who made it all up to be re-housed by their housing association. They failed to realise that the people in question were actually *buying* their house and not renting it; furthermore, *they* requested the anonymity in the book and *they* have since rebuffed all media attention. The authors guess that if those narrow-minded critics had actually read their book based upon the case properly they would have been aware of these facts and consequently not embarrassed themselves. Their point is that not all claims of having a haunted house are false. Some people do live in fear of haunting phenomena and have nowhere to turn; if they live in rented accommodation it is worse ten-fold, as they know that if they do ask to be moved, they may well be labelled liars – and it's just not on. The residents in Maud Street discovered this all too well.

Twenty
TEXTUAL INNUENDOES

One of the things the authors noticed during their investigation at South Shields was that the poltergeist displayed an impressive ability to utilise technology. This would demonstrate itself in relatively simple ways, such as the turning on and off electrical appliances. It had a particular fondness for "messing around" with the TV, and on numerous occasions turned it on or off in the presence of both the principal experients and investigators. One slight variation on this party trick was to leave the TV on but repeatedly change the channels. Its most impressive TV-related trick was to programme the attached digital satellite box to remind the couple when certain programmes were about to start. Inevitably, these would be documentaries or movies with a paranormal or horror theme.

However, the polt also demonstrated a liking for mobile phones. Actually, it was more like an obsession. Within a short space of time it mastered the art of using the mobile phone, and eventually was able to do things that were by all accounts scientifically impossible. The polt could make a mobile phone ring, and then stop it ringing. It then worked out – somehow – a way of making a mobile phone ring even when it wasn't switched on. As its phone-related skills were honed, it began to send text messages – many of them of a vile and threatening nature. On one occasion, the polt sent a series of terrifying text messages to Marianne, one of the principal experients, whilst Mike was on the phone to her. The messages related to things that Marianne had said just a split-second earlier in the conversation. It would have been physically impossible for a human being to compose even the briefest of text messages within such an incredibly short space of time, but the polt managed it.

As the reader will now be aware, one of the principal themes explored in this book is that of contagion; the possibility that, in some way, people may become infected by the polt-presence and, in turn, experience polt-related phenomena themselves. Another aspect of the poltergeist phenomenon that the authors have explored is the bizarre similarity between cases that are geographically – and often culturally – separated. Why would a poltergeist in Enfield display a fascination with children's toy building bricks, and a poltergeist three decades later at the opposite end of the country demonstrate exactly the same compulsion? Just why these "polt-parallels" occur is something that we will explore later. However, for now the authors simply wish to draw the reader's attention to an uncanny parallel between a number of cases – all of which repeated what the authors had already discovered at South Shields; that polts just *love* telephones.

On Tuesday April 29, 2008, Mike and Darren were giving a lecture on the South Shields poltergeist case. Mike had arranged to meet Darren at Newcastle Central train station at 2pm before they headed off for the venue of their talk. Mike – a stickler for punctuality - was well ahead of time and decided to browse through the magazine shelves at the WHS store inside the station. After a minute or two his eyes fell upon the May edition of *The Fortean Times*, one of the world's most respected magazines dealing with strange phenomena. He purchased a copy, and then ensconced himself at a table in one of the station's several open-air cafés with a large Americano. Darren wouldn't be arriving for another twenty minutes or so, so Mike decided to flick through the pages of the magazine to see if there were any stories of unusual interest.

And there was. On page 8 there was an article entitled, *Cell Phone Stalkers Playing Mind Games*. The article dealt with a "reign of terror" that three families had been forced to endure in the city of Fircrest, Pierce County, Washington State beginning around the month of February, 2007. The case involved a variety of non phone-related phenomena, including horrendous banging noises on walls and screams seemingly uttered by disembodies voices. Inevitably, by the time the police arrived on the scene the perpetrators had vanished. However, the worst aspects of the case were those that centred around mobile phones owned by the victims. They would receive voice-mails spoken in guttural, chilling tones which contained death threats. Worse, the callers obviously knew exactly what the victims were doing at any given time. The perpetrators would describe what they were wearing, what they were eating and, often, what they were actually doing within the confines of their homes.

A subsequent investigation showed that many (although not all) of the calls were seemingly coming from the phone of one of the victims, sixteen year-old Courtney Kuykendall. However, it was later proved that when many of the calls were made Courtney wasn't using her phone, and that it had actually been switched off. Conversations made over the phone were occasionally recorded and then sent to the victims as voice-mail messages. As the victims received their phone bills, they were horrified to find that they were enormous, sometimes approaching $1,000.

One of the victims was Taylor McKay, who went with her mother to meet with the principal of her school to discuss the situation. A police officer was present at the meeting. Both Taylor and her mother, Andrea, placed their cell-phones on the table in front of them. They were both switched off. Suddenly, Taylor's phone switched itself on and promptly sent a text message to her mother's phone.

The victims tried all manner of things to rectify the situation, including changing their phone numbers. As soon as they did so, they would begin receiving more voice messages. On one occasion, Andrea McKay was slicing limes in the kitchen when she received a message from the perpetrators telling her that they actually preferred lemons.

There were two possible explanations for the enigma. The first was that the victims were the victim of a highly sophisticated campaign of terror organised by malicious (but very human) perpetrators who seemingly had the ability to hack into the websites of their service providers and effectively "hijack" their phones. Such a thing is possible, but to carry out such a campaign to that degree would need a sophisticated knowledge of phone and computer technology beyond that possessed by the vast majority of people. In any case, why would anyone want to go to such lengths simply to make the lives of three ordinary families a misery? Further, this explanation does not deal with how the perpetrators were able to monitor the exact movements and actions of the victims within their own homes. To do this they would have needed to break into the families' dwellings and install covert surveillance equipment without being seen or apprehended. It just doesn't seem to make sense.

The second explanation was radically different, and involved the suggestion that the perpetrator may have been something far from human; a poltergeist. Poltergeists are well known for creating banging noises and moving objects around, but those who took an interest in the case were astounded at the idea that a poltergeist could actually manipulate mobile phone technology to such a degree – and with such wanton vindictiveness. This didn't surprise Darren and Mike, because they'd seen it all before – at South Shields.

By Monday August 28, 2006, the incessant barrage of attacks had driven the family at Lock Street to distraction and they decided to vacate the premises for the evening and stay with Marianne's mother. Mike asked Marianne to ring him and let him know if everyone was okay later that evening. Marianne did ring Mike, although she still sounded distressed. Marc, she said, had telephoned the landline of their home "just to see what would happen", although he knew that no one was there. No one should have picked up the receiver, of course, because there wasn't supposed to be anyone there. But something did pick up the receiver before immediately replacing it on the cradle. It was almost certainly the polt.

The authors tried to reassure Marianne that things would turn out okay; she just needed to remain calm. Marianne said that it would be difficult, as during the day she'd received a series of nasty text messages from the entity, saying things like, "tonight is the night you will die", and, "I'll come for you when you're asleep".

Marianne was searching desperately for reassurance, and said, "Mike, please tell me that it hasn't come with me to my mum's! I couldn't stand it!"

Of course, this was a reassurance that Mike could not give her, as poltergeists are, as previously discussed, "person-centred" and not "place-centred". It may very well have "followed" Marianne.

This placed Mike on the horns of a dilemma. What should he do? Lie, and tell Marianne that the polt couldn't or wouldn't have followed her simply to make her feel better? Or should he tell the brutal truth and frighten the living daylights out of her? Before he could even begin to consider the problem, the decision was taken out of his hands.

Within the space of one second the polt sent Marianne another text message. It had obviously been listening to the conversation between her and Mike, for the message read, *Please donwt gow now. I will just com with you bich!*

"Mike, I'm frightened to go to sleep!" said Marianne, understandably. Her words were followed by another text message which removed any residual doubt – not that there really was any – that the polt was listening in to the conversation with grim fascination: *I cann get you when you awake and I'll come for you when you're asleep bich.*

This was only one incident of many in which the South Shields poltergeist used mobile phones – and sometimes landlines – to bring terror into the hearts of the people it had chosen to victimise. The messages it sent demonstrated that it, too, knew where the family members were, what they were doing and what they were thinking, what had happened at Fircrest, then, was nothing new. And yet the modus operandi utilised by the perpetrator in both cases was so similar it left Darren and Mike in no doubt that the same, guiding intelligence was behind both incidents.

When Darren arrived at the station to meet Mike, Mike showed him the article in *The Fortean Times*. He was stunned. The authors discussed the ramifications of what they'd read, and it was at this point that they finally realised something incredibly important about the nature of the poltergeist phenomenon.

Twenty-One
CONTAGION: THE DESIRE TO SURVIVE

Earlier in this volume the authors highlighted a number of intriguing parallels between several poltergeist cases that they had personally investigated, including those at South Shields, Jarrow and Ashington. To be honest, these strange symmetries really only scratch the surface. During their research they noted a huge number of parallels between the case at South Shields and that of Enfield, which was ably investigated by recognised experts Maurice Grosse (now sadly deceased) and Guy Lyon Playfair. They also accumulated a host of parallels that are so specific it once again flags up the notion that the same, overriding presence is behind most or all poltergeist infestations.

The authors have discussed the concept of contagion throughout this volume, and also the fact that there are startling "coincidences" that act as common denominators in many cases of poltergeist infestation. To try and understand what may precipitate the phenomenon of contagion, and ascertain just why so many bizarre parallels exist between certain cases, we need to look more closely at some of the terminology we employ as we struggle to come to grips with the poltergeist enigma. First of all, we need to look at the process of contagion itself.

During the rest of this volume, the poltergeistry experienced at "Ground Zero" will be referred to as the *Primary Infestation*. The process of contagion will be described in stages:

1st Stage Contagion

This refers to instances of contagion which affect not the principal experients, but those who have had direct contact with them. For example, the authors had direct contact with the family at Lock Street for a protracted period of time. On one occasion, in Mike's study, a book disgorged itself from a shelf when both Darren and Mike had left the room and landed on the floor with a thump. This is 1st Stage Contagion in action.

In the experience of the authors, 1st Stage Contagion always differs from the poltergeistry experienced in the Primary Infestation in at least one (but not necessarily all) of the following ways:

- *1st Stage Contagion does not last as long as Primary Infestation.*
- *The symptoms of 1st Stage Contagion are not as severe as those in the Primary Infestation.*
- *The events experienced during 1st Stage Contagion are fewer in number than those experienced in the Primary Infestation, and there may be longer periods of inactivity between them.*

2nd Stage Contagion

This refers to instances of contagion which affect those who have only had indirect contact with the principal experients. On one occasion, the mobile phone of Mike's friend rang Mike's mobile phone in the early hours of the morning without any human assistance. At that point, Mike's friend had had no contact with the family at Lock Street, and his only link to them was that he knew Mike, who in turn knew the principal experients. This is 2nd Stage Contagion in action.

In the experience of the authors, 2nd Stage Contagion always differs from the poltergeistry experienced in 1st Stage Contagion in at least one (but not necessarily all) of the following ways:

- *2nd Stage Contagion does not last as long as 1st Stage Contagion.*
- *The symptoms of 2nd Stage Contagion are not as severe as those in 1st Stage Contagion.*
- *The events experienced during 2nd Stage Contagion are fewer in number than those experienced in 1st Stage Contagion and there may be longer periods of inactivity between them.*

3rd Stage Contagion

This refers to instances of contagion where the victims are

distanced from the principal experients by yet another "link in the chain", and whose only "contact" with the principal experients is that they know someone who has been the victim of 2nd Stage Contagion. This form of contagion is extremely rare, and is usually restricted to a "one-off" event or single display of poltergeistry, usually of a relatively minor nature. However, it is not just the terminology regarding the process of contagion that we need to get right, but also that which we use regarding the bizarre "coincidences" that so often accompany poltergeist infestations. Enigmatic parallels between individual cases, weird "coincidences" that inextricably link those associated with a case and other manifestations of what we may call *synchronisation* also need to be broken down into precise types:

Coincidental Parallels

Coincidental Parallels are those which have no ostensible meaning or relevance and may, as their title suggests, simply be coincidences.

To find an example of a Coincidental Parallel, we need look no further than the natural world. Ravens are black, and the gemstone known as jet is black. As far as we can determine, the similarity in colour between the raven and the aforementioned gemstone is nothing more than a coincidence and has no "meaning" whatsoever. There is no "law of nature" which dictates that the gemstone known as jet and the raven need to be the same colour. Life is teeming with Coincidental Parallels: oak leaves are green and one of Mike's dressing gowns is green. Snow is soft and marshmallow is soft. Escaping gas hisses and snarling cats hiss...the list is endless.

Significant Parallels

Significant Parallels are not coincidental, and exist because there is a demonstrable link between one "subject" or set of circumstances and another. Again, we can look to the natural world for an example of a Significant Parallel.

A human being born, say, in Beijing will (genetically-linked deformities discounted) possess two arms. Similarly, a human being born in San Francisco will have two arms. There is a parallel or similarity here, but it is neither coincidental nor meaningless. The reason that both individuals have two arms is that they both belong to the human species, all members of which, under normal circumstances, have two arms. Human beings may differ in terms of gender, skin colour, height, religion and goodness knows how many other things, but they should always be born with two arms.

Person-Specific Parallels

Person-Specific Parallels are not found between separate individuals or artefacts. They are either a) similarities of action, but so specific and unique that they are almost certain to have been carried out by the same individual, or b) similarities of appearance indicating that the persons or artefacts in question are actually one and the same.

Imagine that a man attends a business meeting and introduces himself as "John Smith, CEO of the ScrummyCookie Biscuit Company". Later in the day, if someone attends another meeting and introduces himself as, "John Smith, CEO of the ScrummyCookie Biscuit Company", they are – conspiracy theories aside – highly likely to be one and the same person. This is an example of *Person-Specific Action*.

Person-Specific Appearance can be illustrated by an almost identical analogy. Imagine that the above-mentioned John Smith has an unusual birthmark on his forehead shaped, say, like a starfish. Let us also imagine that John Smith is short, thin, balding and dressed in a green suit. His height, lack of hair and attire are not quite enough for us to say that we are working with an example of Person-Specific Appearance, for it is just possible that two men called John Smith, both of similar appearance, happen to be in the same city or town on the same day. However, when we factor in John Smith's unusual birthmark, we are presented with an extremely person-specific parallel. Both John Smiths are almost certainly one and the same. Both in appearance and action, they are essentially identical.

There is no doubt that poltergeist cases almost always display similarities. Indeed, it is these very similarities that enable us to state with some conviction that a poltergeist is at work. The question is, what *kind* of parallels do we actually see in poltergeist cases?

Without question there are Coincidental Parallels. A poltergeist case in London may be centred in a house with a tree in the garden. Another case may be centred in Oslo – also in a house with a tree in the garden. The presence of a tree in the garden in two polt-infested houses is almost certainly nothing more than a Coincidental Parallel and, unless additional factors indicate otherwise, should merit no further investigation. However, there are simply dozens of Significant Parallels that also present themselves in poltergeist cases, and these certainly do merit looking at.

There are certain "signatures" that indicate the presence of genuine poltergeist activity. No two cases are the same, and it is highly unlikely that all these signatures will be present in any two cases selected at random. Nevertheless, there will almost certainly be enough of these common denominators to enable the open-minded researcher to form a link. Such Significant Parallels may include the translocation of household objects, mysterious bangs and whistles, the opening and shutting of doors without human assistance, strange odours, anomalous pools of water, the stacking of objects in geometrical patterns, and so on. Just as the presence of two relatively hairless arms indicates the presence of a human, the presence of one or more unique poltergeist symptoms may well indicate the presence of a polt.

But what about Person-Specific Parallels – that testify to the "omnipresent, singular polt" idea? Here we need to examine some of the "signatures" or "calling cards" that poltergeists leave behind; these are actions that are so unique and specific that they point strongly to the idea that the same guiding intelligence is behind them. At Enfield, the poltergeist demonstrated a fascination with children's plastic building blocks. The poltergeist at South Shields did the same. At South Shields, the poltergeist repeatedly took mobile phones from the ground floor and placed them on the first floor. The poltergeist at Jarrow did the same. At Ashington, the poltergeist ran its fingers through the hair of its victim and stroked her thigh. The poltergeist at Middlesbrough did the same. In four cases the authors have personally investigated, the polt demonstrated a fascination with pulling the bedclothes off its victims during the night. In fact, Darren *was* one of its victims when he stayed over at Lock Street one night on the settee. After engaging in a battle of blanket tug-of-war with the Lock Street polt he eventually managed to get some sleep – only after *it* decided to let him.

In literally hundreds of cases, including those investigated by the authors, poltergeists have demonstrated an obsession with placing household objects in perfectly aligned geometric patterns.

Perhaps one of the most startling parallels, however is the way in which both the South Shields and Newcastle poltergeists took plastic bottles of mineral water and balanced them bizarrely on edge, even moving or spinning them without them falling over. To deny that there is something more than coincidence at work here is, the authors think, patently ridiculous.

The authors believe that the incubus/succubus and the poltergeist are closely connected, and may even be two slightly different aspects of the same phenomenon. The authors believe that the uncanny parallels between different cases is not coincidental, and may be indicative of the fact that the poltergeist is literally a "hive-mind"; a single, global entity which is simultaneously comprised of hundreds or possibly thousands of "aspects" or "sub-entities". These "aspects" would have a limited degree of autonomy but basically be saturated with the overriding personality of the "hive" or "collective". The poltergeist, just like the demon that Jesus exorcised, could be both *one* and *many* at the same time. This would explain why, on a global scale, poltergeists display the same characteristics and the same obscure idiosyncrasies; they are essentially *of one mind*.

When investigators grapple with a poltergeist, they are, on one level, dealing with a single poltergeist. However, it is also possible that they might be simultaneously dealing with every poltergeist that has ever been and currently is. The authors believe that the "hive-mind" or "collective" concept also helps explain the phenomenon of contagion. In the flesh-and-blood world, it is the disease that spreads whilst the carrier or host remains in the same place. With the poltergeist, it is somewhat different. As every personage within the poltergeist "hive-mind" carries within it the potential to exercise all the symptoms associated with poltergeistry, all that is necessary is for one personality to infect a victim. Other polt-personalities within the "hive mind" can then attach themselves to those who are directly or indirectly connected with the primary victims, although we do not as yet know why secondary infections like this always seem less virulent than the first. There are many, many things yet to be understood about this baffling enigma.

At the end of the day, we can say with confidence that the poltergeist phenomenon is a real one. The related phenomenon of contagion is also real, and there is no doubt that the symptoms of poltergeist infestation can spread themselves outward like ripples on a pond, affecting others as well as the primary victims. Like pond ripples, however, the ripples of poltergeist infestation weaken as they spread. Perhaps we should be thankful for this.

In Chapter 3, *Principles of Contagion*, the authors discussed the difference between passive contagion and active contagion. We simply don't know enough about the nature of the poltergeist to determine how much contagion is passive and how much is active. However, in *The South Shields Poltergeist – One Family's Fight Against an Invisible Intruder*, the authors argued strenuously that in the early stages of poltergeist infestation, the entity almost certainly has no sentience. It is unlikely to be conscious, possessing no self-awareness. However, the authors also argued that in the very later stages of a poltergeist's existence it could actually separate from its "host" and would, once acting independently, enjoy the self-awareness that had previously been denied it. This is an important point, because it may, at least theoretically, help us to differentiate between the aspects of passive and active contagion in the poltergeist's life-cycle. If the poltergeist in its early stages of existence has no consciousness, then it cannot deliberately initiate the process of contagion. Therefore, any incidents of contagion in the early stages would be passive; that is, part of a natural process of contagion and not consciously enacted. However, if the poltergeist is not truly a collective of independent entities, but actually a "hive mind", or singular arch-poltergeist that manifests itself in a multitude of different aspects – that is, as *seemingly* "individual" poltergeists – then the concept of the poltergeist having no sentience or consciousness in its early stages is seriously open to doubt. An arch-poltergeist would obviously possess sentience, and this would almost certainly mean that its individual aspects were sentient from the outset, merely being extensions of the arch or "parent" entity.

If the above proposition is correct, then it would mean that the two types of contagion – active and passive – could only be present in a strictly limited set of scenarios. If the poltergeist does indeed possess the ability to actively and consciously infect others with its activity, then it is possible that active contagion is the only kind. However, it is also possible that both types of contagion, active and passive, both work concurrently. There may be an active form of contagion deliberately initiated by the entity, alongside a passive form which infects people who find themselves interacting with the poltergeist in a certain set of circumstances which make them vulnerable to it. There is a third scenario, however, which is unlikely. The authors think there is little chance that the passive form of contagion could be present on its own without the active kind. This would infer that the arch-poltergeist or "poltergeist collective" possessed no way of consciously targeting its victims and would have to rely purely on instances of passive contagion to achieve its ends. It would also imply that the poltergeist – individually or collectively – possessed so little intelligence that it was unable to manipulate circumstances in any way to bring its victims within the sphere of its influence. The likelihood is, then, that either both the active and passive forms of contagion exist concurrently, or the active form exists on its own.

Working on the presumption that at least some elements of polt-related contagion are active – that is, deliberately and consciously generated by the poltergeist – the question arises as to just what its motivation might be in infecting others with its malign presence.

The almost universal common denominator in cases of poltergeist infestation is the inevitability that witnesses – particularly those at "Ground Zero" - become intensely frightened. It is no coincidence that there has long been a belief – and a well-grounded one, in the opinion of the authors – that the poltergeist actually *feeds* on fear or stress. We may not understand the scientific process involved, but the authors have been involved with far too many cases to dismiss the idea. Indeed, time after time they have witnessed a direct corollary between the degree of fear being experienced by victims and the intensity of polt-related phenomena. The worse the fear or stress, the more active the poltergeist becomes. Conversely, if the fear or stress experienced by victims begins to dissipate, polt-related phenomena almost always become weaker and more sporadic. Even a cursory perusal of these facts flags up a blatantly obvious possibility. If the polt feeds on fear and stress, and spends much of its time acting in ways which are calculated to cause fear and stress in its victims, then there is a distinct possibility that the polt deliberately precipitates stress and fear in its victims to enable it to feed! It is, we would venture, no different to the fisherman who baits his hook with a worm to enable him to catch the fish. Every intimidating poltergeist act is simply a metaphorical worm on the hook with which it can lure its victims into position.

The whole purpose behind active contagion – and the additional benefit of passive contagion – would then be manifestly obvious. The more victims the poltergeist is able to frighten, the more fear it has at its disposal to feed upon. Active contagion, then, may be stimulated by nothing less than the poltergeist's desire to survive.

Twenty-Two
CONCLUSIONS

Essentially, the authors are putting forward a hypothesis for discussion; that poltergeists may not be a collection of individual entities living independently of each other, but rather, a "hive-mind" or collective which to all intents and purposes is one *arch-*poltergeist which simply manifests itself in aspects. Each aspect of the supreme poltergeist may just possibly enjoy a degree of "autonomy", although it likely does not. Each individual poltergeist, we would suggest, may merely be a "tentacle" stretching out from the centre and carrying with it all the traits and characteristics of the parent body.

The "collective poltergeist" theory would also explain the number of astonishing "coincidences" and parallels found in a multitude of separate cases. Why? Because if there is in reality only one, universal poltergeist, then the very same consciousness and personality must be the prime motivator in each instance. This would explain why the South Shields poltergeist chose to balance a bottle of mineral water at a weird angle on a table, and the Newcastle poltergeist did exactly the same. Likewise, the South Shields poltergeist repeatedly took mobile phones from the ground floor of the house and placed them in a bedroom on the first floor. The Jarrow poltergeist did the same.

In their first book, the authors were at times puzzled by the fact that the personality behind the poltergeist seemed to mimic or parallel the personality of its host. On other occasions it would display character traits that were markedly different from those of the host. Our belief was that whenever the poltergeist "took up residence" in a human being a fusion may have taken place between both the polt and human personalities. Sometimes we might have been seeing the "true" poltergeist, and at others glimmers of the host's character shining through.

The authors fully accept that their theories and ideas may not necessarily all gel together or blend consistently. There may be times when, in their offering of hypotheses, a number of statements seem to be inconsistent. There is a reason for this. They believe that their concept of an arch-poltergeist is a relatively new one, or at least has not been examined previously in any depth. The authors do not claim to have all the answers. They simply wish to throw open to debate a series of crucially important questions regarding the poltergeist enigma, and to suggest tentatively some possible solutions. Their desire is that other investigators will go on to fine-tune these solutions, minimise or remove any inconsistencies and ultimately further our knowledge of a truly baffling and terrifying phenomenon. Having had first-hand experience in dealing with a truly vicious poltergeist at South Shields, and an abundance of others subsequently which were not quite so bad but still incredibly frightening to the witnesses, the authors feel they deserve the right to pose such questions.

Even the authors do not necessarily agree on all aspects of the very source of the poltergeist phenomenon, although they do agree to a large degree on the way the phenomenon presents itself. One question concerns the "hive mind" concept. Whilst accepting that the presentation of the phenomenon sits well with the hive-mind notion, Mike now believes that there may be another explanation. As the final draft of this manuscript was being prepared, Mike underwent a dramatic and radical change. Through an extraordinary set of circumstances which intruded upon both his professional and financial lives, the author was led to make a conversion to Islam. Islam is a spiritual path that is grossly misunderstood by those outside its provinces, but there is one doctrine which sits at the heart of the faith which is hardly understood at all; a belief in what Muslims call the *Al Ghayb* or "Unseen World". This book is not the arena in which to discuss this concept in any detail, however, the *Al Ghayb* provides a possible alternative to the hive-mind theory which Mike has now come to embrace.

The hive-mind theory was applied to the poltergeist phenomenon by the authors primarily for one reason; the uncanny number of person-specific parallels that seem to prevent themselves in cases all over the globe, leading them to conclude that poltergeists may simply be aspects of an arch-personality or "super-polt". However, in Islam it is generally believed that the majority of paranormal phenomena - if not all of them - are the handiwork of a race of spirit-beings known as the Jinn. The Jinn, in Islamic history and theology, are believed to be a race of creatures created by God after the angels but before human beings. The Jinn inhabit an alternative dimension and are usually not supposed to "slip through" into the human world. However, as the large majority of Jinn are rebellious, mischievous and even malevolent, they disobey this command.

The leader of the Jinn is Shaitan – the Islamic equivalent of Satan. However, whereas in Christian theology Satan is said to be a "fallen angel" in Islam he is not an angel but one of the Jinn. Shaitan, Muslims believe, acts like a Supreme Commander over his army of Jinn and issues them with detailed and precise instructions as to what he requires of them. All of the Jinn – with the exception of the minority of righteous ones, who still follow God – act in a nigh-identical manner to each other not because they are part of a "hive-mind" but because they obediently – nay, slavishly - follow the operations manual of their malign leader. The instances in which Jesus – or Issa, as Muslims call him – spoke to the "devils" which had possessed a man both in the singular and the plural are also explicable within the confines of Islamic belief.

The fact that the authors individually favour different concepts for the phenomenon behind poltergeistry should demonstrate to the reader that they have no hidden agenda, no axe to grind. Whatever lies at the very heart of the enigma – a hive-mind collective or a race of Satanic foot-soldiers – the authors have no doubt or disagreement about the important things; that the poltergeist phenomenon is real, and it can spread like an insidious disease.

After the authors engaged in many debates and in-depth discussions, and re-evaluated the poltergeist and its mechanics almost to the point of monotony, they stumbled across yet more important questions that seriously needed addressing. If Alexander Fleming had not been inquisitive about the interaction between mould and bacteria on a petri dish we may never have

Conclusions

had penicillin in modern medicine. The authors believe that the same principles apply here. Questions must be asked and evidence *must* be sifted and evaluated before definite conclusions can be made. The re-asking of those questions and the re-evaluation of the evidence must be carried out before we can move forward.

No one has all the answers to the poltergeist phenomenon. It remains one of the world's greatest mysteries. Perhaps the best we can hope for is that painstakingly, inch by inquisitive inch, we can move in the right direction and see the light get a little brighter with each passing year.

INDEX

Al Ghayb; 201.
Alien Abduction Phenomenon; 58.
Alone in the Dark Entertainment (AITDE); 35.
Amazon Basin; 20.
Anthropomorphic figures; 66, 111, 129.
Antibiotics; 27.
Apparitions; 9, 19, 25, 35, 42, 48, 69, 75, 80, 81, 92, 101, 104, 108, 115, 117, 118, 120, 121, 123, 125, 126, 128, 130, 131, 156, 157, 159, 160, 164, 177, 184.
Ashington Incubus case; 135.
Association for the Scientific Study of Anomalous Phenomena, the; (ASSAP); 172.
Atchison, Texas case; 113*ff*;
Atheism; 28.
Auditory phenomena; 21, 44, 47, 55, 59, 64, 73, 74, 84, 87*ff*; 93, 118, 120, 127, 128, 129, 145, 161*ff*;183.
Avicenna; 27.

Babylon, ancient; 11.
Bacteria; 27, 31, 202.
Bartley, Drew; 7, 130, 134.
Beatles, the; 85.
Bigfoot; 20.
Bob Trollop's; 35.
Bottle balance; 127, 134, 177, 196, 200.
Brown MP, Gordon; 149.

Capitalism; 28.
Carbon Footprint; 170.
Christianity, early; 173 *ff*;
Church, Roman Catholic; 12, 138, 146.
Coincidences, poltergeist related; 43 *ff*; 177.
Communism; 28.

Conservative Party; 149.
Contagion; *active*; 31 *ff*; 197, 198, 199; *passive*; 31 *ff*; 197, 198, 199; *stages of*; 191 *ff*;
Cottrell, Lez; 7.
Crystal Skulls; 152.
Cynics; 15, 111, 143, 183.

Democracy; 28.
Demon Child TV programme; 113.
Demons; 11, 12, 76, 136 *ff*;173 *ff*;183, 196.
Devil, the; 174.
Disappearing objects; 25, 26,
Discovery Channel; 110.
D'Morgyn, Rhianne; 7, 36, 45, 46, 47, 76, 139, 140*ff*;148, 151.
Dreaming; 40, 56, 57, 60, 65 *ff*;86, 104.

Eclecticism; 146.
Electrical phenomena; 9, 10, 21, 23, 24, 56, 60, 70, 73, 94, 101, 146, 160*ff*; 170*ff*; 178, 186.
Elemental spirits; 12, 143, 148.
Elves; 12, 143.
Enfield Poltergeist; 10, 71, 110, 176, 178, 180, 181, 182, 187, 191, 195.
Entity, the (movie); 183.
Exorcism; 12, 138, 174.

Faeries; 12, 143.
Fircrest, Pierce County, Washington State case; 187.
Fleming, Alexander; 202.
Fortean Times, the; 187.
Fungi; 27.

Geometric patterns; 195, 196.
Ghost Club of Great Britain, The; 172.

Index

Ghosts; 9, 19, 25, 35, 42, 48, 69, 75, 80, 81, 92, 101, 104, 108, 115, 117, 118, 120, 121, 123, 125, 126, 128, 130, 131, 156, 157, 159, 160, 164, 177, 184.
Gmelig-Meyling, Dono; 10.
Gnomes; 12, 143.
Goblins; 13.
God, gods; 135, 174, 202.
Gorner, Gemma; 126 ff;
Greenhouse gases; 170.
Grosse, Maurice; 7, 10, 180, 181, 182, 191.

Hallowell, Mike; 6, 9, 15, 30, 38, 45, 50, 62, 75, 82, 88, 93, 102, 117, 130, 134,142, 152, 161, 167, 182, 192.
Hallucinations; 120, 155.
Haunted Loom case; 90 ff;
Hepatitis A; 31.
Hinduism; 146.
HIV virus; 16, 32.
Hive-mind theory; 196.
Hodgson, George B; 105.
Hypnopompic sleep state; 120.
Hyslop, Professor James; 13.

Incubus; 11, 12, 135 ff; 183, 196.
Islam; 146, 174. *Mike's conversion to;* 6, 201, 202
Issa; 202.

Jarrow Poltergeist; 7, 38 ff; 43 ff; 70, 75 ff;
Jesus; 173, 174 ff; 196, 202.
Jinn, the; 202,
Johnson MP, Boris; 149.
Judaeo-Christian theology; 173 ff;
Judea; 173.

Kiss (rock band); 163.
Kuykendall, Courtney; 188.

Labour Party; 149.
"Legion", collective noun for demons; 174.
Ley Lines; 142 ff;
Lisbona, Natalie; 182.
Livingstone; 149.
Luke, Gospel of; 174.

Maud Street Poltergeist; 184, 185.
McDonald, Paul; 7, 126.
McKay, Andrea; 188.
McKay, Taylor; 188.
Mediums; 7, 9, 10, 17, 36, 45, 47, 63, 64, 65, 76, 114, 121, 135, 139, 145, 151, 152, 157.
Middlesbrough poltergeist case; 155 ff;

Mills, Liz; 128.
Milne, A. A.; 108.
Mobile phone, and anomalies; 29, 39, 70 ff; 95, 99, 102, 104, 127, 151, 177, 186 ff;
Mormonism; 146.
Murdie LL.B, Alan; 114

New age spirituality; 143, 148.
Newcastle Keep; 126.
New Dominion Pictures; 110.
Nesbitt, Victoria; 90 ff;
New Testament, the; 173 ff;
Night terrors; 57.
North East Ghost Research Tea (NEGRT); 80, 130.

Offshore 44; 35.
Olfactory phenomena; 87, 88, 149, 158, 159, 195.
Olley, Darren; 7, 108, 109, 112.
Ouija Board; 143.

Parallels, *coincidental*; 193, *significant*; 193, *person specific;* 193.
Parapsychologists; 120.
Physical attacks; 14, 73, 165, 177, 178, 183.
Pixies; 12, 143.
Playfair, Guy Lyon; 7, 10, 81, 110, 180, 181, 191.
Poltergeist, case parallels; 176 ff;
Possession, incidents of; 173, 175.
Possession, symptoms of; 175.
Price, Harry; 81.
Protozoa; 27.
Psychics; 7, 12, 17, 20, 36, 45, 69, 121, 142.
Puberty, relationship to poltergeist phenomenon; 79 ff;
Purists; 146.

Racism; 28.
Raps (anomalous); 45, 72.
Red House, The; 35.
Risolino, Jo; 128.
Rituals; 111, 113, 147, 148.
Rosie; 127.
Ryhope case, the; 63.
Ritson, Darren; 6, 15, 19, 21, 36, 38, 47, 48, 72, 75, 78, 84, 97, 102, 104, 107, 110, 115, 119, 126, 129, 151, 154, 164, 181, 192.
Ritson, Abbey May; 19, 49, 75, 107, 108.
Rue des Noyers case; 9.

Sallie's House case; 114.
Satan; 174.
Sceptics; 13, 15, 59, 69, 184.

Serial killers; 81.
Sexism; 28.
Sexually-related phenomena; 10*ff;* 136, 137, 139, 179, 183, 184.
Shaitan; 202.
Smith, Stuart and Lauren; 87*ff;*
Socialism; 28.
Society for Psychical Research (SPR); 110, 172. *Journal of;* 110, 114.
Somnambulism (sleepwalking); 63.
Sounds, (anomalous); 21, 44, 47, 55, 59, 64, 73, 74, 84, 87*ff;* 93, 118, 120, 127, 128, 129, 145, 161*ff;* 183.
South Shields Poltergeist; 9, 23*ff;* 95, 97, 99, 109, 130, 150, 186, 189.
South Shields restaurant poltergeist; 25.
Spontaneous combustion; 149*ff;* 179.
"Stacking" phenomenon; 23, 177, 195.
Succubus; 11, 136, 137, 183, 196.
Sumerians, ancient; 11.
Suzanne, Investigator; 118 *ff;*

Taylor, Steve; 7, 10, 35*ff;* 38, 45, 46, 90, 135, 139.
Telephone anomalies; 95, 126, 153, 187, 189.
Temperature anomalies; 92, 94, 96, 133, 158, 159.
Text messages; 14, 17, 30, 98, 104, 186 *ff;*
Theocracy; 28.
"Tony and Linda" poltergeist case; 8, 155*ff;*
Trewick, Pte. Thomas; 181, 182.
Trigger objects; 122, 130, 132.
TV-related phenomena; 46, 70, 128, 171, 186.

UFOs; 20, 58, 60 *ff;*
Underwood, Peter; 81.
Unseen world, Islamic view of; 201.

Violence during poltergeist attacks; 14, 73, 165, 177, 178, 183.
Vipond, Fiona; 7, 130, 134.
Voices, disembodied; 44, 46, 53, 57, 64, 84, 85, 86, 90, 91, 92, 93, 117, 118, 119, 120, 131, 133, 165*ff;* 177, 187, 188.
Vortex, vortices; 142 *ff;*

Water-related phenomena; 10, 12, 39, 41, 97, 98, 138, 178, 195.
Watson, Jayne; 48, 49, 102 *ff;* 107, 153.
Western Kentucky case; 111 *ff;*
Wicca; 147.
Willin, Dr. Melvyn; 81.

Wilson, Colin; 4, 13, 15, 81.
Winter, Mark; 7, 80, 130.
Written messages, anomalous; 30, 179.

Yorkshire; 10, 118.